Also by Tina Catling

Making Waves	13 May 2011	Wiley
Think	18 October 2002	Capstone

MAY DAY

An impractical guide to giving up everything and sailing away with your husband and dog - a book a bit like a year in Provence except it is more than a year and it isn't in Provence.

Tina Catling

May in the Dingy with S/Y Magic in the Background in Lagos Marina, Portugal
Original Design by Stephanie Maguire
Photography Tina Catling
Thanks also for Art Direction by Dave Easton
And support by Svea Schäfer

ISBN: 978-1-4834-6934-8 (sc)
ISBN: 978-1-4834-6933-1 (e)

Lulu Publishing Services rev. date: 06/08/2017

Dedication

This book is dedicated to the dreamers and all those who dare
to have adventures and keep their sense of wonder.
For the curious and for all lovers of life.

For Gareth, James, James and Sara – We love you.
Never stop having adventures.

For Beryl and Geoff – Mum and Dad - You inspire
us with your wisdom, fun and vitality

Epigraph

"Not all those who wander are lost"
JR Tolkien

Isabelle: **"We could get** into **trouble"**
Hugo Cabret: **"That's how you know it's an adventure"**
From, the must see movie, HUGO

Contents

Preface

This book came into being because we wanted to capture our adventure. Initially the writing was in the form of a blog which was written for our family and friends. As our journey unfolded before us we were honest about all the mishaps, the financial stresses, the fun and the chaos. We were critised and, also praised for our honesty.

Acknowledgement

I would like to thank

May – for being the most courageous, intelligent, beautiful and fun travelling companion

Mark Davies– for being the most skilful sailor and loving husband

Andrew and Susan in Lagos – Andrew thanks for the weather support all across the Atlantic and Susan thanks for all the fun and TLC

JimB – for his support and wisdom when things got tough on the online forums

Simon Philips – for being the most incredible skipper and teacher – experienced, calm, fun, generous and kind. His company, Seaway Yacht deliveries is an exceptional organisation

All our friends in Lagos, Portugal – a wonderful place but more importantly filled with incredible people

All the exceptional friends we met on our adventure those who are sailors and those honest and skilled people who work on yachts to help keep us all safe and afloat. We include, the sailmakers,, the riggers, the engineers, the chippies, the sparks, the painters, the cleaners and the laundry guys

Karen van Rensburg from Lighthouse yachting Antigua for helping us prepare s/y Magic for sale and of course for selling her.

Vision for his unique singing of 'three little birds' whilst cleaning our s/y Magic so wonderfully when we arrived into Rodney Bay, St Lucia – look him up if you are ever in Rodney Bay

The boat boys and people who supply services around the Caribbean that helped us moor up or stock up or clean up.

Chris Doyle – your guides to the Caribbean are the best

Jacqui Byrne

Geoff Davies

Karen Spencer for proof reading and support

The team at outside the box – Stephanie Maguire, Dave Easton and Svea Schafer

and finally to all fellow adventurers on the sea – thanks for the advice, the support, the rescues and more importantly the music, fun and laughter along the way

Introduction

Tina and Mark had been working for thirty years building their families and businesses. They had done well but were a little bit tired. Their four children had all left home and their business interests were thriving without them. They had a moment, they suddenly realised that for the first time in their lives they did not have to live in one particular place. Should they live by the sea? Why not ON the sea?

So that was it, they bought a yacht and sailed away. But how easy was that? Did they know how to sail? What about their dogs? Could they afford it?

What could go wrong?

Everything, as it turned out.

Prologue

Tina and Mark have always been adventurous. Together they have built two successful companies and travelled around the world. They have worked together in Iran, Australia, The Maldives, North America, Africa, Russia and all over Europe. Both have always been bold and brave in life and whilst not thrill seekers – they don't like roller coasters, bungee jumping or sky diving. They are not afraid to jump into new experiences. They have always done things which their friends and family have regarded as brave (or crazy) like buying an old converted chapel that needed 10 years of repair or buying a flooded apartment in central London – when even their solicitor said it was a folly. But they love to surprise their critics and both these property adventures have turned out to be very good decisions.

What greater adventure then than to pack up everything and set sail. To Tina and Mark the open sea meant utter freedom – with a yacht you can sail around the world and with 71% of the earth's surface covered in water – what a waste not to explore it.

Tina and Mark Happy at the Helm of Magic : Sunshine, fair winds and calm sea.

Chapter One

MAKING A LIFE CHANGING DECISION

I blame the pork scratchings!

October

It has been an incredible journey. But who would have thought that making a lifelong held dream come true would be so hard? Personally, I blame the pork scratchings.

We had a moment and it went a bit like this: "The children are thriving and building their wonderful lives, the rest of the family are all well, so let's not grow tomatoes, let's get out on the Ocean and have an adventure of a lifetime – why not?"

Perhaps I should explain how we got to that point. We were experimenting with how we wanted to live. For the first time in our lives we found that we didn't have to live in a particular place. The first step was to realise that we were getting too comfortable. We were taking root. So first we had to prise ourselves out of our beautiful, soporific nest –a cosy converted chapel in North Yorkshire that has been our perfect home for 20 years.

Next, we had to consider what we really wanted. That is always the first step to making changes in your life – asking, "what do I really want? What would make me really happy?" It is the hardest part. We talked and talked and realised that to answer the question we needed to do some research. We needed to experiment with different ways of living. To begin with we both agreed that we would like to give living in a village a go. When you are really clear about what you want it often doesn't take long to make things happen. We quickly found a perfect cottage to rent in beautiful Nun Monkton, a very special village. We were there for a wonderful year. I have never lived anywhere where I felt so loved. But once again we found we were putting down roots and my falling in love with the green house and growing tomatoes was the last straw! We had to go!

The next thought we had was to go and live by the sea. Mark (that is my husband) and I both love sailing and we thought that if we lived by the sea we would sail more.

We went to the pub to talk more about our plans and over a packet of pork scratchings (don't judge me) and a pint of Theakston's in the Alice Hawthorn, Nun Monkton, we started looking at yachts for sale – that is when it struck us – "Clang - why live *by* the sea when we could live *on* the sea?" So that was it, we had our moment and we decided there and then – let's buy a yacht and sail away.

Buying and choosing the boat and making plans

The process of deciding which yacht and then actually buying the yacht is a very long and really rather dull story so I will spare you all the spreadsheets and endless deliberations. The point is that we finally found the perfect yacht – an Oyster (sailors love those). She ticked all the boxes, a very sea worthy yacht and perfect for crossing oceans. She had all the right equipment and everyone said that was a sensible yacht to buy.

Then we bought a Hanse because we liked the interiors better. We knew she didn't have all the right equipment like the Oyster but the spreadsheet was forgotten, we just fell in love with the Hanse, she was ours. Having posted this irrational and emotional decision on a sailing forum we were instantly doused by wave after wave of criticism. Luckily, we are not people who care much about what people say about our choices so we carried on with arranging for our new boat – il Sogno, re named "Magic" to be delivered from Holland to Portsmouth.

The plan was that we will be living onboard Magic from 1st November in sunny exotic Portsmouth, then in early December, we will set sail, initially to the Algarve then on.
      Perhaps we will be having Sardines and not Turkey for Christmas. When I say we... I will be 'sailing' on Brittany Ferries and Mark will be travelling with our amazing professional crew –

Yes, they will be crossing Biscay in December – a journey of 12 days (or more dependent on the weather). We were told by many more experienced people that sailing across the Bay of Biscay in December was bonkers – so that was what we planned to do. We are building our sailing experience so we are taking a professional Skipper and crew. We know that it is important on more challenging crossings to ensure we have fun and we are safe.

We have decided that we are not retiring we are, um – adventuring – to us it's a new way of living – not stopping work – just working differently – for us it is a more exciting and innovative way to live life.

So, back to the plan? Well, it is only broad right now – which we love. Up to now in our life we have had to do so much planning so it is wonderful and thrilling to have plans –that are ish! Rather than absolute

We will be tootling around the Med until October next year when we will go to Canaries in preparation for crossing the Atlantic to St Lucia in November– We have already booked our place for ARC next year (that's a sort of race across the Atlantic) so we are committed.

We will still be in London until the 30th October, and then we are popping to Manchester to say hi to family. Then we are heading to our beloved Nun Monkton for few nights and finally we will be driving to Portsmouth where "Magic" will be delivered from Holland. We have renamed the yacht, as although its original name 'il Sogno' is a beautiful name meaning 'the dream' in Italian – it sounds horrible in an English accent! 'il SOG no'. Also, we wanted a name that meant something to us. Our beloved Cocker Spaniel – Magic died just a short time ago and we miss him so we thought – what better than to call your yacht after a dead dog.

We were going to call the yacht 'Beryl' which is Mark's Mum's name but then we thought she wouldn't like that!

Of course, our gorgeous dogs Bear and May will be joining us for the Adventure – they will soon be *Salty Sea Dogs*

Here we go!

Getting ready and hanging about in the UK
Shopping? It's not Shopping its investing
OCTOBER

We knew that the purchase of the boat would only be the beginning of the spending – or as I like to think of it "Investing". Of course, as you know we did not buy a boat that had lots of what we needed already on board! So, we have had to buy ALL the safety equipment – it's a long list of things some of which we have never heard of Epirb, Dan Buoy, Jon Buoy and some we understand Life Raft, Fire Extinguishers, Flares and First Aid Kit. Also, as we are still learning about sailing we need books on all manner of things from Weather to First Aid and Navigation.

We need Oilskins and Charts, and despite all the protestations from advisors we did not buy a boat with a Generator and a Water Maker and we will now need these too! We also do not have air con or a washing machine – the list goes on and on.

The night before …
OCTOBER

This is the night before the week when all our plans start to come together.

I have had a chat with our dogs Bear and May and they are concerned but going with it!

Next week we finalise the purchase of "Magic", the money will be exchanged into Euro's and sent to the Dutch notary – our son who is a lawyer is travelling in Peru on holiday so we will have to go it alone on this. Our surveyor has been excellent, we watched his sea trial video and reviewed the hundreds of detailed images he took of our new home. He is going to be the one that checks that all the work has been done to a professional standard and that she is good to go. On the 27th October, our delivery crew arrive in Bruinesse, Holland and on the 28th they set sail for Portsmouth. We are planning to meet them on the 29th or 30th and get stuck into the business of stowing our gear and buying more stuff – this will include getting Magic measured for her smart new Bimini (sun shade) which will be designed and created prior to Mark's departure across the Bay of Biscay to Lagos on the 28th November.

We are excited to have our Oilskins – we bought them via the Cruising Association – Henry Lloyd Elite – grey and very smart. We unwrapped them and immediately both put them on and walked around the kitchen. I was tempted to get a pan of water and chuck it over Mark – you know to test the new gear- But thought better of it! We are going to get personal Epirbs (safety equipment that sends a message for help if you fall in the water) and Spin Lock life jackets and harnesses. We want to get the best safety gear we can. Bear and May have their life jackets too. A huge order with all manner of safety gear is being sent from Force Four in the UK to Holland for our delivery crew's trip across to Portsmouth. The previous owner used our boat for trips around the coast of Holland to entertain clients – for who, we were surprised to hear, needed no safety gear. We had to buy the flares from the chandler in Holland, as we could not ship those. As I mentioned before we are doing the ARC in November next year and so we are diligently following their enormous list of safety equipment – not only so that we do not have to buy twice – but also so we are sure we have the right gear for our crew and for us.

It is a strange feeling – being on the cusp of such a big life change. We have some doubts but mostly we have extreme giddiness and there is much spontaneous dancing and laughter.

Tomorrow more lists! We now have lists of lists. Fingers crossed the Euro works in our favour next Thursday … Oh, and must order more dog food and water tight containers, and …

The week of the final purchase

Well this week a lot is happening – we have just paid a big chunk towards the final payment and paid the Dutch solicitor. A lot of really boring stuff also has now to be done, like the boat has to be de registered in Holland before re registered on the Small Ships Register for the UK – we need evidence that there is no outstanding finance on it from the seller and we need proof that we have paid the VAT – it's all pay, pay, pay and paperwork at the moment – the list seems endless – the lettering on the boat – the solicitor – the lifting out on a crane for a survey – the survey and the survey of the works following the survey! The new Bimimi (sun cover) the delivery crew, the insurance, the marinas in Portsmouth and Portugal, the Dogs' injections, the safety equipment (£5k and counting) the sailing clothes – Henry Lloyd Elite Oilskins x 2! Dog and People Life jackets, Charts, Van Hire to move our stuff out of London to Leeds, Flares, all that and still no Bacardi – good thing the owner left a bottle on board.

I have just booked the ferry from Portsmouth to Santander for May and Bear and me – one way!! Brittany Ferries do a dog-friendly cabin where we can all sleep together – I will let you know how that goes!

5 Days before our boat leaves Holland for Portsmouth

I have been having a ball – filling in insurance forms and registering the boat with the Small Ships Register, dealing with the banks and managing the exchange rate!! No really, it has been wonderful and to me even the graft and realities of dream making are fun. It all means we are getting there. Of course, everything has cost more than we had planned. I think someone on the Cruising Association forum said they spent £50,000 on everything – I thought 'wow, how did you manage that!?" – Now I understand how!!

There are several lists and even the lists have lists!

1. Safety Items – must have now and must have in November next year for the ARC
2. Day-to-Day Living – Must have – Now and Later
3. Luxuries – Must haves – like Bacardi and like to have – you know like the Port and Starboard Socks!

The Day Before Magic Leaves Bruinesse for Portsmouth

As I write – we are still finishing all the bits on the boat! For example, she has no gas bottle as the previous owners never cooked aboard! We are going to really show this boat what she was built for! Simon our trusted delivery skipper and crew are all travelling to Bruinesse and should be there tonight. They will pack her with provisions and gas! and head off tomorrow. We were thinking that saying we live on a yacht in the Med sounds pretentious and have decided that in conversation the best thing to say would be that we live in a mobile home.

This is it The Dream Begins!
Tonight, we have our first night on our yacht (aka Mobile Home)

Neither of us could sleep last night! We had been tracking 'Magic' across the sea as she has sailed towards us. She left Bruinesse on Tuesday lunchtime but only got a little way before she had to pull into a port. She had issues with her autopilot. The skipper, Simon said he didn't want the autopilot to be playing up whilst they were crossing the busy shipping lane! – good call.

The Auto pilot fixed they headed out again yesterday at 11am they were just off Ostend – Belgium. Their estimated time of arrival at Portsmouth is 4pm. We have used our dishwasher for the last time and made sure we have washed all our clothes in the washing machine – I am sure I should have had a dishwasher and a washing machine fitted in the yacht!! We have packed what looks like very little to go on the Yacht. Our trusty Landover Defender is stuffed to the roof and we will be driving to Portsmouth at lunchtime – yes, I know we will get there before 4pm but we want to have part of our dream fulfilled – that of seeing our own Yacht sailing into harbour towards us! – Thanks to our neighbours – we can leave the dogs at home this trip and delay their moving into the boat until the 6th when we all move in together.

Tonight, Mark and I will sleep on Magic for the first time. We are both so excited and full of anticipation, doubts and fears – it does feel great – alive – visceral. Our heads are full to busting with things for work, logistical things, exciting hopes and dreams things, lists and lists and all manner of other stuff!

However, we are both just having coffee and eating toast and jam as if this was just another day – but it really isn't. This is the day we move off the land and onto the water.

We know that we will work it all out and take each new challenge as it comes along – we are happy and healthy and positive. We are not delusional however and we know there will be challenges – not least of which is the health and well-being of our beautiful dogs May and Bear. We are going to keep an open mind about if this new life will suit them. We are sure May who is a Maltese Terrier will be fine – small and white! But Bear who is a Bernese mountain dog, huge and black is not perhaps the best design for a yacht in the sun.

For now, we will focus on getting ourselves to Portsmouth and fulfilling the bit of our dream where our boat comes home!

Here we go…

NOVEMBER

Well that's it – we've done it now! We are living aboard…and the verdict – We LOVE, LOVE, LOVE it!

We are so very happy – we have made a fantastic decision – we didn't always think we were doing the right thing – but "Phew!" We have.

We have talked about this dream coming true so many times – and here we were standing together in Portsmouth Marina looking out at the setting sun as our yacht sailed towards us – just as we had imagined.

I felt so overwhelmed I felt sick. We watched as she got closer and closer to us and as she did she looked larger and larger. Other people gathered and some of them said 'what a beautiful yacht' we had to quietly agree!

We ran along the quayside like small children. We watched Simon, our skipper, as he moored her gently alongside and stepped calmly off the boat onto the dock. He walked slowly towards us to shake our hand and say hello. We were speechless. Simon then took Magic through the lock to her berth – we ran along the jetty– what a happy, happy day.

It really isn't every day when a dream comes so spectacularly true.

Simon and his crew moored up expertly and we went on board – we both had the same feeling – that of overwhelming incompetence – what were we thinking – we have forgotten how to sail – how will we manage this boat?!

Both Mark and I had very heavy hearts as the creeping realisation sank in that Bear could not come with us. As we climbed aboard I know we both had the same thought at the same time. There was no way we could manage to get a 6 stone Bernese Mountain dog on and off the boat and up and down the steep ladder in companion way.

Neither of us spoke about what we were both thinking.

We went for dinner and a beer and then back to the boat for a cuppa before bed. Simon had made a list of things that didn't work – one of which was the heating – we were cold and damp, anxious and excited and shattered and worried – so under 2 duvets we had a cold and restless night – we finally gave in and at 5am, left Magic in Portsmouth and drove to London.

This new day felt odd – our new home was a boat! It was sinking in.

What a day it turned out to be – in short – 5am depart Portsmouth – 7am arrive at our London house and completed the work of packing up. At 11am Mark got the van and we packed it – leaving for Yorkshire, finally at 1pm. We have an office in Leeds and that is where we were going to store all our stuff. We had to drop the van off in Leeds at 6pm after unpacking. But as it was Halloween night and the end of half term there was gridlock on the M1 and we ended up driving for 7 hours to Leeds.

What do you want after a 2-hour drive – 6 hours of packing and 7 more hours of driving – Yes, you guessed – you want another 1 hour of unpacking and 2 more hours of driving – to Manchester!!
Making this dream come true is exhausting, expensive and emotional.

We finally arrived at Mark's Mum and Dad's house in Stockport to find that Mark's dad had just had an operation on his eye. We had been so self-obsessed with our logistics we didn't know.

We were also deeply sad, as we had made the difficult decision that Bear would need a Foster Home. But as if fate had held our hand again – Bear's family in Wales said – "Yes of course we would LOVE to have her stay with us and our other 12 Bernese Mountain Dogs"!! The family includes Bear's doggie Mum, Dad and brother – it is the right decision and the perfect solution for her. Her breeders are amazing people who have 12 Bernese as well as a very innovative smallholding in a beautiful part of Wales. Bear will be having hikes in the Welsh mountains with her family while we are sweltering and teetering around in a tiny space on Magic.

We focused on Mark's Mum and Dad all weekend and caught up with lots of family – lovely. Wednesday night was the 5th November and Nun Monkton put on a wonderful bonfire night with huge fire, a Guy and lots of fireworks and hotdogs – then we went to the Alice Hawthorn to drink hot whisky Macs with the homemade Parkin – transcendent!

Our beloved Nun Monkton – the village we love but have made ourselves leave. Being there was like surrendering into a big hug – safe, familiar, loved.

What a way to set off – Bliss.

The next morning, we are heading off with the Land Rover bulging.

We drove towards Birmingham where we were meeting Tony to hand over our Bear. I knew it would be hard but the pain was searing –

Tony said, "Let me take a picture of you all" The picture looked like we were smiling but we were crying.

Mark walked Bear for a bit as I handed over her lead and Life Jacket. Mark then brought her back and Tony asked me if I was alright? – that was a mistake – the pins of tears jabbed at my eyes as I let her go I kissed her warm furry head. She went with Tony happily jumping into his car. I watched her watch us as they drove away – then I let the tears fall.

We drove on arriving at Portsmouth in pain-filled silence. The tears just flowed down my pain-filled face and onto May who was sitting quietly on my lap. We were giving up a lot to follow our dream. We made ourselves move out of a village we loved, we gave away Rasputin our cat and Bear our dog. What a weird mix of emotions the pain of letting go mixed with the thrill of moving towards our new home.

But the reality is it's November we are in Portsmouth on a freezing, damp boat – we have left our friends and family and our home – we have left our beloved dog Bear

"Oh, my God, what have we done?"

Our most important job was to get the heating working. Magic has central heating in every space so it should be toasty not icy.

I am quite technically able and so I set about looking for the manual – found it! – oh – it was in Dutch! So, I went on-line to find an English one – couldn't – so-called the manufacturer Webasto, they found one and emailed it but even though Mark and I tried we couldn't understand it so, feeling a bit stupid I phoned them again and – *their* engineer didn't understand it either! Finally, after hours of trying to get the heating to work we hit on a solution.

Go to the pub for a meal and to get warm. As we walked down the jetty I laughed to see May trotting ahead of us as if she now owned the Marina – she will be a fine salty sea dog.

To get warm and dry out we decided to get into our Land rover Defender as it has heated seats. We drove to Old Portsmouth and found a lovely pub. When we told the land lady we were cold – she offered to give each of us a hot water bottle to take with us – how lovely is that! – we have our own, so we politely declined but that is what I call customer service.

When we got onto the boat we were delighted to meet our 'next door neighbour' who also lives aboard. He brought us a heater – unfortunately we now had a problem with the electrics so none of the sockets worked to plug it in! Still cold.

That night there was a gale but it was lovely snuggling up on the boat under piles of quilts listening to the wind in the rigging and the rain pounding on the deck.

We thought – this is crazy and we love it!

The next morning, we set to work – more unpacking (there really is nowhere to put anything)- a rigger and a spark and a sail maker were on board. …what a strange new world we are entering.

We have some wonderful adventures ahead –
> Good Decision?
> Good Decision!

What a lot has happened in just 14 Days – Getting used to living aboard…

The view I am enjoying as I write is one of Mark and his two sons at our Saloon table watching Man U v Arsenal – warm and cosy with family on board – lots of laughter and Man U are 1 – 0 up which delights all. This is the first time we have had family on board and it feels fantastic.

I am writing from the chart table on my Mac and the boys are watching the game on Sky Go on Mark's Mac – Sky Go on a Mac is a revelation – great service. We have a fantastic TV but currently the sound doesn't work – which is a shame as we have just invested in MacTV and a Free View box – so we have more entertainment than we could wish for – just with no sound!!

This leads me to 10 new things that we have learned (things that those who live aboard already know):

1. **Whatever can break will break and just when you need it the most-**
Everything breaks and needs fixing. The TV you know about and our central heating has not been working for the last two weeks and it seems that engineers are hard to find – one is coming on Monday …. Possibly. My hands were so tired that when I picked up my external hard drive I dropped it – it smashed onto the beautiful saloon table chipping it and then hit the floor – 14 years of stuff – lost –

But yes – I had a mirror of the hard drive PHEW – PHEW PHEW – I must find out how to put all my stuff on the cloud.

2. **All your muscles will hurt and you will be tired all the time.**
Another new experience is the sheer physicality of living aboard. Every muscle hurts – especially – and this might seem weird – my hands. I am using muscles that I haven't used ever or certainly for a long, long time. This – I have decided is a great thing as I hate the gym and now I will tone up and get fit just with the everyday living things on board. Just climbing up and down – lifting and pulling – carrying and stowing things away, crawling in and under things…. Fantastic.

3. **However, much you think you will need to spend – quadruple it.**
We have been so surprised at how much new stuff we have needed – some of it we still don't know what it is or why we need it! If I hear one more person say, *"what your boat needs is a …."* Or " *Oh no you bought that from 'them' shame – you could have bought it MUCH cheaper from x or y"*

We have met some wonderful people who have helped us – and some not so great people who have hindered us, confused us and even some who have ripped us off. As we are on a very steep learning curve and as we are here only a short while we are feeling rather like a carcass that is being picked over by vultures.

4. **However, much stuff you have – cut it by half.**
There is lots of storage on our yacht compared to other yachts but compared to a house there is about 90% less – have a think about down-sizing everything you own by 90% – clothes, jewellery, cosmetics, shoes, bags….

5. **You can work on board (rats!)**
So, I have found that it is possible to conduct our businesses from the yacht (mobile home) and we have been working with clients and using SKYPE to great effect…so this really *is* just a different way of working. Mark and I are already booking work into the New Year. Turns out that

Faro airport in Portugal is easy to use and creates a journey that is cheaper and faster than taking trains in the UK to see clients. Rats!

6. **There are two main modes of living aboard – at sea and in the Marina.**

At sea, everything is put carefully away – including May! In the Marina, we can set out our rooms like any smart home with accent lighting – pictures – plants and fruit in bowls – we like having two modes of living!

7. **Learning a lot of new things fast is wonderful.**

Even though we discuss doing new things often with our clients – we only have done a few new things in the past few years. In the last few weeks we have done literally hundreds of new things – and the learning continues. Navigation, electronics, yacht maintenance, weather, fixing TVs, fixing Webasto heaters...... fixing everything – all the time.

8. **There are some wonderful people who live aboard.**

There is an entire community of exciting and interesting people who live aboard their yachts. This is a lifestyle choice and one that is tough to make. So, it is great to discuss the ups and downs with others who have also done it.

9. **The new toys you get are FANTASTIC!**

There have been some purchases that leave you cold – rubber buckets, bilge cleaner, deck brushes, storage solutions for the fridge and freezer, but there are some that are exciting – two foldable bikes, a transceiver, a new OLYMPUS touch stylus camera, MacTV, Free view Box, A Go Pro4 Silver, Cool Henry Lloyd Oilskins and we have also invested in Jackets, T-shirts, Polo Shirts and Hats with 'Magic's' name on them – and of course we have got a T Shirt printed for May!!

10. **Finally – this is the best decision we have ever made – even though it hurts – emotionally, financially and physically.**

It has been hard – at times brutally hard. We have been sad, tired and grumpy. We have been mentally and physically exhausted – we have been cold and damp – we have had a lot of minor injuries – my legs look like a Dalmatian's legs – my head has dents and bumps – banging it on the spray hood – the chart table (which is heavy slamming on it – twice!) my fingers have been burned on the oven and we are tired – tired. And we miss Bear so much that our hearts hurt too.

But despite all of this we know we have made one of the best decisions of our lives.

We cannot wait for the next phase – Simon, the delivery skipper, and crew arrive on Wednesday and then we leave the cosy safety of Port Solent Harbour for the sea.

I asked him what route he is planning and what food we should get for our 8 – 12 days at sea – thought you might like to see his reply:

"Dependent upon wind direction either staying closer to the UK coast and then crossing shipping lanes in the western approaches, or crossing the channel sooner and following the French coast. I would like to stop in Camaret, which is a pretty little French fishing town just west of Brest. Here we can obtain the latest forecasts before crossing Biscay. After Biscay, dependent upon fuel / food supplies, a nice place to stop is Baiona, which is just in Spain. Earlier places to pull into if weather is no good are Vigo and surrounding rivers. From here it is a relatively straight trip to the majestic Cape St. Vincent, where we turn towards Lagos! The nearest airport to Lagos is Faro, approx. 50 miles away.

Food wise, I do not have a specific list on paper, however items which work well are usually quick meals with little input or preparation time – especially if it is bumpy! Just the normal type food eaten at home is fine. Porridge for breakfast is always nice especially at this time of year! Cup-a-soup / sandwiches for lunches / larger meal for dinner – pies / pasta / lasagna / stews etc. Some of these can be made beforehand and frozen, so all that is required is to heat up in the oven. Bottled water / fizzy & still. Energy drinks such as Gatorade is about the best for keeping hydrated properly.

Lots of snacks – cereal bars, chocolate biscuits / energy bars etc. are good. Ribena or similar for hot drinks is always good! Ginger biscuits and ginger cake help with seasickness (and morale!!)

Foods to avoid would be greasy / fatty foods as these are harder to digest and stay in the stomach longer which quite often make people feel unwell!

Grab bag foods would include cereal bars, energy bars and water / Gatorade / electrolyte type drinks.

I would imagine it would be around lunch time when we will be arriving next Wednesday.

I am very much looking forward to it, I hope you have a waterproof video camera to record the journey!

Best wishes,
Simon
Simon Phillips
Managing Director
RYA Yachtmaster Commercially Endorsed & RYA Instructor

Our first day out on Magic and thinking about crossing the Bay of Biscay in November!

We have been moored up in Port Solent since we moved on board on the 6th November. Big Brother House voice – 'Day 18 on the Magic yacht'

We decided to take Magic out to test systems – we haven't got our Main Sail back yet – we are having a third reef put in that is to make the sail smaller for high winds – thinking about the Bay of Biscay at this time of year. If we can make the mainsail small then it is easier to handle.

We got Magic ready – and put May into her new life jacket – she looked smart. As we moved out of the marina into the harbour I realized that we would always have to take extra care with May. Portsmouth Harbour is interesting with lots to see – Spinnaker Tower, Navy installations, The Marie Rose… it made me think of all the sailors over the years and how they must have felt leaving safe harbour.

We were thinking of the Bay of Biscay. It is thought by sailors to be one of the most treacherous stretches of water in the world – so of course it puts fear and dread into most amateur sailors hearts. The reason for the jeopardy is something to do with the power of the Atlantic Ocean cramming into a relatively small horseshoe shaped area.

I was told – "*oh no – you should **definitely not** cross Biscay in November – wait in the UK until the Spring*" and "*You won't get insurance to do the crossing at that time of year*" and "*you are mad!*" But – being a classic polar responder – those sorts of comments make me even more determined that we should go.

The Cruising Association recently ran a course on crossing the Bay of Biscay but as we are going with a professional skipper – we thought that would be the best training course we could get! Simon has done the crossing many times at this time of year and the key is to is creep around the coast and then when you get close to the Bay of Biscay you wait for a good weather window and go for it!

We have all the safety gear on board and the right clothes – There will be four humans sailing – and of course May – we thought that someone should always be on 'May watch!' to make sure she is safe and happy. The challenge for May is that she has no idea what is about to happen. At least we can discuss it and mentally prepare. We will make her a priority with one of us holding her if we are sailing in rough weather.

No Main Sail, Heating STILL doesn't work – May has tried to eat our neighbour's Parrot and Mark has lost his Passport!!

To be honest we are now exhausted and stressed out of our heads – overwhelmed, cold and sleep deprived –we are working 15 hour days.

We have so very much going – I am sure that my brain will pop – it is all exciting but also it is too frantic and intense – somehow this isn't what we signed up for…..yet

Tuesday now and we are both on the boat – there are workmen and tools everywhere – Mark has lost his passport so we are now adding that to the list of things to worry about.

I am not sure what time we will set sail on Thursday morning as that will require some planning and checking tide tables to get out of the harbour!

I say 'we' because having looked at all the options for me to drive to Portugal it seemed easier for me to join the crew. We didn't want to take the Landrover with us and you cannot hire a car in the UK and drive it to Portugal. So, decision made. May and I are joining the crew. I am anxious about the journey but relieved as I would rather be with Mark on the crossing.

We cannot wait to pull out of the Marina and be on our way as at least it means we will not be rushing around in cars and trains seeing clients and doing last minute shopping and planning.

Some funny things have happened today– the heating engineer arrived and pronounced he couldn't do it – the mainsail guy still hasn't confirmed if it will be ready – and during all the chaos May found her way onto our neighbour's yacht and tried to eat their parrot!

Mark heard loud squawking and had to go on their boat and grab May – there were a few feathers about the place and the parrot looked quite cross but was fine.

There are 50 essential jobs still to do in the next 24 hours but our electrician has decided that the LED coloured lighting is the most important —this is just madness. But we are getting used to madness.

My dear friend Claire in Ireland wrote to me with some warm, kind wisdom:

Darling heart.

First, remember to breathe. Also, when I am stressed out I go outside and look at the sky and try to hear some bird song. If there is no bird song then I look at roof tops or tree tops or clouds.

By now you will be in full flow. And by the end of today – Monday will be over . But that means only two more frantic days till you are on the open sea.

Beginnings are exhausting and endings are the same but you can't have one without the....other. That bit should be sung to the tune of Love and Marriage by Frank Sinatra. I have helpfully attached a YouTube link of the song

Massive hug to my brave sailor.

It's so good to be loved! Having the support of close friends seems as essential as food and drink now – that and being an optimist helps.

I am sure that the heating will eventually be fixed, I have faith that the mainsail will arrive and that the 50 other jobs will be completed, Mark will find or replace his passport, the weather will be fair for our crossing and I am sure the Parrot will recover perfectly from May's visit!

Penultimate night and what a night ...where is Mark's Passport

What a day...there are so many jobs to do and the heating is still not working – Mark's lost Passport was the major form of entertainment and gave us about 24 hours of gut-wrenching stress – until I finally figured out in a moment of unusual clarity that it could be in the loan car we had handed back. When we had our Landrover Defender serviced they had lent us a car. I thought – I am sure the Passport is in that car. We called the Garage and they said the car would be back at 5.30pm – At 5.15pm we were there but the manager said that the loan car would now not be back until noon tomorrow – OMFG!!!! The delivery skipper, Simon and crew are arriving tomorrow – what would we do if Mark's passport is not in the car – call them and cancel and delay by 5 days to get a new passport? (We know it was 5 days as we had called the passport office earlier in the day).

The manager in the garage told Mark that he would not call the customer who now had the loan car as he did not want to disturb them – great customer service but another sleepless night of worry for us. When Mark told me what the man in the garage said – I decided I could not have another sleepless night and I hopped out of the car and into the dealership to plead with the manager *"Please could you call the customer and explain our situation we are about to set sail and we really need to know if Mark's passport is in the loan car..."* Thankfully he said yes, called the customer and their customer checked the car ... **YES** Mark's passport was in the loan car – so we CAN go on Thursday morning after all. I do love having good persuasion skills! What a relief.

We both feel literally sick and tired of all the stress it has been such a roller coaster.

Today we had one of our indulgences delivered on board and it cheered us up –
Baseball caps – jackets – polo shirts and T-shirts with our boat name on – as well as
helm covers, the sail bag and of course a T-Shirt for May all with "TEAM MAGIC"
printed or stitched on. Essential? I think so.

It keeps hitting us in waves what a VERY BIG adventure we are about to embark
upon – we cannot believe that we are finally ready.

Here we go…finally

So, this is it, our last night in Port Solent, Portsmouth – we leave the harbour at
noon tomorrow. There has been some (ok, a lot of) stress but also lots of fun and a
steep learning curve – which we love.

We were advised to stay the winter in the UK to get to know the boat and ensure
we had all the work completed – We chose to ignore that advice and stay for only 3
weeks then head out and cross Biscay – don't do this at home as 'they' say - I have
always wondered who 'they' are.

Having a deadline *has* meant we had stress and pressure but it has also meant that
we got what we needed doing, done – we even managed to get some things we
didn't 'need' doing – our TV, our Team Magic Gear, our LED coloured lighting –
fun things that will ensure that it really will be home from home and not a
compromise.

As for getting to know the boat well we will get to know her crossing Biscay
and during the whole of our 8-12-day journey to Lagos. We are delighted to be
travelling with the very calm and experienced Simon Phillips from Seaway – he is
a Yacht Master and RYA instructor and a pragmatic and intelligent leader. For us it
will be like an 8-12-day training course.

We also think that the added benefit of *not* staying in the UK during November,
December and January can be summed up by the thoughts of our Christmas lunch
in the sun– Sardines on the push-pit BBQ with some Port….. I do think we are
making a good choice.

Christmas without our family will be a first, ….the kids are all busy with their
fantastic careers and happy lives – they all have plans for Christmas this year – so
this is the first year that we will have Christmas on our own after 25 years of family
rearing. I am not sure how alone we will be however as the Cruising fraternity in
Lagos is already welcoming us – they have a membership called 'The Navigators'
and we already have invitations to the Christmas Carols and Portuguese lessons.

In the morning, I will swap my work clothes for Oilskins and boots and switch planning trains and tubes for doing a passage plan and checking tide tables not time tables.

Mark wants to slip the lines – that was the prominent moment in his dream of going sailing. Then, we will sail out to sea – past the Isle of Wight and away. The passage plan is dependent upon wind direction we will either be staying closer to the UK coast and then crossing shipping lanes in the western approaches, or crossing the channel sooner and following the French coast. I would like to stop in Camaret, which is a pretty little French fishing town just west of Brest.

So that's that – we leave at noon.

Mark and May enjoying some time relaxing in Magic's beautiful Saloon.

Chapter Two

SETTING SAIL FROM THE UK

Five Days of Adventure – dolphins and stars, fun and frustration
and a rather nice man called Stig with a volt-meter!

We had shared our MMSI number (that's a number that is unique to Magic) with
some friends and family so they could track us on ship finder Apps. We were
surprised and delighted at how many of them were following our journey. We felt
looked after.

During the night, the wind crept up and the swell built and soon it was
uncomfortable. To stay on the deck was to be cold and blown about and to go below
was to feel disorientated and randomly fall about, bashing arms and legs against
all the unfamiliar objects. I even crawled about on the floor to obtain items from
cupboards! Our crew is fantastic – Peter is hard working and knows his stuff. We
feel we are in safe hands but we are anxious wondering 'what have we done!?' May
wasn't at all sure and we took turns to make sure she was alright. We found that
holding her really helped – she felt reassured and it was comforting for us in return
to feel her warm little body in our arms.

After five hours of being bashed about Simon gently suggested that we 'could'
spend a more comfortable night if we went into Portland and sheltered. By 11pm
we were working together on docking – it was a very tricky affair in the dark with
the wind howling and waves crashing around us but by midnight thanks to Simon's
skill we were tucked up in safe harbour listening to the wild wind whistling through
our shrouds – good decision we all thought.

May had been wonderful the whole time – a little anxious and shivery but really
a trooper. Our main concern was that she had not used her toilet since we had left

Port. As soon as we docked Mark took her for a long walk and she was relieved – Mark came back on board and announced "May is empty" so we entered that into the ships log.

Day one of our new way of life was over and we all had a glass of wine at the saloon table and went to bed, wind-swept with red faces and exhausted. We had only travelled from Portsmouth to Portland but it felt like we were on another planet and had travelled hundreds of miles. We slept well.

Friday 28th November Portland for the night

Waking in Portland Marina was interesting – the wind was howling through the rigging making it sound scary. Seals were bobbing up to have a look at us and the seagulls circled overhead. In the distance people were windsurfing and paragliding – proving the meaning of "it's an ill wind that doesn't blow someone some good". We all went to shower and then had a breakfast of porridge and toast aboard.

The wind was wild and even in the protected marina the sea was choppy. It made us so relieved that Simon had decided to take us to shelter. All showered and rested we set to on small tasks like putting markers on the anchor chain and doing a small repair to the shore power line. Simon also created a new line for our third reef to ensure we could use it easily when we crossed the Bay of Biscay.

At around 11am we decided to take a walk up into Portland – a very steep walk up and out of the marina into the town on an adventure to find a bakery – The co-op seemed to be the only shop so we got bread there and Peter, one of our able crew – who is also, rather usefully, a chef got the ingredients for Chicken à la King – one of my favourites for dinner that night.

The light grey Portland stone cottages overlooking the sea were beautiful, this Jurassic coast is stunning.

One thing that we love about our new life is having time to talk and listen! During one of our chats Simon had been talking with us about the many things that had gone wrong with Magic since we had bought her – a lot always needs fixing on yachts all the time but Simon thought we had had more than our fair share of problems.

He suggested that perhaps a de-naming and re-naming ceremony was required. I did some research on the proper manner of this ceremony and we decided to create a modern version. In brief – Neptune and Poseidon keep a log of all the ships and their names and allow them safe passage. So, basically, we had to tell them to update their database!!

We also had to remove all references of the boat's previous name from anywhere on or in the boat. After a, thorough inspection we found some traces of her old name. There were two stickers with 'il Sogno' on the helm and in the chart table there was a Cork key ring with the previous name written on – all were removed off the boat.

Another part of the ceremony is to write the old name on a small ship and drop it into the water. Where to find a small ship? In a quirky shop in town – a lovely man was meticulously painting toy soldiers and displaying them in cases, we found the perfect little model boat – it was £2.50 but with my famous negotiation skills I purchased it for £3.00! The man asked us where we were sailing to (he knew we were sailors as we were wearing all posh new gear with 'Team Magic' on) when we told him The Algarve – he screwed up his face and said – "Hum… Biscay in November" we were getting used to that response.

May helps me to drop the little boat into the sea from Magic's bow as part of our re-naming ceremony. Simon and Mark look on at the very serious proceedings

Back to the boat for some 'down time' and some vital weather and passage planning. The wind had only been a force 6 but at night in the rain and near to Portland Bill the 'wind over tide' had whipped up a nasty sea state. We planned to make up the time by heading out the following morning and heading straight to Portugal without stopping. The weather looked perfect and Mark and I were excited by the prospect a non-stop passage.

That evening the five of us went to the Marina bar for a couple of pints – 'Proper Job' beer, it was delicious and, we thought it had an appropriate name – then home for the much anticipated Chicken a la King – I love this dish, as it was one of the staples I was brought up on. I usually make mine with a roux as a base but Chef Peter used cream and it was quicker and better – a revelation. So – onions sweated down, chicken fried in them until brown then chopped mushrooms and red pepper – cooked in fresh cream with salt, pepper and garlic. Served with Basmati rice. We enjoyed our meal together in the lovely, cosy Saloon of Magic with a few glasses of wine – pretty civilised!

Then a walk for May and bed.

Reflecting on the past days as we fell asleep we reviewed how the heating still doesn't work, nor does the TV, and the LED lighting throughout the boat is not right (some are out altogether, some way too hot) and the auto pilot is still not functioning. It is infuriating how many things need fixing on a boat all the time.

We can get some help in Lagos. The critical thing is that the boat sails well – she is safe and she is fast!

Day Three: Saturday 29th November
Set sail from Portland to Portugal

We woke up to calm water and beautiful sunshine – time to go!

We got the boat ready for 4 days at sea – extra gas and water on board. Ever vigilant, Simon asked that we prepare a grab bag (to grab if we must abandon ship!) – The Epirbs – Mars Bars – bottles of water, seasickness tablets and hand warmers. It is important that we are prepared for any issue. Then we ran though the health and safety elements on the boat – fire drills, MOB and use of all the safety equipment – professional and careful. Then we kitted up – we are getting faster at putting on our thermals, oilies, boots and life jackets!!

We made a nest for May – portside deck, by the companion way under the spray hood! Then we carried out our de-naming and re-naming ceremony from the foredeck. I asked the gods of the sea to remove 'il Sogno' from their records and add Magic – affording her all the same rights and privileges of safe passage. Peter took photos to mark the occasion. Then we picked up our steps and slipped the lines, brought in and stowed the fenders and were away into the Channel.

As we are at sea all the time we have a watch system. When I learned to sail, we did four hours on and four hours off – 24 hours a day but that is exhausting. Simon prefers watches of 4 hours in the day and 2 hours at night. So, for example – Simon does 06.00 until 10.00 then it's me 10.00 – 14.00 then it is Mark 14.00 until 18.00 then Peter 18.00-22.00 then Simon 22.00 – 00.00

Then I do 22.00 – 02.00 and then Mark is 02.00 – 04.00 etc.

Now it is my watch 10 .00 – 14.00 and we are sailing in 1m waves and light winds with the sun shining what bliss – this is our new life. From the helm, I watched May sleeping in her little on deck nest and beside her was Mark smiling and I imagined many more happy days like this to come.

Perfect sailing all day and all night – we crossed the shipping channel under Simon's watchful eye – wow those tankers are HUGE – I thought one of them was

Guernsey! We watched the sun go down and were then given quite a display as the orange waxing moon rose.

By morning we will be North of Roscoff.

We took some time to think about our plan: Sunday lunchtime we predict we will begin crossing the infamous Bay of Biscay. That will be on my watch and I am excited and anxious. Simon is with us and we literally trust him with our lives. It is a crossing of 350 miles so we will have completed the crossing by Tuesday lunchtime. Then Wednesday or Thursday we will be moving down the coast of Spain and Portugal – we may even pop into Bayona for Tapas – then we should arrive in Lagos around Friday.
That is not your usual week, is it?

We had lasagna and baby broad beans for supper – I cooked – well what I mean is I put the water on for the beans and put the lasagna in the oven and served!!

I take over the night watch from Simon and walking from the dark saloon up the companionway stairs towards him in the cockpit was like walking up the stairs into a sparkling heaven. The night air was warm and there was not a single cloud in the sky, only inky blackness and thousands of stars. As my eyes became accustomed to the darkness I watched in rapture as Simon pointed out the 12 dolphins surrounding our boat, whizzing along beside us like some magical, inky-coated, honor guard. I could see their dorsal fins as they surfaced in turns and their grey shiny backs were flecked with magical phosphoresce – green sparkles. I imagined them playing beneath us.

The main sail was up fully and the perfectly sliced half-moon cast a silver shadow across the sea. The swell bulged making the horizon appear as if there were hills in the distance and Magic sailed effortlessly over it all. We were navigating by the stars, which I find impossibly romantic. You make sure you are on the right course and then rather than steer to the compass or the electronic instruments – you pick a star that is in just the right place between the shrouds and keep it there.

Dolphins beside me and under my feet and steering by the stars – I was so very happy. This is what we came for – I reflected on how little of the outside I have seen in the last few years and now the sky is our roof. It is such a wonder and a privilege to experience such magic.

Day Four: Sunday 30th November
Reluctantly in Camaret – Beer, Batteries and a
rather nice Swedish guy called Stig

As is usually the way of things every silver lining has a cloud – today we had hoped to be able to grab the excellent weather window and keep going South but we have more issues – the heating still doesn't work and the LED bulbs are still a problem – but those are the least of the problems – the new and altogether more important issue is that the batteries are not charging. This is potentially dangerous as without them we them we cannot pump out the bilges, have navigation instruments or lights. This is an issue that Simon highlighted to us following his delivery trip from Bruinesse to Portsmouth. So, checking the batteries was one of the first issues we had looked at in Portsmouth and the declaration from the 'experts' was that all was well and in working order – not so.

This is bad as it could literally have put us all at risk – we are not happy.

We have had to turn everything off including the fridge and freezer so we preserve the power for the instruments – we are going to be navigating some tricky waters in the infamous Chanel du Fort which is North of Camaret and if we have no navigation instruments it would be very dangerous.

We crossed our fingers that the battery power would last as we passed some enormous and vicious looking black, jagged rocks with waves crashing up on them. The batteries are supposed to take on a charge as you motor but they were not. We cannot risk the Biscay crossing with no electric. So, we are now reluctantly heading to Camaret to make a stop, but as it is Sunday and as we will arrive late we will not get help today. So, in the morning once the engine has cooled we can look at the issue and consider if we can fix it or if we need professional help. I guess this is what sailing is – fixing things, spending money on fixing things and changing plans so that things can be fixed!

We had so hoped we could just crack on as we were getting into the rhythm of the watches and being at sea full time – it is an irritation to have to call into a harbour. However, that is sailing and we will enjoy Camaret and even stock up on wine and cheese for our trip across Biscay, which now looks like it will be Monday or Tuesday – that is *if* we can find another good weather window.

Having just completed my 4 hours on the helm I am tired. May and I have gone to our cabin for a break and I am sipping hot tea and cuddling my hot water bottle and eating a slice of ginger cake. May is by my feet and seems cheerful enough, she doesn't get sea sick and has generally good sea legs. The only issue is once again she hasn't been to the toilet since we left Portland and I hope it won't make her ill, she is such a good dog I am sure she cannot face the prospect of going to the toilet in our home. It is a challenge for her to figure out what is inside and what is outside.

We have put a dog toilet made of Astroturf on the 'Poop Deck" (and that is the proper name for it!) and we even had her use it ashore– but now she refuses to go.

As for me well, everything aches. I have a cold sore and a spot! I know my body is telling me it is running on empty when I get a cold sore – and I haven't had a spot for about 20 years! I am looking forward to taking time off in Lagos and repairing mind, body and boat.

Mark is a trooper – but then he does look after himself better than I do – he takes breaks and rests and doesn't let himself get exhausted or stressed. He was a little nauseous earlier today but thankfully that seems to have passed. Perhaps the problem with me is not exhaustion and stress but that I haven't had any alcohol for over 24 hours as we are ' a dry boat' when we are night sailing and running a watch system.

I was sound asleep when Mark rushed into our cabin. *"Where is the French Courtesy flag?"* he asked. I was bleary eyed and honestly couldn't think what the hell he was talking about — France? Flags? What day is it? Where am I? Then I woke up more fully and could tell him. I got up and quickly dressed so I could go on deck to help with fenders and lines as we pulled into Camaret Harbour.

It's a horrible situation not just because we are missing the perfect weather window to cross Biscay but also because we feel we have been let down – these batteries had been checked in Holland and in Portsmouth – both on land and sea in each case. They were declared fine and they are not fine.

All the flooring is lifted to review the batteries and Simon is doing his best to identify the problem but we don't have a battery tester. He suggested that Mark and I go ashore to see if we could find one which presented another challenge for us - It is Sunday night and we are in in a small French town searching for a battery tester. All the shops were shut except for a bakery and an Irish Bar. We considered that the bakery would not have a battery tester so we thought we would use our initiative and bought bread and cake for the troops and then went to the Irish Bar to see if we could find someone to help us.

We found Stig – an ex Swedish Navy man who was sailing his small boat single handed from Sweden to the Canary Islands and then on to the Bahamas. He is a wonderful guy, a true adventurer. Like us he was stuck here. His problem is worse than ours however as his Yanmar engine had completely ceased. He was hoping he could replace it for an old one at £5k but thought he might have to purchase a new one at £15k, we felt for him, we were all stuck and longed to be making the most of the fine weather to cross Biscay. He is lovely – a salty sea dog – we swapped tales of the sea and then we asked him if he had a volt meter and of course he did, so he walked with us back to his boat, even though he was about to have a pizza in the bar (he told us they do a pizza which has a croissant dough base and seafood topping which is very strange but out of this world!) As Mark and Stig left the bar I gave the bar tender ten euros, which is the price of a pizza for Stig.

Back on Magic Simon is doing his best to see what is wrong as every hour that passes we watch our precious weather window disappearing– perhaps he can fix the issue or perhaps we will have to wait until Monday morning and stay here. Either way it is frustrating as we had a survey in Holland and then some fixes then paid for the surveyor to return to check all was well – we had a sea trial and we had the batteries checked in Portsmouth and we were told all was well….. we have been let down. After some further diagnostics, our batteries have been pronounced dead! So, we are currently stranded in Camaret.

You may think, 'ah that's ok, just change the batteries' – but it is 10 batteries and there are none here in Camaret – there are two in Brest and two elsewhere in France – we have to order them and then have them fitted – it is Monday now and they won't arrive until tomorrow afternoon at the earliest – then we have to have them fitted. By then the weather will be bad again – force 8 and rain, so it seems the new plan is that we will set sail again on Wednesday afternoon, that should enable us to get to Lagos on Monday or Tuesday!! I suppose it's only a 3 or 4-day delay and it all adds to this adventure. Then there is the rising cost – the delay costs us more days of Simon and Peter's time and of course the 10 new batteries

The cost of the new batteries? Well that is only €2,000…..!

I thought it would be good to note the highs such as last night, under the stars with the dolphins and the lows to ensure this whole adventure isn't romanticised.

No Advent Calendar and still waiting for a weather window – but the spot and cold sore are gone!

Monday 1st and Tuesday 2nd December and we have no advent calendar.

Mark and I remembered that neither of us had brought an advent calendar – that must be the first time ever that we have not had one, it doesn't seem like the run up to Christmas. It is odd – this journey is so all consuming that nothing else is on our minds.

Waiting…

When you are given, Lemons make Lemonade. Simon, is busy rigging in a third reef and helping to fix the VHF and the TV, so as we sit we are improving the yacht . We were surprised, again, at the price of things – the line (in sailing speak you call rope – line) for the third reef was €297 and the block was €80 – the time invested in this new rigging would have cost us even more but as Simon is on board he is doing it as part of our delivery package – so in the end the waiting is a benefit.

It isn't all tough. Whilst waiting we have been forced to eat more light and delicious Bretton Pastries, and enjoy the delicious butter and out of this world cheese and pâté. Also, we have also had to drink the local cider which is AMAZING – There is an artist's quarter here too and the work is exciting and very classy.

As I write, cosy and sipping café au lait in the Hotel Styvel on the harbour front, the wind is howling a gale. We walked May along the harbour wall and she looked like she was being tested in a wind tunnel! When Simon looked at the sky he said – "Mackerel sky's and Mare's tails make tall ships use small sails". It is a force 8 here and a force 9 in Biscay – we are happy to wait!!

I have noticed that when the seagulls take flight in this wind they seem to just stay in one place – suspended in the air as if tethered to the ground like a gull kite. The spray is being flicked off the breakers over the harbour wall giving us blasts of surprising sea water spritz as we walk into town.

The engineer guys are on board fitting the new batteries – Never thought I would be excited about spending nearly £2000 on batteries –"whooo hoo we have 10 shiny new Bosch L5013's"

Mark and I decided to get out of the way. We did some washing in the Launderette (€10 to wash and €6 to dry – excuse me but that seems a bit much!) we had lunch in a small bar – odd but delicious   tartiflette pizza! And we met Stig again – he really is a cool guy – he lived in LA for years working in the film industry – producing films and writing theme music. His boat is beautiful with a dark blue hull and classic lines. Stig is thinking of going sailing without an engine!! all the way to the Bahamas – his only other choice is to stay in Camaret until they find a replacement engine, which he is not sure will happen in a hurry. He said " well the only issue will be getting into safe harbour in a storm under sail, with no engine it is very, very tricky" Brave man!

We have a delicious beef stew on the go for this evening's meal, which we will eat after a short visit to the Irish Bar which is compulsory. Then tomorrow, Wednesday we will continue to sort, tidy and fix. Today is Tuesday – we keep looking at the weather and it seems that we cannot leave until Thursday morning – meaning we will arrive Monday 8th or Tuesday 9th December

Wednesday 3rd December .
Still stranded in Camaret…a bearded lady and an electrician called Christophe

Now Camaret Sur Mer is lovely – but I wish we could leave.

Of course, when you stop you notice more things. Here in Camaret, the grey mullet swim in their hundreds by the harbour wall and the little jellyfish float in drifts. Local people gather on the harbour wall and fish for squid – the gray concrete is splashed with black ink – it made me feel sad for the frightened squid.

Everyday seems to bring more jobs, more broken things and more expense. I cannot remember when I felt more ignorant – a fast learning curve and a draining bank account is exhausting.

Today's surprise was that even though we invested £2,000 in new batteries – they are still not charging as the alternator is now broken – the electrician has been on board for hours and is still tutting! His verdict – *"the problem comes from the little box"* whatever that is. He says,
   "I don't know where I can find it or how long it will take " – great!

It is now 5.30pm and we were hoping to leave tomorrow morning at 8am . There is another good weather window opening. I just don't want to miss another weather window, as I am not sure how many more there will be. The appeal of the Bretton croissants, butter and cheese is now waning as we just want to leave and we wish that things would 'just work'. I know more experienced 'live aboards' will tell you that fixing things is a constant as is spending money – but really – this is running at around £1,000 a day – surely it must at least slow down soon. I had roughly packed my Buddha and my lucky bamboo plant under the bed last time we were out at sea so they wouldn't get damaged – I have just taken them out for some TLC and to wish us some luck.

I have just glanced at the electrician who is still tutting and now reading a manual – urghh this is not a good sign. The alternator is working now but the regulator is now the thing that is not working and needs parts – Christophe (the electrician) says that there is a 'work around' that he can rig up tomorrow morning so we can go. It is so challenging to keep up with all the technicalities.

Crew Check:

Mark is coping better than me – he is so calm and centered. He keeps reminding me that we don't have to be anywhere for a particular time.

   Tina, I don't know why but I just need to let frustration out – feeling a diva foot stomping coming on. But at least I got to go to the hairdresser where a bearded lady cut my hair – not a bad cut and it feels better.

May is calm and looking lovely. She needed her hair doing too and I finally brushed her to a point where all her knots are gone. I also trimmed her so we now both have our hair cut.

Simon is a super star – he is fixing everything and looking after everyone. He never stops and is consistently polite, calm and softly spoken. Nothing seems to faze him in the slightest and he plans for everything to ensure we are safe.

Peter is not only our first mate but also chef – he has planned all our meals for the next 5 days at sea and done the shopping. He is funny and interesting – he has travelled a lot and worked in the Bahamas as a chef.

Equipment check

No charge is going to the batteries, The TV and The Heating are still not working and now also we have no internet – the card that was fitted to the Wi-Fi that was fitted to the boat in Portsmouth is a phone card and not a data card and we need a data card for internet in main land Europe – who would have known. The LED lights still are not the right ones and the coloured LEDs that were fitted in Portsmouth have all fallen off where they were fixed and some of them have gone the wrong colour as they are broken. Simon is not happy with the position or the lighting on the compass as it is difficult to steer by. Two new bulbs have just been fitted to the compass and both blew!

I think how spoilt we were in our on-land home where everything worked and if, on the odd occasion it didn't then someone who we trusted was on hand in minutes to fix it. Also, if we wanted to go somewhere, we just did, no weather window watching. The other thing I wasn't quite prepared for was how physical it all is. That is of course a good thing as we will both be leaner and fitter! But now everything hurts – we walk miles every day and when we are not walking we are lifting and fixing and scrubbing and hauling.

I think the things that we are both struggling with the most are:-

1. **Ignorance is not Bliss.**
    We are not sure how a lot of things work and so cannot fix them when they are broken or indeed understand if we are being ripped off.

2. **We are out of touch**
    I cannot get the Internet on and it is weird and not fun – we miss our contact with the outside world and looking things up when needed.

3. **We are not in control**
    Ok, now we know how much control we had of our lives before we lived aboard and now we don't – things break, the weather changes and people let you down.

But this is what we came for – the challenge, the change, the experience, the adventure, the unknown. We are learning to adapt but it is harder than we thought.

And guess what – we ARE sailing tomorrow – we will leave at lunch-time and will not be stopping for 4-5 days until we are in Portugal. Well that is the plan

Chapter Three

BISCAY BOTHER

Sailing across the Bay of Biscay in December with a Dog, a broken autopilot, a piece of grass called 'Le sod' and learning that I can fly....

I started my day awoken by excited voices, wooden clunks and metal clanks coming from near our deck. It was the people on Belle Poule a beautiful square rigger that had pulled in last night – a French sail training ship. That's one of the lovely things about sailing – you never know who you are going to wake up beside. It brought back many happy memories of my time at sea with the Ocean Youth Club – sailing from Northern Ireland to Scotland and from Wales to Norway – good times.

We started the day with chores – I set out on one of the foldable bikes. They cycle better now that they are adjusted correctly and the tyres are pumped up! However, the handlebar was not fully tight and I fell off – lucky escape – body intact – ego bruised! I fixed the bike and carried on. As I am becoming fitter and better at fixing things these knocks are not so challenging.

I cycled to the chandlery to collect the block for our third reef. Did they, have it? "No, or rather "Non!" They had sent it to the wrong town so 'that was that', as we are planning to leave in a couple of hours. I cycled back to the boat – we are becoming used to being let down and we just move on.

We cleaned and sorted the boat. Our electrician turned up to quietly and professionally finish the work he had begun yesterday. Only another few hundred quid!! His 'work around' would fix the issue of our new batteries not charging. I wasn't sure how and I wasn't able to ask as I knew I wouldn't understand the answer! Not because of his French but because it was technical.

We ate a breakfast of delicious fresh Bretton crusty bread and golden yellow butter and then it was time to get changed. I am getting used to putting on 3 thermal layers – oilskins, boots, a life jacket and gloves. It was raining, grey and very cold – again. I do wish we had managed to get the heating system working. We probably won't even need it in the Algarve!

I was on watch when we departed Camaret at 11.00 until 14.00 after which it was Mark's turn. In four more hours, we will reach Biscay. The weather was good – a heavy swell but only a light wind. The sea looked very strange like hammered lead. Four hours doesn't seem like a lot but when everyone else is down below resting and keeping warm and you are alone on deck in the cold and the driving rain it is a long time. Our watches are made even more challenging, as the autopilot doesn't work. It engages but then goes 2 degrees of course every couple of seconds – that is not good! So, we all had to manually steer. Good experience I suppose.

Coming off watch I was cold in my core, my toes were numb. As I always do when I travel I had brought my trusty 'hottie' so I boiled the kettle poured the hot water carefully in the 'hottie' and cuddled in my bunk to warm up. I took May with me as she is still a little anxious – the swaying and all the bangs and crashes disturb her. May had not enjoyed the morning and had been a little bit sea sick – a cuddle and a rest with me would make her feel better.

It is important that all the crew are rested, warm and well fed and watered as we have 4-5 days at sea ahead of us. I do hope May will learn to poo and wee aboard this time – she will have to! We had the idea to cut a sod of grass and put it on her dog toilet in the hope that might help her. Mark went and got a sod of earth this morning. I thought he would return with a neat little square but instead turned up with a huge sod of earth with long grass on it. We put it on the poop deck on top of her dog toilet.

May was not impressed. It was named "Le sod"

Friday 5th – December
Moonlight and singing to whales

We are getting into the rhythm of the watch system. Waking 30 minutes before you are on night watch to get dressed in all the gear and go outside, clip on the safety harness and receive handover instructions from whoever is on the helm. We sailed happily though the night – sailing by the stars, with a full bright moon (running out of ways to describe how beautiful the moon on the water is – silver on black is so cheesy but at least it matches our boat!) and the dolphins and waves. It's all so breathtaking. I finished my watch and handed over to Mark. 14.00 I had noticed that the wind was getting up and noted the change in the barometer.

It was Mark's watch from 14.00 until 18.00. With the auto pilot broken it is tiring having to actively steer for four hours – keeping the wind in the right place for the sails and keeping on course means you cannot lose concentration for even a moment to sip tea or put on warm gloves.

At around 16.30 a squall hit us hard and too quickly to prepare, there was some very loud and violent banging and slapping, the preventer (a rope that is used to secure the boom in place when the wind is coming from behind) had broken allowing a crash Gybe (that is basically not good – it is when the boom flies over from one side of the yacht to the other) This snapped the battens in the mainsail and damaged one of the blocks. A crash Gybe is feared by sailors because when the boom whips uncontrollably across the boat at a great speed people can be killed.

There was a lot of unfamiliar noise and in the dark and the increasing swell Mark, May and I were feeling very anxious. Simon however was calm and professional as always. He sprang into action – threw on his life jacket and went on deck. His demeanor had changed, he was still calm but now with an acute focus. He took the helm and Peter, who by now was also up, was dressed and ready for action. They began to take the main sail down. Although reefed (reducing the sail area), we had too much sail up for the strength of the squall that had hit us.

Peter and Simon worked to get the mainsail down fully but it was still catching in the wind and would not fully come down into the sail bag. Simon and Peter hooked their safety harnesses to the jack stays (safety lines that run the length of the boat) and went on deck. Then they climbed onto the coach house roof to pull the mainsail down and lash it for good measure. The wind was howling through the rigging. Mark was on the helm – he told me later he was thinking which of the man over board pieces of equipment he would use, and in what order, if one of the team had fallen from the deck. We were anxious but in good hands. As I had been off watch I was on 'May watch' – that is I was down below holding May so that she did not fly around like some of the other objects such as the footrest and the charts, the kettle and the bin. We thought we had stowed everything well but you don't know until the sea and the wind get up and you are in the middle of Biscay. If I was needed on deck I would have put May in our cabin but the team had everything under control. I knew where my life jacket was – I was beginning to understand the importance of keeping everything on a boat in the same place at all times so you can find stuff in a hurry or in the dark if needed. Imagine being in the dark and inside an enormous washing machine which is full of large objects flying about – it's a bit like that.

By around 18.30 order had been restored – the Mainsail was down safely and we were sailing with a very small triangle of Genoa (that's the sail at the pointy end), using it as a storm jib. Even with very little sail up we were doing 7 knots - 7 knots is fast on a handkerchief!

Peter had taken the helm for his watch. It was dark now and very cold.

Mark had been fantastic during the last two hours of his watch – he had been anxious and was just about to act himself when Simon and Peter had come to help. This is Biscay in December and it is raw. We are so happy with Simon – we are learning so much about our boat and our own skill level.

Mark told me that the wind instrument had been saying 40 knots (this is classed as a Gale) and then its alarm started sounding and it just said HIGH WIND – no kidding! Gusting higher to 50 knots (this is classed as a storm). The waves were close together and about 16ft.

You can hear the big waves – they have a low growl. We found that with some of the waves we could surf the boat on them and some smashed into us hard jolting everything and everyone on board. Some you looked up at (a bit disconcerting!) and some seemed to slip under the boat powerfully raising us up as if a giant was cupping us in his hands.

It was very cold, wet and windy crossing the Bay of Biscay in December. All our specialist equipment was needed. This is me squall dodging.

I came down below and sat with Mark and Simon as Peter was still on the helm – I was sitting in one of the starboard seats holding May when suddenly, we were hit by a massive wave – it slapped our starboard side hard and literally knocked me clear out of my seat and into the air. I flew several feet up and across the saloon. I dropped May and then landed hard on my bum on the floor at Simon's feet. I was winded and afraid and I immediately knew that I had done some damage to my lower back – it hurt a lot. I was in shock but was desperate to get up, I had that thick ache of bruised bones and I was disorientated at the sensation of how one moment all was well and the next I was flying through the air and crashing into the floor. I was so lucky I didn't do more damage. I knew I had injured my coccyx as it is a very specific pain. I have had an injured coccyx before from a car accident, so I knew it would take months to heal.

The weather eventually settled down and we were all a lot happier. Peter had made a delicious stew with Veal and Bretton smoked sausage. Simon is always ready to eat but Mark, Peter, May and I passed on the food. The hours of storm battling anxiety had taken its toll. I went to bed wanting to get some rest before my watch at midnight. Although I was nursing a very sore back I enjoyed the movement of the boat now gently rocking me to sleep as the water sloshed and whooshed past my head – our cabin is at the very front of the boat and I love the sound of the water parting in front of us so close to my head.

May was now getting her sea legs. It is interesting to watch her move her little body to steady herself and she knows how useful corners are to stop slippage. She has even learned to use the heads (the toilets) and I am delighted with this as I was getting concerned for her. I had put an old smelly towel down and encouraged her – this is a good place for her to go to the loo as we can easily clean it and it is safe and out of the way. Clever little May.

When I awoke at 11.30 to take my watch I could hardly move, my back was so sore and seized up. I moved carefully to the end of the bed – which took some gentle wiggling – then there was the matter of standing and getting on more layers – including oilskins – thermal socks, boots and life jackets. The boat was moving about erratically (not good for an injured back). Dressing in this environment is hard to describe – sort of like trying to get dressed into unfamiliar clothing in a small damp fridge, which is also a tumble dryer, which is also in the dark.

Then add to that being in agony and tired, wet and cold and as you are attempting to put your boots on someone comes up and shoves you hard on the shoulder so that you stumble and fall on the floor– and this happens every time you get dressed. Being jolted about is not easy at the best of times but with my bashed lower back it made it all the worse.

Being at sea for days you must work on your personal resources – you need large quantities of perseverance, tolerance, patience and tenacity. You need Grit!

Out on watch alone under the stars in the middle of the Bay of Biscay and still with high winds and big seas I admit to feeling a little anxious. But also, enjoying the experience always under the watchful eye of Simon. Simon's eyes were not the only benevolent eyes watching over us. As I took the helm a pod of Pilot Whales joined me, it really felt that they were coaching me along – amazing.

I decided to sing to them and they seemed to like it as they stayed alongside me for miles. Bliss.

There are tales to be told: Gale force 8 and Attacked by a Portuguese fishing boat

Mark writes:
The weather was calmer, the cold not so challenging. An hour into the watch and I saw lights way in the distance, the radar picked up a large boat.

Simon had shown us the way to look on the horizon for other ships, in between the waves, sometimes in the mist or the haze. From several miles, away there's only a glimpse, a suggestion of something on the horizon. This was more obvious. I could clearly see the green starboard sidelights, not on our course, plenty of room to go starboard to starboard.

But something wasn't quite right. We were sailing through moderate to rough seas, large swells, gusts, not difficult but not easy to move around because the wind was directly behind us and once again we had the mainsail fixed by a preventer.

I couldn't keep my eyes off the boat; it kept coming and coming closer.
I know I could only see the green starboard lights that meant that we were not on the same course, but I didn't know how close it would come. I looked at the radar and it looked like it was getting closer.

From the glimpse of lights in the distance to bright lights in front of me has taken 20 minutes. If you see just green lights you are sailing parallel, if you see just red lights they are passing in front of you – if you see both red and green they are sailing straight for you.
I'm watching and watching.
Then suddenly right before me red and green lights then a bright white light – full beam lights straight at me. She had changed course and was coming straight at me.

This was a Portuguese fishing boat – probably 120 feet long, a working boat, lights on everywhere, seagulls surrounding it like flies, I could see everyone. This was a rough, tough boat. The noise was powerful, aggressive the boat was crashing through the waves towards me and it forced me to change course. It passed so close.

The shocking thing was from seeing nothing close to us for so long and then so close – the noise, the power and everyone else was fast asleep.

I know fishing boats have the right of way. They go where the fish go, so I guess the fish were under our boat that night, however it's a big ocean out there and they didn't need to come so close.

May has become increasingly happy and settled – she loves being on deck watching the sea birds and keeping an eye on us. She has learned how to steady herself whilst walking around. And I love watching her tilt her head and breath in the sea air though her shiny black little nose.

We are doing well and think we will arrive in Lagos on Tuesday. We have been doing between 7 and 10 knots all the way in 15 – 30 mph winds so we are cracking through the miles.

Monday 8th December
An unexpected Detox and being an alien
Following almost 5 days at sea we are running low on water and we have no fresh milk. UHT should only be used in dire emergency, as it is horrid! The sun is shining and we can even feel it's warmth – finally! We were just passing Cascais in Portugal so, we call in to fill our water tanks.

Good idea – we all wanted to feel that we could use more water as scrimping on water was becoming a bore. Mark took us into the Marina and as we moored up with the four of us getting ropes ready and fenders I wondered how Mark and I will manage when we are on our own. Mark is great at parking and did a super job. As we filled up with water I went to the nearest shop and got milk, chocolate and salad!! I noticed that people were looking at me as I walked passed, as if I were an alien that had landed – then I realised I had my full sailing gear on. I had just got off the boat without even taking off my life jacket and harness – they were in their normal clothes and they looked as odd to me as I must have to them! May enjoyed running around on the grass for a bit and we had lunch while the boat was still and steady.

I had a cracking headache when I awoke the next morning – it felt like a hangover – which was impossible, as I have not had one sip of alcohol for five days. (I know that my friends reading this will not believe me on this one!!) I thought I was perhaps dehydrated so drank a lot of water but Mark thinks that as we have not had tea, coffee or alcohol for days it is a detox. It certainly has been a dramatic detox. No booze, small portions of healthy food, no caffeine, no news, Internet or email and lots of fresh air and exercise. Weird.

Our ETA into Lagos is just after lunch – we hope to get into the Marina, get all ship-shape then sleep for a few hours before getting tidy and going for cocktails (oh yes! oh yes! oh yes!) and then dinner out.

Chapter Four

LAZY LAGOS

Phew we made it

9th December

We did it. We have arrived into Lagos –a surreal moment. We first of all dropped our anchor just off the beach. There we took down our sails and made the deck tidy. At Lagos Marina, there is a harbour entrance that then leads into the river. It is a beautiful way to meet a new place. The sun was shining on the palm trees that fringe the promenade. People were waving to us as we made our way to the reception. I was so happy – we had made it. We were tired but so relieved to have completed our crossing from Portsmouth to Lagos and we were all safe and well – except for our bumps and bruises. We checked into the Marina office but we were asked to wait as our berth was not yet ready – so guess what we did – yup cracked open the wine and had lunch.

We are reflecting on what a good decision it was to leave Portsmouth and come here. How can you regret the decision when we learned so much, had such a great teacher and ended up in the sun? Now every morning we are waking up to the view from our windows on board of blue sky and palm trees – oh yes, and a lovely stork family on top of a nearby abandoned chimney!

As I write we are sitting in Lazy Jacks bar in the sunshine – listening to a rendition of 'Chestnuts roasting on an open fire' . It is odd thinking of Christmas when you are sitting in warm sunshine.
  We have been thinking about what gifts we can send – Sardines for everyone?

I have now caught up with some important things – cleaned the boat, done our laundry and had hair and nails done – human again. When I was putting some of the laundry in the bag I noticed a brown stain … I just said *"is that poo or rust?"* – it seemed so matter of fact – and then Mark and I both fell about laughing … it is so weird what you deal with living on a boat. You may think living on a 54ft Yacht in the Algarve sounds glamorous but it is a caravan at sea really – ask any person who lives aboard and it comes down to maintenance and toilets and supplies. Of course, all the Magic moments are worth the inconveniences you must live with.

We have been talking about how much weight we have both lost since we left London for our new life aboard – about a stone each!! We have no car, we are living a much more physical life both on board and walking everywhere and we are eating salads and delicious fresh grilled fish – fantastic!

Lagos is lovely – a pretty town with lively bars and classy restaurants. We have not gone to the beach yet but we plan to soon. Time is already slipping through our fingers – bliss! We are going to take Magic out and run some drills – MOB (Man over board), mooring stern to and bow to – we are going to anchor off and take the tender to the beach….but perhaps – tomorrow!! Today we are going to build our BBQ on the Push Pit and cook fresh fish on it for our supper.

Reflecting on the trip I was thinking :
    How amazing that I did Portsmouth to Lagos in December and kept on a full set of nails!

It's good to be a girl aboard – we used some of my red nail polish to colour the new bulbs on the compass and we used my silicon hair scrum to stop the squeak at the end of the boom! Both worked brilliantly.

Our mainsail is another story – we managed to do £1000 of damage during our Biscay crossing – we have ripped the sail, delaminated some of the tapes and broken every batton!!

Whoops!

We now also need a new Main Sheet – Mark went to get one and brought back one – in …Red! RED!

I have taken it back and asked if they can do a special order of the same rope (line) specification but in BLACK – of course – on Magic most of our lines are black or marl or plain. It's odd but the older I get the more and more important aesthetics are to me and I could not have coped with a Red Mainsheet right in front of me as we sailed!!

We are happy and having the time of our life!

Ups and Downs and why Acetaminophen is my friend
Saturday 13th December – Monday 15th December

We awoke to a howling wind and driving rain. The halyards were banging on the mast and the noise reverberated – clanging and banging into our cabin: Today and tomorrow is rain again – grey clouds and cooler. But that is ok as Monday and the following 7 days will then be clear blue sky, sunshine and 18 Degrees – nice.

We are not coping very well with chilling out – we keep making lists of things to do. Today top of the list was to wash May and brush out her knots – she really is one salty Mat! I have booked her a groomer's appointment for the 19th but she was grey and salty so a bath is required!!

One thing that we are finding weird is being unrestricted in that we can just leave and sail away anywhere any day – but being restricted in terms of resources – lots of things we took for granted living on land – like power and water must be managed with more care – but the oddest thing is living without unlimited internet. This doesn't feel like a luxury lost but more of a day to day necessity lost.

Let's go sailing! – Urm perhaps we should wait until the ice melts off the Deck!
DECEMBER 21

Lady May in the Algarve Sunshine with Alison her personal hairdresser

We are getting into the way of living aboard and have figured out many important things – like what semi- skimmed milk is called in the supermarket (Meio Gordo – should you ever need to know!) and how to get Radio Four and the internet – it's interesting to know what is important and as it turns out fresh milk and the internet are right up on the top of the list.

Yesterday May had her haircut – the mobile dog groomer came to the boat and May had her hair cut in the sunshine! It was funny watching May with the blue sky and Palm trees behind her! She seems to be taking all this change in her stride.

Now, just listening to Van Morrison on a Sunday evening everything seems not just normal but better than normal. Mark is looking at the Sunday Times and a photo of a child in a riot in the Ukraine leaps off the page – what a world of contrasts – hell and happiness. We are so lucky and we appreciate what we have. Yesterday we awoke to find ice on the deck – the extremes of temperature are weird.

But we can't sit around in the Marina – we came to sail! Then we realised that this would be the first time we were taking Magic out on our own – so we had a briefing session about lines and fenders – we checked the systems and got on our life jackets – May had hers on and we put on her harness so she was secure.

Mark took the helm – suddenly the yacht felt enormous – I was on the fore deck and we slipped the lines. I had a fender at the ready, as our berth is tight. Mark gently reversed and used the bow thruster to maneuver a three-point turn.

We had a good day out on the ocean – the view from the sea back to the town is better than the reverse and looking down the coast I had a longing to keep going. Mark said, "you know – it's a weird feeling – we have everything on board so we could just keep going. We could go anywhere!" And yes, that is how it feels to be cruising. After sailing for a short while we brought Magic into the marina again. We were very anxious as this was the first time we had moored up with only two of us on board. We need not have been concerned as the weather was calm and there were some very friendly and experienced hands on the dock side to help us with our lines. Calm organisation, plenty of fenders, calm weather and friendly help ashore – perfect.

Today we had another adventure. We set off in our Tender to go and see the caves and go to the beach, there was an onshore breeze and I recalled my father only letting me take out my small boat and outboard out when there was an on-shore breeze. We motored out of the marina and down the short stretch of palm tree lined river to the sea. We turned in the direction of the caves and it suddenly felt very splashy.

May, who had previously been happily looking out to sea from the front of the dinghy was now not at all sure. And we were not either. Those rocks and waves looked a lot bigger from low down in our small inflatable dinghy.

We enjoyed the view but decided to head the other way towards the beach where the idea was to go up on the beach and pull the dinghy on the sand to have lunch at the beach bar — Ha ha ha….those of you reading this who know about onshore wind and waves and landing small boats on a shelved beach will need to read no further!

Relaxing in beautiful Lagos, Portugal. Mark looking smart and May strapped in with Life Jacket on ready for our dingy adventure.

We got within about a metre of the beach, turned the engine off and figured out how to tilt it forwards – well almost! Then I jumped out – thinking I would just pull the boat towards the shore. Err, no it was a lot deeper than we thought and, I stumbled as a large wave hit the back of my knees. I was knocked forward and into the sea – completely soaked. As it was only about 11am I was still wearing layers – everything wet! I laughed but Mark and May looked concerned – honestly it took me back to being a teenager – learning boat handing. I stood up and pulled the boat in further towards the beach and Mark jumped in too. We pulled the boat up the beach a little – but it was MUCH heavier than we had thought and the waves much stronger! We put May onto terra firma and she was so relieved she ran and rolled about in the golden sand. May really loves sand and gets a bit giddy – skipping and jumping about.

It really is a stunning beach – a perfect arch of fine golden sand reaching for a couple of miles. I wanted to walk May and look at shells – chill out and then go for lunch – but no!

We fought with the dinghy and realised that there was no way we could leave it and that our only option would be to go back out. I thought we needed to get the water out of the boat so I headed up the beach to look for some empty bottles but it was immaculate. In the distance were a couple of bins and I opened them to retrieve two empty water bottles! No shame – bin rummaging …there is a first time for everything and needs must! May was still happily playing in the soft sand, her nose covered in it! Mark was holding the dinghy and we both started bailing out the water but with each new wave it filled up more. I was thinking that we needed help here; it's funny but I seem to have lost the courage I had when I was younger. Mark was much calmer and suggested we just had to get beyond the beach surf and then we would be fine. We had one go at that and got it wrong, we twisted sideways and the boat was filled with a large wave which then washed us up the beach – we had both been paddling the same way!! May was not impressed as she was now soaked and nervous and didn't understand why we would choose to leave the soft warm sand and go on a rubber boat into the twisting waves. She looked at us as if to say, "humans are crazy"

We recovered and planned a more coordinated approach – May and I would get in first, I would secure May with a tether and then I would begin paddling, Mark would wade out as far as he could then jump in. This plan worked except Mark was up to his armpits in water before he jumped in – and it was hard to do. A big wave washed over the bow of the dinghy soaking May completely and then as Mark finally managed to get onboard the boat tipped and May fell overboard, luckily, she was strapped onto the boat and had her life jacket on so she was fine and back aboard in seconds – poor May!! All aboard and we both paddled like mad. I was singing the theme tune to Hawaii 5 O – Mark had never heard it before and thought I had gone mad!! – but if you sing along now you will feel the moment more!

Once we were out several metres from the shore Mark worked on getting the engine started whilst I paddled. There was a very strong current and although I was paddling we were not moving, and worse - I broke a nail! Honestly 8 days across Biscay and not a single nail issue then a few hours in our dinghy and I have a nail disaster. Mark eventually got the engine working (phew) and we motored home. …bailing out all the way. Another adventure!

We went back to Magic to dry out and change. Then, to recover, we went to the Marine Bar to have a full Sunday lunch with wine – coffee and dessert!

May and I then slept for two hours – we girls needed to re energise after adventures and fine dining!

Tomorrow is Christmas week and I think our adventures will only be as much as fixing the boat. The carpenter 'Stitch' is coming to fix some drawers and the table, David the engineer is coming to fix our heating (we hope) (not that we need it now but we are on a mission to fix the damn thing)

As I reflect on the last two days I admit that am a little disappointed that I seem to have lost the courage for adventures I used to have when I was younger – must work on that.

An Antiquarian Book Seller, a Neurosurgeon, eating dragon's claws for Christmas lunch and an encounter with a portable Didgeridoo

It's Sunday 28th December and I am listening to the Archer's Christmas omnibus whist sitting at the chart table. The news from home is of snow, ice, blizzards and train delays caused by Network Rail … I was watching it all unfold on SKY News now that we can get Apple TV through the Internet. These images underline why we are happy to have made the decision to be in the Algarve. I have been thinking that I am not keen to live above 45 degrees latitude ever again and 30 or below would be better. Mark is still pondering!

Mark is at the gym in the Marina Hotel Spa – a month's membership was one of his Christmas presents. Mark goes stir crazy if he cannot go to the gym – something I will never understand!! There is a perfect beach and sunshine and even an outdoor gym in the town but he loves to go to the indoor gym… very odd behaviour. We have been enjoying settling into life living aboard. There are frustrations but the joy of our new life outweighs those.

We were planning on having Sardines on the boat with a good bottle of wine for our Christmas Lunch but then we had a lovely invitation from two fellow live aboards to dine with them on their yacht. Tony and Clare are extraordinary people – intelligent, warm, funny, generous and talented sailors. They are in the process sailing their boat 'Hai Mei Gui' from Thailand to the UK via a long spell in Portugal.

Our Christmas morning began on board Magic with a delicious breakfast of scrambled egg and smoked salmon (a favourite). May enjoyed some of that too. Then we opened our gifts – Christmas jumpers from Mark's mum and dad – two new tops for me from Mark and sunglasses for Mark from me.

Then, off to the beach. Going to the beach is something that we both wanted to do on Christmas morning. It was the first time either of us has been in the sunshine for Christmas so the idea of being on the beach was exciting. It is a funny thing – but the blue sky and sunshine really wakes us up and makes us want to jump out of bed and enjoy it. I think that is born out of the rarity of sunny days at home – we have been programmed to make the most of each sunny day.

It was beautiful – the beach here at Lagos is stunning. A perfect arc of fine golden sand stretching for miles. May loved the sand and skipped with joy. It was so warm we even had to take our Christmas Jumpers off!!

Going to Tony and Clare's boat for our Christmas Lunch we didn't know what to expect but we had such a fantastic time. We came aboard and were greeted so

warmly. We were introduced to their friends – an antiquarian bookseller who has a shop in Mayfair and his wife Fran, a neuroscientist who specialised in Alzheimers – what important work.

Tony and Clare's boat was stunning – a beautiful classic and classy steel yacht all hand built and finished inside with cosy beautiful wood, a much more traditional

On the beach in our New Christmas Jumpers

yacht than Magic. They have sailed from Thailand and are on their way home to Burnham on Crouch in Essex.

In the cockpit we were served, our starter, Goose Barnacles – they tasted like prawns but looked like dragon's toes – very odd… but delicious.

Then we went down into the cosy nest of a salon and enjoyed a delicious fish stew – apparently, the key to deliciousness is to ensure that every trace of blood is removed from the fish prior to making the stew! We had lots of lovely food and drink and great fun with this very educated and well-travelled crew – we thought it was such an honour to have been invited into their Christmas Lunch but that is what happens in the community of live-aboard sailors.

We have allowed the days following Christmas Day to blur – last night was lovely – each Saturday night some of the people who live aboard and who love music gather in the Marina Hotel Bar and play. There were singers and guitar players and one guy even played both his Clarinet and his Saxophone – whist his partner brought along a portable Didgeridoo – it was a wonder. Mark and I joined in and it was easy, as we were once again made so welcome. I even managed a solo of 'Summer Time' which is one of my favorites. I love to sing and although I am confident at a lot of things – singing in public makes me feel like I am standing naked in front of strangers who are all laughing at my wobbly bits.

But here amongst my new friends, somehow, I felt supported and safe enough to experiment with singing. What a gift.

We are already planning our route for when we depart. My two children, Sara and James are coming out on the 2nd of April and we must figure out where we will be and what would be a lovely cruising area and fun port as well as easy flights from the UK. Part of the fun of this adventure is to share it with friends and family.

Happy New Year – here's to a new year and all who sail in her!!
JANUARY 6

Happy New Year

Well it is a new year and we are now really settled into living aboard.

We did hit a wall where we thought – "what have we done?!" It happened to both of us at the same time. The heating still wasn't working, we had lost some more things – the VHF needed replacing and we had just found a long scratch on the side of the boat…It's often the smaller issues that tip the balance. We talked it all through and then thought – No, we are in the right place at the right time and we are going to learn not only to manage but to thrive. This is an adventure and it is a challenge we are going to rise to.

We both feel out of our depth most of the time and the learning curve is not a curve! But we are going with it because this is a way of life we have chosen and we want to learn to deal with the changes.

We are never bored and are surrounded by fantastic people. There is so much to do as the community in Lagos is so welcoming and fun. There is something to join in everyday and we have all fallen in love with the beautiful beach. Although we think in the Summer it may not be so lovely! Mark has been going to the gym and doing yoga (I did one class !!) and we are still eating well. A diet of grilled fish and salads is wonderful – a revelation really. We have let the days between Christmas and New Year slip by and it was lovely. We decided to have designated "not fixing things today" days and that works well!

We had a lovely New Year's Eve – Indian Meal with 20 people then into the main square in Lagos for a performance by one of Portugal's biggest stars, Aurea Sousa who is a really world class soul singer. Then we were treated to some wonderful fireworks and back to Lazy Jacks bar for some live Jazz and dancing. It was all great fun and so lovely (and weird) to be walking around in a strange town bumping into friendly and familiar faces.

We still have no main sheet as we are waiting for the black one to arrive. So, when the guys went out dinghy racing we decided to have a cocktail cruise on Magic and took her out for a motor. Mark took the helm and there were 8 ladies (including May) for Crew. I think Mark was rather pleased with himself!

One of the girls brought a water bomb sling on board and we interrupted the champagne cocktails from time to time to fire at the racing sailors!

So, life aboard continues – we think we may have our heating finally fixed (cross your fingers as the nights are very cold), we have found a new VHF at a good price and a reliable electrician to fit it, we have new paint to work on the scratch and we will soon have our new mainsheet on board.

We have itchy feet and so we may move on before March. We are both thinking - Life is Good

An accusation of Culpable Homicide, an overnight guest who looks like Jesus and turns out to a Cannabis expert, learning to always bring something yummy and wear slippers

It is almost the end of January and I am sitting on the Easy Jet flight to Gatwick – moving away from 20 degrees and sunny towards wet, cold, snow, grey and windy. I have time to do a little writing. I am on my way to work with one of my favourite clients, so that is good but I am already missing being on the sea! I love our new life with its quirky new challenges, amazing vistas and incredible people.

During the past week, I have had an adventure stuffed full of 'ings' –

Planning our voyage by running a workshop where I encouraged people to become living pilot books. Sailors tell their stories of where they have been and what they liked and didn't like.

Drawing I joined in an extraordinary drawing class and to my huge surprise produced something quite good – even if it was a bit of a surprise that is was a life drawing class and a rather beautiful naked man was in front of me at 9 in the morning.

Rehearsing We now have a cool little gathering on Tony and Clare's classic boat on a Tuesday morning at 11am to work on the singing we are developing for Friday night's music sessions

Performing in our music evenings. I am now loving singing as I am becoming more confident and I am even developing my own set of jazz numbers

Rigging with a team of our new friends who helped us run all sorts of mouse lines and sorted out the reefing system on our main. How generous and warm they all were.

Nursing Mark (who I had to take to hospital in the end with ear and lung infections) Poor Mark it's horrid to be ill and man flu is serious.

Hosting is a constant and wonderful thing on the boat with people coming and going all the time – tea, coffee, wine, beer and food . On Friday night, we offered a bed for David an extraordinary guitar player who specializes in Rag Time.

Listening to our overnight guest David who looks like Jesus and is a Cannabis expert. He turned up at the music evening and was a mesmerising guitarist.

Driving all over the place as we have hired a car for a while and it is great fun to see more of the area than we can reach on foot.

Grooming May as she fell in the water attempting a leap from our steps to our deck. Poor May – she loves being with us but is still getting used to negotiating the space.

Skyping (is that a word?) I have been in touch with the kids and work colleagues – it's fun to Skype

Pampering – As I had the car and Mark was healing by sleeping all day for days on end, I escaped to Portimao the nearest 'big town' and had my nails done and my hair – lovely treats

Teaching – it was great to work with a team from Morgan Sindall on the psychology of Impact, Influence and Persuasion one of my favorite topics

Healing – following the training – I totally lost my voice (a first for me) it's a shame as I was really looking forward to singing – but that will have to wait.

Winning – we joined in a race with Magic – it was a fun day with perfect weather and it was our first race. We were lucky to have an ace crew with Melwin at the Helm – she was Aaaamazing and we won – by 14 minutes – despite having a handicap applied (and yes for you purists we should not have had our ensign up whilst racing – but then it was a fun day race and as you know we are still learning!)

Writing – I am enjoying keeping notes of our journey

We had a rough time on internet sailing forums. We were criticized for most of our decisions (some of the comments have been annoying and some upsetting) – we have been criticized for lots of things including the purchase of Magic as she is not the '*right*' boat

She is:

- **A Hanse and not an Oyster**
- **54 and not 45 ft.**
- **Black and not White**
- **Wide and not Slim**
- **Packed with 'gizmos' and not stripped back**

But we love Magic, all the live aboard luxury we have – lots of space, clean modern lines, TV, DVD player, Music and Internet and of course silent electric fresh water flushing toilets!! She is a sound boat and sails like a dream – as our racing results now show. We love Magic and she is the right decision for us.

Some of the people from the forum have been in touch directly to say they do not agree with all our decisions but they respect our individual choices. But some seem to continue to enjoy continually poking holes in every move we take.

I have decided that we should stay clear of forums. The most recent comment was one accusing Mark in writing of culpable homicide – not nice! It was a complaint about how Mark handled the encounter with the Fishing Boat on our journey into Lagos. We are not rising to any of that – we are learning and happy doing it.

We are taking Magic out and sailing around the bays along the Algarve coast from Lagos. This is enabling us not only to work on the finer details of handling her under sail but also to check the rigging and all the electronic systems carefully.

We are booked in Lagos Marina until 9th of March and plan to leave then – weather permitting, of course.

We do remember to think about what a good decision this was – every day brings new challenges and new reasons why this was one of the best decisions we have ever made.

If you live aboard or are thinking of living aboard – do it!

Love and Lists Make the world go around
FEBRUARY 14

Today is Valentine's day and the girls in the marina have been talking about it ranging from 'it's a stupid thing' – commercial etc. to 'why not have a day to celebrate love and consider how romantic gestures are important?'

I used to be disappointed by romantic gestures that either never transpired at all or that were less than my very able imagination would conjure up. So, I have learned that the best way to ensure happiness for all is to make subtle and not so subtle suggestions to help Mark out!! I sent him a menu of ideas – writing in the sand, writing a poem, flowers, dinner, making something...I left off diamonds and gold as if we are investing money then I would rather have a generator and a water maker – no really – what has happened to me !!

Last night Mark brought a beautiful and exotic bouquet of flowers – Proteus and Anthurim they were so beautiful – and this morning we exchanged cards – Mark's had a beautiful poem that he had written – then he made me breakfast in bed – perfect!

Tonight, we are going out for a lovely dinner with friends at a local restaurant in the old part of Lagos – so Valentine's Day is a big success. The cruising life does place a strain on a relationship – and it is as vital to ensure that is as strong and sea worthy as the boat.

Meeting extraordinary people is a striking feature of being one of the live aboard community:

I like the wandering musician, a bearded man who lives in the hills and whose sparkling music career came crashing down when he was arrested for Cannabis Cultivation and spent years learning law to defend himself in court.

With each new encounter a new world of wonder, pain and adventure – each new person an incredible book. Each one of them on a unique journey. There was the man whose successful music career was ruined when he was accused of cultivating cannabis so he taught himself law to defend himself in court. There was the courageous woman who sailed from Turkey to America to be with her injured dog. Their stories inspired us and amazed us. What a privilege to have a front row seat to all these incredible lives.

We are enjoying thinking about where we are going to go next the plan now looks like this:

Lagos to Cartagena via Gibraltar and CADIZ (9th March to 15th March)
Valencia – early May
Ibiza – June
Menorca – July
Corsica – August
Lagos – September
Canaries – October
Caribbean – December

Then

Month	Details	Miles
January	Saint Lucia to Santa Marta, Colombia	815 NM
	Santa Marta – San Blas, Panama	295 NM
	Transit Panama Canal	
February	Cruise Panama	
	Las Perlas to Galapagos	850 NM
	Cruise Galapagos	
March	Galapagos to Hiva Oa, Marquesas	2980 NM
	Cruise French Polynesia	
April	Tahiti rendezvous	
	Cruise Society Islands	
May	Raiatea to Suwarrow	690 NM
	Suwarrow to Niue	540 NM
	Niue to Vava'u, Tonga	230 NM
June	Cruise Tonga and Fiji	
July	Fiji to Tanna, Vanuatu	450 NM
	Cruise Vanuatu	
	Port Vila, Vanuatu to Mackay, Australia	1150 NM
August	Cruise the Great Barrier Reef	

Then who knows where!!

Chapter Five

MAST HYSTERIA

Take it to the Bridge
FEBRUARY

Lagos has a lifting bridge. Yachts with masts must call the bridge operator to open the bridge before they can pass.

This is the official report of our Accident.
 We are now stranded on land for up to 10 weeks

In preparing to sail during the day Mark reviewed current and forecasted weather conditions, wind, sea state, and time of sail, distance and choice of course. The wind was 14 – 25 knots from the NW on our Stern exiting the marina. As it had been the previous time we had sailed. These were quite normal conditions. There was a strong outgoing tide.
 After the normal preparations with the experienced crew on board who had sailed Magic with us many times previously, we left Lagos at 12.45 for a fun sail in the bay.
 We called on Ch9 to ask for a bridge lift the moment we left our mooring. The normal procedure is to radio the bridge at this point.
 We had the response from the bridge operator: "Yes, 3 minutes"
 This was the usual response. We checked our time because we normally take around 3 minutes to reach the river from our mooring.
 We have passed through this bridge more than 20 times since we arrived in Lagos; we therefore know that it is essential that the bridge opened in time so we had a time check before we entered the river on 3 minutes. This was our recurrent normal procedure.

It was unusual to find the bridge had not opened. Having entered the river we called on Ch9 again more urgently requesting that the bridge be opened immediately because they had failed to do so – the time had passed 3 minutes. They responded by saying it will be a further two minutes before the bridge will be lifted.

With the wind behind us and the strong tide under us it was difficult to control our speed so we used precautionary speed by putting the throttle in reverse to counter the forward motion of tide beneath us and the wind on our stern.

Our speed was under 2knots.

After a further 2 minutes the Bridge still didn't lift.

We again asked for the bridge to be lifted urgently as we were finding it difficult to control the boat.

They responded by saying there were people on the bridge.

We responded by calling on the VHF again – this time more forcefully telling them in no doubt that we needed the bridge to be open immediately.

We put on more reverse but the result was more kick to port turning us starboard side on to the wind, we used the bow thruster but it was not strong enough to control the direction of the boat.

The bridge still did not begin to open.

As we got closer to the bridge, it was apparent that it was not going to open in time. At this point, we tried to turn the boat around (using reverse with full port rudder to take advantage of the prop kick, forward with full starboard rudder and bow thruster pushing the bow to starboard). Given the very narrow channel and strong wind and tide, this maneuver was not possible. We were eventually pushed sideways into the bridge, just as it started lifting.

The impact happened 8 – 10 minutes after the initial call to the open the bridge (when we were told it would take 3 minutes). We had never had problems with the bridge opening previously.

The Port rigging hit the bridge – the rigging on the Port side took the initial impact – ripping off the Lower port spreader completely and cracking the top Port spreader.

The rigging also knocked down a sign, which hit the deck causing some damage to the coach roof. Ironically it was the sign that said 'Call Ch9'

As we were twisted around with the current and wind the rudder hit the rocks at the Port side, the port side of the boat was touching the pillars of the bridge, although we fended off the bridge as much as we could there was still some surface damage to the chrome and paint work.

A local tourist boat observed what had happened and offered us assistance to pull us from our starboard stern line off the bridge. We accepted their help to tow us and reversed back up the river against the wind to the point where we could turn our nose into towards our mooring.

To make the mast safe, it was secured by attaching the main and spinnaker halyards to the port shroud base.

We immediately emailed our insurance company to tell them what had happened and we were told not to worry and that we are covered.

Around 10 minutes after we moored up we were visited by two people from a neighbouring yacht. They said "so sorry about the accident – we think it was our fault" We were shocked – how could it be their fault. They told us that they were in the Marina office chatting with the only member of staff on duty. They told us they were with him when our call came in. They heard him say '3 minutes' in response to our request to open the bridge. But then he kept talking with them – it was only when our more urgent cry for a bridge opening came later did he then say to them he had to go and open the bridge. They said to us they felt responsible for delaying him and that he was on his own. He had to leave them and go upstairs to then open the bridge.

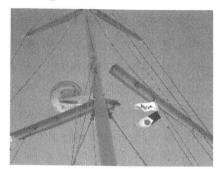

Looking up at our very sad broken Port Spreader and damaged mast.

After we were all tied up securely in our berth we were all in shock. I had stocked up for lunch at sea so I offered the crew to stay. I wasn't sure what to do or say and usually when that happens I eat! As we ate we reviewed what had happened. In only 20 minutes we had gone from the jolly anticipation of a lovely day on the water to disaster. Our beautiful boat was broken. Mark and I were really upset and concerned about what the next steps would be. Everyone was saying "I think you are going to need a new mast" This is serious.

We have learned so much about our boat and ourselves as sailors. We have listened to all the comments and views from those more experienced and we continue to learn. It is of course not always easy – like all adults we love to learn but we hate to be taught.

We are members of several online forums for sailors and this has mostly been a great experience. We shared our accident report on one forum and got a lot of helpful advice and support – and there was some bashing as well

But also, there were some wise and supportive voices – one of which was Jim B whom we have come to admire and respect. Jim was an RAF pilot who later became a test pilot and tutor. This is what he said following our post about our accident:

"Almost all mishaps have two or more causes. First, an un-anticipated event or events create conditions you've never met before. Second, your training did not prepare you to handle this situation. Third, your ingenuity or experience may (or may not!) have rescued the situation. So, there are usually two or three ways of avoiding accidents or mishaps.

(1) Prevent the situation. Don't cross Biscay in Winter. Don't insist on operating procedures for a bridge which put users into difficult situations. Don't try to sail around the world. Don't sail at night. Don't go to sea in F5 or more. Don't exceed the speed limit. In other words, accept limitations on what you attempt.

(2) Train people to handle more likely situations. Colregs, reefing, alongside maneuvering, dragging anchors, going aground – the list is endless, and cannot cover unlikely needs. Such as the need to do a tight 180 in a narrow waterway because a bridge won't open and the current is behind you. So:

(3) Learn through experience. Otherwise known as pushing your limits and making (or nearly making) mistakes. And then sharing them with others so they can learn too.

But please, no blame culture. That'll shut the door on learning through other people's mishaps.

I live by the mantra of my Alma Mater: "Learn to test; Test to learn". It makes for an exciting life . . . discovering limits. More fun than just accepting others' opinions.

JimB
Thank you, Jim, if you want more wisdom from Jim just Google JimB to see his web site.

Amongst other things we have learned that we are strong – Mark and I work well as a team and we have worked together to get Magic back in the water. We moved into an apartment and we moved Magic on the hard. We worked with the surveyor, the yard, the rigger and the insurance company –to get everything moving.

Once all the surveys were complete it was declared that a new mast and standing rigging were required – the bad news was that it would be 10 weeks. I had to make the painful decision to call my kids and cancel their trips out to see us in Cartagena, Spain. We had been due to leave Lagos on the 10th March and move West.

Now that the ten-week delay was settling in our minds we worked our way over the disappointment and though to thinking of ways we could improve Magic. There are literally hundreds of jobs that need doing on a yacht all the time some big, many small. Everyone who cruises talks about their list of jobs and how when you knock things off the top more get added to the bottom.

So, we thought we would use the time to work on our list!

Little did we realise that doing this would be a potentially lifesaving task. We have been doing everything as mundane as scrubbing fridges and bilges and clearing out food lockers. But also, we have been running through our safety equipment. For example, we have checked our emergency tiller and our emergency bilge – good thing too. The emergency manual bilge pump which enables you to pump water out of the yacht was set the wrong way around. From the factory, it was set to pump water IN

Can you imagine being in a situation where you were having to pump water out if you were sinking and the pump was pumping water IN

Next up was the rudder – the rudder was taken off for examination and it was found to have had no damage. However, the rudder bolts which secure the rudder to the yacht were found to have only been finger tight – that is when they removed it they did not need spanners they could just easily undo the bolts – this is scary as if your rudder falls off you can be in big trouble.

As we are sailing across the Atlantic later in the year we can't help thinking that this frustrating situation was a blessing in disguise.

We will have all new Standing and Running rigging, our rudder and all our safety systems will have been thoroughly checked.

The other good thing is we have what we seemed to always have none of when we were at 'home'. We have time

Bliss, Swimming in the Sea with the Sun shining

Time to play – I love the sea and swimming and Lagos has the most amazing beach
Time to reflect on what happened and what we have learned.
Time to consider what Magic needs for our Atlantic Crossing
Time with the people we love hanging out with in Lagos
Time to work – Mark and I have both done some consultancy work
Time to research – we are considering what we need for the ARC and considering our equipment including a generator and water maker
Time to be creative – we wrote "The Lagos Bridge Blues" and our fellow 'live aboards' joined us to perform it – that's what I call therapy

You must sing this like a classic blues song and when you see a * you sing

"Da Da Da Da Da"

The Lagos Bridge Blues

I woke up one morning *
Sun was in the sky *
Who wants to go sailing?
I do said I
I'm singing the Lagos Bridge Blues
Let's make a little Magic *
Let's go to sea *
Let's play with the dolphins
And just be free
We were a little hungry *
We packed the fridge *
We heard voices calling
Let's take it to the bridge
I'm singing the Lagos Bridge Blues
Called Channel 9 *
Please open the door *
3 minutes only
Why was it 10 more?
The river was running *
The gulls in the Sky *
The bridge wouldn't open
Why oh why
I'm singing the Lagos Bridge Blues
The barnacles crunching *
Our rigging was bashed *
Oh holy shit
I think we just crashed
Now we're staying here *
Our boats on the yard *
And now we find out
why it is called the hard
I'm singing the Lagos Bridge Blues
So, we'll see you round *
Cause we'll still be here *
In fact, we may be here
For another year
We're singing the Lagos Bridge Blues
Yeah
Channel 9 (spoke!)

So, we will be here in Lagos until around the middle of May. We plan to live aboard again as soon as her body is repaired and painted. Then we can be amongst our friends again in the Marina. That should be around the end of March or early April.

When the mast comes on May 12th (not that we are counting!) We will need a week of rigging and sea trials. Then we will leave Lagos and go west. Our plan is to do a modest amount of sailing in the Med and return to Lagos in September to begin our ARC preparations. We will then sail down to Grand Canarias via Madeira. We will berth in Las Palmas from the 9th November until we leave for Saint Lucia on the 22nd November. at 13.00 (ish)

APRIL

Mark inspecting Magic's mighty hull before she is re-sprayed.

Happy Easter Magic

We will move back on Board Magic on Easter Monday – a lovely gift. Her keel and rudder have been checked and she has had a total re-spray and polish. We can't wait to see her and move back on board. Of course, we then must wait until the middle of May before we have our new mast fitted and all new running and standing rigging fitted. Once everything is checked we will then sail out of Lagos – it is a wonderful place but we now have seriously itchy feed and want to do what we came for … Sail

While we have been working on 'Project. Fix Magic' I have been pondering.

Luxury aboard…

When you have been lucky to feather your nest on land with the luxuries you enjoy – fabrics and cushions and 400 thread count Egyptian cotton sheets, paintings and ornaments and books – you notice that when you live aboard you miss some of these things.

But of course, we are sailors who love to get out and sail and we put our boat to the test. So, fine fabrics would stain or get wet, cushions escape overboard, paintings fly off the walls, ornaments crash and break and books are best kept on a Kindle.

It is interesting to notice that we miss these things but equally interesting to notice that we don't need them. We cherish the luxury that we are fortunate to have. Of course, these are things when of course the greatest love of our life are family and friends. Here I am talking – Stuff. I have always loved stuff and as I get older I am increasingly aesthetic and find ugly things difficult! The restriction of a life living aboard is good for me – I do love shopping but find it is not so much the acquisition of more stuff but the joy of looking and enjoying the things. If I see something I really like now when out shopping I take a photograph of it and enjoy it for a while. It is interesting how soon I don't look at it any more.

There simply isn't enough room on board for one more thing!

And now we have our crew for the Arc the Atlantic crossing seems more and more real. We are going to have to downsize the amount of stuff already onboard so we have room to stow the gear of four more people and all the food and safety gear we will need….urm

Magic, the Hanse 540e we live in is beautiful thing in itself – I have totally fallen in love with so many things I thought I would share:

From a technical viewpoint, she is a safe and seaworthy sailing yacht – her hull, deck and rigging are all designed to near perfection. I love the teak deck and the clean lines and space as all the running rigging on the deck that goes under the coach roof to the cockpit making lots of clear space to walk on deck as well as looking better. I trust this boat with my life.

Then there is the look of her – Magic is dark grey – which is unusual in yachts and looks fantastic. (I know we may get hot but then there is always air-con! – ok ok I know we don't have air con and all we have is full central heating but then I never said I was practical.

Her overall shape is beautiful – lovely lines, as they (who every 'they' are – say) the interior is genuinely like a smart, modern apartment and so different from many of the boats that we visit – we love the ceiling height and the light and the space. It works for living aboard and we can have up to 10 people around our saloon table for drinks and games and fun. The finish on the wood is warm and stylish and the pale floors and furnishings add to the light bright interior (even if they make me a bit OCD about cleaning!) The Galley works so well and we have a large fridge and a good-sized freezer – we are going to need those when we are taking 15 – 18 days crossing 2700 miles at sea with 6 people aboard!

Another luxury aboard – are the 'facilities' each of our 3 double cabins has its own 'head' or bathroom – two of the rooms have their own electric fresh water flush toilets and each has a shower.

When water is plentiful it is lovely to wake up and shower in our own space rather than having to walk to the Marina showers.

So, life is good! It has been a challenging time but now we are looking forward to getting Magic back on the water and sailing to the Med. As we do this we will also be preparing Magic and ourselves for the ARC – The Atlantic Rally for Cruisers. We now have our ARC file and will fly our ARC flag with pride. There is a lot to do but that is part of the fun of it all and all the time we are meeting people who can help and support us.

Paint, Parties, Planning and Partings
APRIL

Paint

The days have been whizzing by as we wait for our Mast to arrive in mid-May. We have spent weeks of detailed and technical project management whilst staying in an apartment. Then two weeks ago we eventually got Magic back in the water. We were so excited to see her and get back on board. As usual with the wonderful live-aboard community here in Lagos – friends bearing gifts arrived – wine and cups to celebrate her homecoming. Of course, as this is Portugal, she was late …but the wine kept flowing and our friends stayed with us until she arrived. I was overwhelmed to see her arriving into the safe harbour.

It was Easter Monday and the weather was foul but the company that had been carrying out the repairs wanted to get Magic back to us so the boss of the company sailed her single handed using his iPhone to navigate! We were so happy to see her that we forgot to be angry that he had potentially put her at risk. It is strange with boats as they are not just incredible equipment – they are also your home and you feel emotional about their well-being.

At first, we thought the paint looked good – We were so happy to be back on board and then when we started to look closer we were very disappointed. How gutting that this work was done so poorly and not checked before she was delivered back to us. We have waited so long for her return and now we must manage the paint defects.

At the moment, we can't say too much about the finish on the paint apart from the fact that we are not happy with it. The supplier agrees with us that it is not up to standard and they have so far had two guys for a full week making it better. We will have to wait until they are finished and then review it.

If we had our mast and could sail away then the paint issue would be very challenging but as it is we are stuck here so it is just disappointing and irritating and we have the time to manage the situation.

We are ever optimistic and hope that the remedial actions they are taking will fully fix the issues. In the meantime, we happy living in Portugal and the sun is Shining!

Party…

Of course, we love to have fun so to celebrate Magic's return to the water we had a party – we invited everyone in the Marina and beyond and ended up with around 55 people on Magic for a party that was described as "legendary!"

It was certainly fun …everyone brought food and wine – the theme was Black or Magic or both! We had Magic mushroom Stroganoff and Magic Mushrooms on edible earth with toadstools – we had Magic wands with chocolate and popping candy – and Magic dips and lots and lots and lots of Chocolate cake … We made a huge black cocktail of rum and black vodka with Blue Berries and Coke… better than its sounds….

We hired a Magician to entertain our guests "The great Martini" and he was fantastic – close up magic on the deck and in the galley amazed all and became the subject of amusement for days.

Also, days after we were still cleaning ….it turns out that black food and black drinks are not a great mix for the teak deck!!

Everyone had a fantastic time and the last guests departed at around 4am. Later that next morning we had a couple of local residents ask if we had enjoyed our party!!

Planning…..

It is exciting planning for our ongoing adventure. However sometimes I feel like we will never leave Lagos – we have been here for so long!

We are also planning what we will do from the end of May until Mid-November. We hope that the Mast and Rigging will be complete, all the paint issues resolved and all our new equipment will be fitted by the end of May (see I told you we were optimists!!) Then the next fixed date is 9th November to be in Las Palmas before our departure to St Lucia on the 22nd November. So, from June to October we have a plan – Currently we are thinking

June – July – August – Out of Lagos and turn left – Cadiz, Gib, Ceuta, Valencia, or perhaps directly to Barcelona, then Menorca, Majorca, Ibiza then back to Lagos for September

September – November – Madeira, Canaries, Las Palmas

We would love to see my daughter Sara while she is in Barcelona 18th to 24th June but as we have learned to our cost it is not a good idea to have a fixed agenda as sailing is a fickle business and it is much better to relax and go where the wind takes you. (Although I am sure that we can get to Barcelona in 18 days from Lagos!!)

Partings....

Something we had not considered was the sadness of seeing new friends leave. You get close to people when you are sailing because you instantly have a lot in common. But then everyone leaves and that is sad.

But for now, we are getting on with the planning and partings and parties the project and the paint ...– fixing our beautiful boat, enjoying Lagos and having fun with friends and family will have to continue.

20 days to go (ish)
MAY

After 4 months of planning and waiting we can now see the end of the tunnel. It has certainly been a significant challenge. We have needed all our project management skills and we are not finished yet but we have our crew and we are planning to leave in early June to sail around to Barcelona.

Magic will have new Running Rigging and new Standing Rigging and totally new paint – the paint has been a nightmare and is still not resolved – but we stick to our trusty mantra that "the only way out is through"

The sustaining things have been:

1. Remembering that this is one huge middle class problem – *"oh my yacht is being repaired and we are stranded in the Algarve!"*
2. Being grateful we had the skills and the time to deal with this
3. Our friends and family at home
4. Our friends in Lagos marina
5. May
6. The weather and the beauty in the Algarve
7. The Music – It has been wonderful to build courage in singing and enjoy music with so many talented musicians – Karaoke holds no fears for me anymore!!
8. Learning more – about the boat, about sailing, about resilience, about each other, about Marina life, about living aboard, about navigation, about first aid, about project management, about being on the hard, about rigging, about paint, about repairs....., about people
    about resolve
    about focus
    about holding on to your dream even if you think it is getting way too hard
    we are nearly there
    20 more days
    (ish)
9. Insurance, thank goodness that we were fully covered

Disappointment comes with the territory
MAY

So, being positive people we have rolled with the punches for months – waiting
  waiting for the paint
  waiting for the mast
  waiting for the repairs
  waiting for parts
  waiting for news
  waiting for paperwork
  waiting for the mast
  waiting to leave
  we have worked hard to remain calm and professional and polite always.

Today we were filling our time here by doing our RYA First Aid Certificate – another step for Mark in his Yacht Master program and for me a useful reminder of my St John Ambulance days!

Today was the day before our mast was due to leave SparCraft's Factory in France and head towards us. Had we counted down the days until tomorrow – YES!

However – even though we are realistic and we understood that not only could the mast be late it probably would be late we had still hoped it would not be late.
WRONG

Sparcraft have cruelly left it until the day before it is due to be transported to tell us it will be a week late:
Sailing teaches you resilience and grit

All About Resilience:
Resilience is that ineffable quality that allows some people to be knocked down by life and come back stronger than ever. Rather than letting failure overcome them and drain their resolve, they find a way to rise from the ashes. Psychologists have identified some of the factors that make someone resilient, among them a positive attitude, optimism, the ability to regulate emotions, and the ability to see failure as a form of helpful feedback. Even after misfortune, resilient people are blessed with such an outlook that they can change course and soldier on.

So, we focus on our leaving date of the 6th or 7th June and we think about meeting my daughter in Barcelona – leaving all this far behind us

But ouch
today was a body blow

PS We still remember that this is a very middle class problem and that there are others much worse off than ourselves. But this is our home and it is challenging.

New Shorts
JUNE 1

Well here we are Monday, and the first day of June. The weather is fantastic and Mark has gone off to play golf – for the first time in the Algarve. It's bonkers – he has only just brought his clubs over from home and we are going in a few days.

Yesterday I drove to the 'Big Town' to Jumbo the supermarket – to begin the food prep for our journey to Barcelona. I went with the amazing and fantastic Susan and of course we had to go via a few other shops including Primark! One of our friends commented on Primark that – it makes you feel like a millionaire – I know it's a guilty pleasure but to have new things for less is lovely.

Growing up in chilly Northern Ireland and then going to a boarding school has ensured that I have enough body phobias to last several lifetimes. So, the wearing of shorts is a thing that in 52 years I have never managed to feel comfortable with! But when it is over 40 degrees on the boat there really is no way around it! So – having experimented with several types I have finally found some in …. that fit and according to Mark and other trusted friends look ok.

So that's it Shorts is the way forward and to hell with the wobbly bits and cellulite and body issues! – well of course I don't really mean it but at least I am working on saying it! and I am in those shorts as I write – determined to get past this stupid – "omg my legs are out – thing!"

Tomorrow is the day that our Mast is due to arrive in Lagos – will it or will it not – who knows

The Paint on Magic is still not in a good state and the painters have not shown up – again!

There are still a few jobs to do – a list of them in fact but are we worried about it – 'No' – well 'Yes'

We are packing and cooking and shopping and generally getting ready to set sail

The plan is to go on Saturday and head straight to Barcelona – however the weather I ordered has not arrived yet so we may have to adjust our plans

By adjust what I mean is that we still MUST LEAVE on Saturday even if we must call in somewhere to wait

I have to GO

Chapter Six

LEAVING LAGOS

The Great Escape
JUNE

Lagos to Barcelona
We did it! We finally left Lagos 15 minutes later than planned on **Saturday 6ᵗʰ June**.

It is hard to put into words the condensed actions and emotions of the past few weeks. Here is a flavor:

The Mast was finished but the transport was not booked – we were then told it could be weeks before it could be delivered – then transport was found
    The Mast arrived a week late but all the parts were there
    The Paint was still not completed
    There were about 20 other jobs to do on Magic – companionway door, Lazerette door, prop, anode, and outboard crane….

As always, the list of things to do was growing and the amount of time left was reducing – therefore cruising sailors say you should just go with the flow and not create deadlines. But following our delay in Lagos we were determined to leave and travel to Barcelona so we could see Sara my daughter and Yvonne our friend. Also, we are deadline type people – we seem to be addicted to deadlines after more than 30 years of following them.

Over the past seven months our experience of boat ownership has been mostly challenging, stressful and expensive. The people we have met have been the best bit. But we had come to sail – so we must admit that we have thought about giving up and going home but NO! We came to sail and we are going to sail…

We booked Simon Philips our delivery skipper to come with us on the trip to Barcelona. He is sailing with us to give us the extra confidence we need on the trip to Barcelona. I know we should now be sailing ourselves but the Straights of Gibraltar are not the best starting point following our delay.

Simon can also run though Mark's Yacht Master Practical course which he is working on now.

Knowing that Simon was arriving on the evening of the 5th June we had to focus even harder on getting Magic ready:

Thursday 4th June

Our deck and stainless steel were being cleaned to a very high standard and just as this work was finished at 2pm Magic was taken out onto the Hard. But then no work was done on her for the rest of the day – weird! But at least we got to stay overnight in the air-conditioned luxury of Sopromar's new accommodation. We all enjoyed the air con – particularly May. It is one of the many ironies that it is now over 30 degrees and our central heating has finally been fixed.

Now that it is fixed we cannot see why or when we will use it again and all we want is aircon!

Friday 5th June

Everything happened at once – every job on the list that we had been pushing to get done was done within 9 hours …It was intense and stressful the Mast was stepped*, the standing rigging was tensioned, the sails were put on the running rigging was moused, the Lazerette door was fixed and the paint was repaired. We went out for a test sail in the bay and got in at around 7pm and then went for good bye drinks with our Lagos friends.

At 10pm our companionway entrance door was delivered to Magic and at 11pm Simon arrived.

What a day

We were exhausted but we were ready to leave.

Bed at 1am

- A short note about the mast stepping: As they moved the mast towards the crane we watched and held our breath – then we were open mouthed as we watched in slow-mo the mast slipping off the supports and falling towards the concrete. No… no… no… Please no, don't let our new mast get damaged – I was standing with Jeff our surveyor and a friend - Andrew and Mark – the boys ran forward to help to support the mast and gently put it back on the supports – the surveyor and I just looked at each other in disbelief. May sighed

But all was well and the crane lifted the mast up and up and up and then the guys on the deck held it and swung it towards the right positon. Then carefully they dropped (stepped) the mast down into the right place. It would then be resting on top of the silver coin we had placed on her step – a coin that we had polished and made positive wishes over to keep Magic and all who sail on her safe and well.

May thought all this was crazy but she was just glad that she was not sailing.

What a day
Saturday 6th June

Up at 6am – head buzzing with excitement and anticipation and a long list of things to do:

Susan and Andrew came on Board with their gear and helped to get the dinghy and outboard stowed

Then we had to
- Walk May
- Shop for Water and Fresh Fruit and Veg
- Pay the Marina
- Drop the Hire Car off and
- Prep the Boat for Departure at 9am

We called for the Bridge to be opened and as they have not rationalized their protocols for this procedure they said – "ok, we will open the bridge soon or in 1 minute!!" Not clear, and we were not going to take any chances. We called back and asked for more specific clarification on when exactly the bridge would open as we could still see people walking over it!!!

Incredible that the Lagos foot bridge is still unclear in its procedures! Following our accident and all the meetings we had with them.

Ho Hum

We departed at 09.45am – friends cheered and fired 'water cannons' (a hose) as the bridge opened and we sailed through *safely* on our way to Barcelona.

As I write these reflections from 36.06.360N, 5.54.92W we have

Just entering the Strait of Gibraltar. We have motored all day with the Easterly wind on our nose and it has been almost complete cloud cover (8/8) – get me with the technical. Cloud cover is counted out of 8 so very little cloud would be noted in the Log Book as 1/8 and total cloud would be 8/8. We spent last night in Cadiz. A beautiful place with the most horrible marina. A dust bowl – concrete dust created by the construction on the new bridge whirls around in the sky blowing all over the deck and all over us.

We walked into the town and had both the worst and the best Tapas I have ever had – we were hungry, tired and disorientated and just needed food and drink. We rejected a few places and then eventually sat down and ordered – we should have noticed the signs - white plastic chairs and one euro Tapas in a main square was always going to be low grade – it was funny – the Sangria came in Pint glasses and all the "Tapas" was beige – all small fried things that all looked and tasted the same. We ate and drank and feeling a little better we then decided to look for the Tapas we had set out to find.

Trip Advisor came to the rescue with the Café Royalty – if you go to Cadiz go there – it is an elegant place with guilt mirrors (not ones that make you feel guilty – ones that have gold on them!) and beautiful paintings of cherubs and exotic birds – The Tapas was the best we have ever had and the service was world class – first they handed us napkins with tongs! Then served up thin rare roast beef slices with horseradish cream and delicious stuffed red peppers and perfect beef stew a sticky, delicious reduction – wow – 3 Tapas each with a glass of wine and a divine chocolate Cake and ice cream for only 16.95 Euro a head…. perfect! and May was made welcome too which was a refreshing change from Portugal where dogs are strictly not allowed in Bars and restaurants. We have devised the perfect plan for 'No Dog' places. As May is small she fits perfectly in an over-sized shopping bag and so we have a few of those and she just curls up in the bottom of the bag and sleeps. At first, we weren't sure if she was happy in the bag until one day when the bag was left on the floor she crawled in and fell asleep – May is a great traveller and the perfect companion.

I am finally allowing myself to reflect on what we have managed to get done on Magic in the last few days.

As I now write it is dark and we have watched the sunset over Malaga. We spent the night in Gibraltar and are now en route to Cartagena (only 4 months late!)

The Straights were windy but fun and the crew were enjoying taking turns on the Helm—we had reefed the main and we were tacking all the way with over 30 knots of wind on our nose – a challenge – The wind was howling in the rigging and there were white crests on the waves. I must admit the conditions made me a little anxious but I should not have been – Magic is a strong and amazing yacht and we were a competent and happy crew.

May wasn't thrilled but I held her on my knee where she feels safe and warm.

It is wonderful to be sailing again.

Evening of the 12th June

We had thought that we would be in Barcelona this morning but we stopped in Javea overnight to refuel and fill with water. We had hoped to go to go to Formentera but the wind changed so we changed our plan and headed towards Benidorm – None of us really wanted to stay there so we made towards. Javea a lovely Spanish town.

With our lovely crew settling in we sailed on with style – Sundowner cocktails Curry and Chips and Ice cream!!

Finally, the wind came in the right direction and we made 11kn moving our ETA (Estimated Time of Arrival) closer to us!! If you talk to cruising sailors they will often tell you that the wind seems to veer around and end up on your nose. This impedes your journey and it is frustrating when you want to get somewhere as soon as possible. This is where you learn that it is the weather that is in charge of your schedule. So, different from home where when you want to get somewhere you just get in the car and go – no need to check if the wind will be with or against you.

On our watch system, again we hoped to arrive in Barcelona – Port Vell at around 11am on Saturday 13th

On Sunday I am going into the city with Susan for some well-earned girl time and on Monday I am going to Paris for work, on Tuesday I am meeting Coke in Paris and then I will be back home on Magic in Barcelona Tuesday afternoon. I am still working and have work in London on the 29th and 30th meaning that in June it will be Barcelona, Paris and London for me!!

What a fantastic life full of adventure, fun, challenge and interest!
We are so fortunate and we recognize and appreciate it.

We are LOVING Barcelona and some of our neighbours. They have the most enormous super yachts we have ever seen. We are tiny in comparison and we are still not resolved if we think they are ugly or beautiful.

May is delighted to be in Barcelona – this is her kind of town! She is strutting around the Marina and city feeling like a millionaire pooch – this suits May!

liaison with a French Tart in Paris
JUNE 24

I enjoyed my trip off the boat to Paris. Having been in Lagos for 6 months being in Barcelona and Paris and London all in one month is amazing. Three incredible cities. In Paris on the eve of our meeting with Coca-Cola I was waiting for a colleague to arrive and I was just people watching. I had my trusty 'laptop' with me – the sort of Old School paper note book that is easy to navigate, is very light and portable and doesn't break if you spill water on it! I took out my pen and began to write.

A Liaison with a French Tart in Paris
18.30 Comptoir D'Issy, Issy-les-Moulineaux:Paris 15th June

A beautiful man in an elegant business suit with perfectly shiny shoes has just walked into the Brasserie. He sits next to me, opens his laptop and dives into to work. The waiter approaches him and he orders, not from the menu, he knows what he wants. The man is consumed by another world until the waiter returns with a glass of cold, golden beer and a plate on which is a very Parisian Patisserie. The tart looks delicious – thin, crispy pastry is the foundation for pale creamy crème Anglaise which makes a soft pillow for perfectly ripe, plump, juicy Strawberries in a light pink syrup that oozes just enough onto his plate. He leaves his work and his beer and turns to the tart. He gives this indulgence all his attention – he eats it like a greedy little boy, fast and furious until it is gone.

I wonder at the combination of Beer and Tart…

The man is wearing a wedding ring and I wonder if perhaps his wife does not approve of such indulgences as this. He looks fit and slim so I imagine this liaison with a French tart is his guilty pleasure. What joy!

He has all the armour he needs for his business battles – his Mont Blanc fountain pen and Mont Blanc leather folder lie waiting for him on the table. His laptop and phone – holding his world. The waiter takes his plate away and I was sure I noticed he seemed a little sad as he turned again to his work.

I wonder about him..I wonder about me – strange as I seem to be of an age where I am on the cusp of appreciating him as a beautiful man and feeling deeply maternal.

I love Paris

Chapter Seven

MESSING ABOUT IN THE MED

Fried Green Tomatoes and a Naked one Legged Man
JULY 22

Its official I love Barcelona

I haven't been writing because I have been so busy living and enjoying so many things. Food – Wine – Friends – Family…

It is always lovely to have visitors on Magic and as we were in Barcelona for a month it made it possible. When you are cruising, it is very tricky to meet up with visitors unless you know you are going to be in one place for a while. Being sure that you can meet them from their plane and get them back one on time it is the tricky part! But it is so lovely – we have had my beautiful daughter Sara and my dear friend Yvonne to stay in Barcelona and now I am writing from Menorca. Our crew gone we have been sailing just the three of us – that's Mark, May and me.

As I write I am aware that I have a sort of queue in my head – a crumpled muddle of all the senses and experiences – the tastes and emotions. It is reminding me of what the lines look like when we bring our main sail down.

I know if I keep pulling it will unravel. I want to recall so many things but now that I have allowed the time to slip through my hands the recollections are more like an impressionist painting – colours and blur but with emotion threaded through. Reflections:

Barcelona – its people, the energy of it, the food the art, the fun

Magic – getting to experience a world class Super Yacht Marina – Port Vell (and Yes – May and I did like that very much)

Sailing – feeling proud of our first overnight crossing on our own – Barcelona – Mahon (Menorca)

Cala Hopping – Our first time in Magic dropping and lifting 'the pin' (the anchor) in perfect little, hidden sparkling bays

Parking – its official I hate parking – Mark is excellent at it, but it is always an anxious time and every Marina is different.

I love being 52 and still having lots of first time experiences – I can feel my brain dancing about and doing giddy clapping!

A Riggers Eye View of Magic in Barcelona waters. We had our rig checked before our sail to Menorca.

But before I move on to our adventure back to Barcelona for some reflections.

Barcelona is such a special city. It is young and fun, anarchic and creative. It is hot and sexy, it is charming and intelligent. When we were walking down the beach one sizzling day I saw a sight that I have never seen – a one legged man, totally naked and having a shower – I thought how fantastic – that's Barcelona. A city that accepts everyone. The flavours of the city are exciting too and the three that I must recall in detail are the Fried Green Tomato Tapas we had in a Bar called Benedicts in the El Born area (a favourite) The delicious snails in a small Bar, in a small square in Barcelonetta – (if you go to Barcelona – don't bother with Las Ramblas at all – got to El Born, The Gothic area and our favourite – Barcelonetta. The latter is where the fishermen used to live and where it is still a local community)

But back to those Fried Green Tomatoes – The juicy Green Tomatoes are sliced thickly and then coated in some dusty delicious ness then they are deep-fried until they are brown and crispy. These are stacked and between them is spicy and delicate Guacamole – then some tiny cubes of feta and finally – on the side…. light and luscious strawberry jam!!

So, creative and exciting it was an amazing feast of taste and texture.

Next – I never knew I liked snails but in the little Barcelonetta bar we had several yummy things delivered to the table and the snails were amongst them. To my surprise, they tasted like game and were served in a deep, dark sauce that my tongue's memory can still recall. The little bar in the little square was rammed with locals and the wine and vermouth was served in jugs straight out of the Barrels that lined the back wall – amazing. Barcelona does great sweets – walking around the El Born area you are guaranteed delightful surprises – one such surprise was the delightful and adorably named – Papabubble …They describe themselves as making 'caramels artesian' – they make traditional hard sugar sweets – but the flavours and the art in them are incredible.

Back to Menorca.

As I write we have just spent two lovely nights on anchor in Cala Santa Galdana. The visit with my dear friend of 37 years, Claire from Belfast was glorious – it is wonderful when friends can come and share our adventure. Claire, May and I are having a ball. We are being ladies who shop!

We have been swimming and snorkeling and enjoying the perfect weather. This little bay on the South West coast of Menorca is very sheltered and has a sandy

Blue Blue warm water in Menorca – Clare and I catching up

bottom so you can see all the way down through the azure blue, warm, crystal clear water.

I know that last paragraph sounds idyllic and it is, but of course when you are cruising it isn't all straight forward and as I have said in other posts things break and get lost too frequently – Currently on the "Lost List" is my Kindle and on the long "To Fix" list the Dinghy has now been added as it has managed to acquire a slow puncture. There are other things too but I am so bored of the lost and broken lists that they make me grumpy to recall so I will stop!

We are still getting waves of emotions … high – sailing under the stars and swimming in perfect bays and low – another lost or broken thing.

The honest thing is that we have not finally decided if the highs and the lows are in the right balance to enable us to live this life for years as we had first thought we would. It is hard a lot of the time. You get too hot or too cold – things break that you don't know how to fix, you get anxious and sometimes even scared when sailing or parking.

I have discovered that May and I don't want to get anxious and we hate to be scared.

Perhaps it will get easier with time?

We have decided that we are going to do the Atlantic crossing with the ARC and we are looking forward to that.

We visited the perfect little town of Cuitdella which is a gem – beautiful, old, great bars and great shopping! The Marina was achingly expensive but we still decided to indulge and stay two nights – two nights is so much better than one! It means you can really relax.

Ciutadella – Tina, May and Clare – girls who shop!

15 Pringles and a Red Bull…. does that constitute a Breakfast?
AUGUST

Sadly Claire's visit was over too soon and as she left for the airport we prepared Magic to leave for Formenterra.

Strong wind – again meant that mooring up at the fuel dock was a challenge – May and I were anxious (again) even the fuel dock manager commented that it was a difficult day. But Mark was a star.

When we dock well in 'interesting' conditions we 'high five' each other – corny

Full of fuel, water and food we set sail for Formenterra – It was to be a 24-hour journey and we were looking forward to it. Mark and I love night sailing. We love the team-work and the challenge – the planning and the adventure.

Something I have found that I have always done in my life is to imagine the perfect scenario of a future situation and then – as my imagination is especially good – the reality inevitably falls short of the dream. I have tried to curb my ambitions of how situations should be – to avoid the ache of disappointment but it seems I am an eternal optimist! So, it was with our trip from Mahon to Formenterra. I had imagined the perfect winds in the right direction, a gentle sea state, stars, dolphins and arriving at noon to drop anchor in a crystal bay to swim and then eat lunch.

Well – there were stars and dolphins and a gentle sea state – a magical combination but no wind so we had to motor all the way – always disappointing when you love to sail. Then, as we got closer we got strong wind but right on our nose and in the totally wrong direction so slowing us down quite a bit. (That seems to happen if you decide in advance you particularly need to be somewhere!)

As a result, we didn't get in at noon – it was 5pm and there was a lot of haze and a strong wind. We picked a spot in a sheltered horseshoe bay in the lee of the island

and dropped the anchor only to be woken in the night as the wind had moved around and it was choppy. So, following our 28-hour sail (motor) we had a sleepless night … not what the dream had promised!

And what of the swim on arrival in the perfect lagoon? – well I did get a swim but that was at 7am the following morning with a rope tied around me. It was very choppy and I was swimming through the waves with a mask and snorkel to check on the hull as there was some antifoul that had come away and we were monitoring it.

I thought – how very Lara Croft of me! And all before breakfast…. I do have fantasies of being Lara Croft which is hilarious. If I made a list of all her attributes such as long silky brown hair, a tall slim body, muscles and gun skills… I have all the opposite!! It makes me chuckle in my head …

So again, the reality was very different from the dream but we pressed on. You know us and deadlines. We wanted to be in Gibraltar for the 1st August.

So, we set a course for Cartagena – another 24-hour journey.

Up to this point I had been enjoying the catering – I love to have good food on Magic – I enjoy treating people and it is lovely to hand a perfect bacon sandwich to Mark when he has completed his 4am – 6am Watch. We even dressed for dinner on the crossing from Mahon to Formenterra!! But as we had battled all night with wind and wave I couldn't face making the 'perfect' breakfast and opted for the remaining 15 Pringles and a can of Red bull –

Mark made toast! I could feel the standards slipping!

We arrived into Cartagena following 27 hours of sailing– exhausted we went straight off the boat ate in the nearest café and went back to Magic to sleep. What we didn't know was that friends from Lagos were in the same Marina – they saw Magic but when they noticed that the sails had not been stowed and the boat not washed down they knew we had sailed through the night and must have gone straight to sleep – that's sailors – they knew!

I said to Mark *"Squeeeek Bump!"*,

"What's that?" he said

"Oh, that's just the sound of the three of us sliding down Maslov's Pyramid and landing at the bottom pride not intact!"

Hot, exhausted, dirty, hungry, thirsty– washing hanging out on the boat!

I guess we have fully embraced this sailing thing!
Now all we must do is get to Gibraltar

SEPTEMBER

Once again, I find that I am catching up on a span of time for my writing. I like writing but it seems that the time just whizzes past. I am not sure what happened to the cruising life I imagined of lazy days in the sun, reading or making jewellery with lots and lots of spare time.

I think you sail as you are and we are very goal orientated busy people and we are constantly setting ourselves lists of tasks and working to get them all done.

As I write this time I am sitting on deck watching the sun go down in Gibraltar – I have a very intriguing view of the airport runway to the stern and forward is The Rock – we are in Ocean Village having a long list of works done – Steel work, Generator, Water maker, Satellite phone…I am enjoying the project management and the technical challenges of knitting the boat full of wires and working out where to fit the new digital panels. I know that means more to go wrong …but it also means we can cruise oceans with more confidence and that is our aim.

All jobs complete and Gibraltar is now behind us – what a strange place and what a weird month – too dull to talk about! We have a crew now for our trip back to Lagos.

Sunday 6th September 2015

Now we are under full sail doing 7 knots with 11knots of wind in perfect sunny weather. We have just left beautiful Rota where we spent the night and we are now heading from Spain to Portugal .. our destination is Lagos and we are looking forward to arriving 'home' to see our friends there. We have friends aboard – John – an old friend of Mark's – we make a good crew and are having a lot of fun. John likes to fish and we have just caught a small Tuna – 10lbs – a perfect size for our lunch.

Reflections on Gibraltar.
I am taking time to sit in the sun beside May to reflect on the time we had in Gibraltar – what a strange, strange place. I honestly do not know how to describe it. Most people who do not live or work in 'Gib' do not stay as long as we have – we were there for five weeks. Five weeks and we didn't go and see the Monkeys or take the Cable Car! I like that…a small rebellion? I once went to Memphis and did not go and see anything to do with Elvis!

Gibraltar has many layers – like the rock itself. On the one hand those who live there are viciously proud of their 'land', their piece of rock – 'Gibraltar shall always be 'free' the flags say. They love where they live and so they should, as it is their home. But we must be honest in our reflections and we did not love Gibraltar.

We left just as the National Day celebrations were beginning. We are going to miss out on the concerts and the red and white flag waving and the special offers on fish and chips.

We made the best of our stay and got Magic in great shape with her new Generator, Watermaker, Satellite phone and Downwind sail – our list of things to do is now down to one missing screw and squeaky floor boards.

When our list had 30 things on it and we thought it would take weeks – but we had a boat fixing dynamo and most things were fixed in the first day. He flew about the boat often fixing two things at once – Mark followed him around in awe and learning like a sponge. This guy is like Simon (our delivery skipper friend) they create a wake of repaired things behind them – everything aboard gets tested and oiled and repaired and polished.

Mark and I are both reluctantly giving into the fact that we must learn to fix everything on board.

I wish Gibraltar was a wonderful shining testament to the UK. So many thousands of people from all over the world visit Gib so it would be fantastic if it made us proud. But instead we were disappointed and even embarrassed by it. We hope that people don't think that it is representative of what the UK aims to be.

Before I continue however we want to say that in Gibraltar we met some great people who have helped us and the place is not a reflection on the people. I don't like to be negative but also, I like to be honest about what we have experienced and seen.

Here are a few reflections…

The narrow Main Street with its Dorothy Perkins and BHS is often bloated with up to six thousand people who have poured out from the cruise ships. They shuffle up and down the main street in search of bargains on sunglasses, booze and perfume. The main street is one massive, claustrophobic, duty-free shop dotted with mediocre English pubs with offers on all day breakfasts and fish and chips.

The streets are filthy – dotted with black disks - discarded chewing gum covered in grime. The rubbish swirls around on the streets with the wind. They do brush and wash the streets but without care.

The weather is dirty too – in August the Rock has its own cloud – the grey Levanter cloud that rains rust coloured dust which has been carried on the wind from Africa.

There are small beaches crammed with people enjoying the views out to sea of giant moored up oil tankers.

There is a tiny bit of colonial architecture and the rest is soulless blocks of flats and offices.

There is a tourism fight carried out on the streets each day an ugly and aggressive war between those selling trips on the yellow Dolphin tourist boats and those selling trips on the blue Dolphin tourist boats – the sales representatives from the Yellows seem more predatory than the Blues and their game is to mark the blues and pounce first at key strategic locations where unsuspecting tourists walk by.

There are lots of places to gamble or eat junk food or get to drink 2:4:1 cocktails but if you would like theatre or fresh salads or live music you will be disappointed.

Having said all that Gibraltar is fantastic for a day…

There is a Morrison's where you can fill your boat with food from home and you can get a great pint of Speckled Hen. You can get cheap alcohol and cigarettes and sailing around the huge oil tankers is fascinating. You can get help with most repairs and maintenance and the people are helpful.

The staff at Marina Bay Marina were fantastic – Tony and Mini were stars – they helped to make our stay safe and fun. It was odd where we were moored – right in front of a cruise ship that has no engine and is a hotel – The Sunborn – locals call it the Sunburn. We never visited it in the five weeks were there. We have one special thank you to make and that is for that diver who saved the day by finding my purse from the bottom to the sea! Mark was doing some Yacht Master training and we had taken a lot of Euros out of the Bank to pay the trainer. I was carrying my purse which had all the money in it and as I stepped on Magic I just dropped the purse in-between Magic and the harbour wall – urghhh

So, we are sorry Gib but we didn't fall in love with you and we think you could do better – perhaps if the new Governor coming in would bother less about the Spanish and more about Gibraltar it would help…just a thought?

Chapter Eight

BACK IN LAGOS

Now where shall we put the Wild Bore Game Pâté and the Pink Moet?
OCTOBER

Lagos feels like home. It is lovely to meet up with people who we had loved spending time with over the Winter and Spring. The activities are just beginning and even the Christmas lunch is booked. It all feels quite animal in one way – some making safe nests for the winter and others packing away stores to survive (us!)

We have had a buffet of emotions about crossing the Atlantic – the overriding one being bloody minded determination – we said we are going to do this so we doing it! Then there are others …. anxiety – what will it be like? How long will it take? Will the equipment hold up? Will the weather be kind?

Some years' people have a wonderful time crossing the Atlantic and other years it's horrendous. This is an El Nino year – what will that mean to our crossing? Our brains are churning – we envy May who just relaxes on the deck in the sun wondering about what all the fuss is about. We are also experiencing a healthy dose of fear. The fear that is driven by respect for such an incredible Ocean and for the weather.

We know we have an amazing crew with hundreds of thousands of sea miles and an exhilarating range of skills:
>   Qualified Professional Plumber
>   RYA/MCA Commercially Endorsed Yachtmaster
>   RYA/MCA Master of vessels up to 200ft
>   Psychologist
>   Expert Fisherman

World Class Dish Washer
Cleaners and Cooks
RYA & St John Ambulance Resuscitation and First Aid
Certificated Sextant and Celestial Navigator
PADi Open Water Diver
MCA Sea Survival Certificate
MCA Fire Fighting Certificate
SPSA Rock Climbing Certificate (hope we won't need this)
7th Kup TaeKwon-Do
Mountain Bike Instructor
Clipper Race Crew Trainer
Open Canoe Instructor
VHF and Radar Certificated Users
Swedish Yachtmaster
Architect
8 languages
and
23 Atlantic Crossings (5 of which were races with 3 firsts and 2 second)
Total nm experience of the Crew =
285,000+8039+7800+34 000+12 000+2 000
= 348 839 nm (nautical miles)

Our crew is very experienced. We make an incredible crew with wonderful skills and Mark and I are so happy and honored to be able to sail with them. Another interesting thing about our crew is that each of is an entrepreneur that currently runs their own business…. fascinating

But today the only fear is – a fear of cupboards and organization – what would that be called ?

Listening to Van Morrison and Queen is helping …and so is Jacqui – we have been following each other's blogs for almost a year and now she is here to overwinter in Lagos. Jackie is so organized and I am the complete other end of that spectrum so Mark suggested (as kindly as he could !) that we should ask Jackie to help us. It took us from 8am to 5pm to complete the stowage of the food and drink and that was 3 of us – so 24 hours. Then – as all this has taken up so much space we had to spend another 16 hours the following day sorting and stowing all the displaced stuff. Mark and I have been happily nesting on Magic for almost a year but now it is time to make room for four other people and all their gear and the food and drink for all of them for the Atlantic Crossing. But what to do with that wild boar pate?

We really didn't understand the size of the task – when we bought Magic we thought – how amazing we are going to sail our yacht across the Atlantic. What we didn't know was that it would take us 12 months of preparation and A LOT of money to prepare. Everyone who sails will tell you that it is harder work and costs more than you could ever plan for – so there is no sympathetic ear in the sailing community – "oh well – that's sailing!" Is what you get....But we all stick with it. Why? Because as I have blogged before – those perfect sailing days are our 'high' and they are worth it.

So, it feels like the adventure has really begun now and my greatest hope is that Mark, May and I will enjoy it more – there certainly has been more pain than pleasure or as Van Morrison says, 'too many problems and not enough bliss'.

Today, 7th October we will go to the airport and collect one of our crew who is sailing with us – we hope until we get to St Lucia. The plan is to moor Magic on the visitor's pontoon tonight and then set sail at 6am on the 8th – although we may leave tonight. We are heading for Porto Santo and then on to Madeira – it is a journey of 435nm and that should take us around 2 or 3 nights. It will be wonderful to be heading South and making our way to the start of the ARC.

As today is a 'prep to leave day' – we have hours of work to do – more stowage, sails prepped, fresh food, safety equipment checked, engine checked, Log Book ready, instruments ready, Jack Stays in place, Life Jackets and tethers ready, Grab Bag ready ...drop hire car back, pay marina fees

Say good bye Lagos 'we love you'!

Now we understand why Lagos really is a 'Velcro' Town
OCTOBER 8, 2015

I feel now like a petulant child – "I want to go ... I want to go.... Why can't I go....?"

But when you are planning to sail for 3 days you need the right weather and setting off this morning as planned would have meant a very uncomfortable journey.

We were all ready and excited – We moved Magic at 3pm, Wed 7th and did some final preparations. Then we went to visit some friends to say good bye. We had a lovely meal out and an early night. We checked the weather before we slept and it looked perfect. At 6am we were up and ready to go.

Just one more update on the weather before we go.

"Nooooo!" the weather had changed and a decision to go would mean 25k of wind on our nose – not today but tomorrow. It would have been rough and splashy and horrible – so we made the decision to wait. When we are on land we are all so used to going when you want to go and arriving when you want to arrive. But when you are a sailor it is different and we are learning – that when it is safer to wait – you wait, even if it is frustrating.

We were as ready as you can be and that's frustrating also a shame because our crew had flown in especially for the journey.

We will now have to go back to our berth and wait. It is the right decision, 24 hours of bashing into the wind would have been miserable and so we must 'put up with' lazing by the pool and reading a book – perhaps tweaking a few things on the boat

… and we can get ready to get ready, again

Watching the weather, we think that perhaps we can leave on Saturday night or as our friend Andrew had advised – Sunday might be the best day to leave.

You must love it when one man can fly and the other can sew!
OCTOBER 13, 2015

Note:
(It is a mad, bonkers, crazy, stupid life living aboard a yacht! – there, I have got that out of my system. Now, where was I?)

Friday 9ᵗʰ November

So, having tried to leave 'Velcro town' and failed, we decided to make the best of things and enjoy Lagos – an early morning walk on the beach then back to Magic to take her from the visitor's pontoon back to her berth on J11, then a swim and chill out in the sun by the pool and dinner in town with friends. We were happy with our 'delay bonus'.

Our new friend Pam, who loves dogs, said she would be happy to take May for a few hours and she was so professional about what May was like and how to care for her.

We relaxed – a break from 'May sitting' and the boat.

Mark and I packed a towel, put on our swimming costumes and headed to the pool – only a few minute's walk away. I had taken my phone with me; it rang just as we left the security gates. I noticed it was a local Portuguese number. The voice said, "Hello, is that Tina Davies from sailing yacht Magic?"

"Yes, it is" I said – then the person said, "is that Yacht Magic on J11?" again I confirmed the information "Yes, that is correct"

I was thinking, how odd – then the voice said – "this is Marina de Lagos we have to tell you to return to your yacht immediately as Magic is taking on water and is sinking in the Marina now" – just take a moment to let that 'sink' in.

How would that feel?

You are standing moments away from your home, in your swimming costume about to have some relaxation time and suddenly you are told that your home is sinking!

I turned white and told Mark then we both started running back to Magic. We could see from where we were that Magic didn't seem any lower in the water. I still had the woman from the Marina on the phone. I told her it didn't look like Magic was sinking and she confirmed that it was a reliable report, a person from Blue Water had called it in – they are respected chandlers near where Magic is moored on pontoon J11. The man had called the Marina office and said that Magic on J11 was taking on water and was sinking. I said to her that Magic clearly was *not* sinking and then – she started to laugh! I couldn't believe it … I thought, surely this could not be a joke, and nobody we know would do that, as it is not at all funny. At that point, the Marina staff arrived in their small boat at great speed with walkie-talkies chattering. They were looking at us and at Magic – they seemed very concerned and confused. "Magic isn't sinking?" they said. "No, she isn't" we said, stating what was obvious for all to see. Then someone called them on their radios and they were gone. And that was it – we didn't hear anything from them again that day – no explanation, no apology, nothing. As it turns out the report to the Marina office had been that a boat called, Big Blue on G1 was sinking. Portugal at its best.

We went swimming.

Saturday 10ᵗʰ October

We waited for a new set of weather information before we could leave Lagos. It rained and rained but it is interesting now, understanding the weather more and more each day, rather than complaining about the rain I found it interesting – and I could relate it to the weather forecasts we had been tracking for days.

This was the 'tail' of the Atlantic low that had been curling its way V=Northwards. There is so much I must learn about the weather but I am enjoying it and it helps to feel more secure at sea. Mark and I even find ourselves casually chatting about weather systems – weird.

Mark was like a caged bear. One minute he was frantically prepping the prep he had prepped for our journey then was sitting quietly looking into space. "What are you doing?" I said when I saw him trance-like – "I am waiting!" he said.

After lunch – just as forecast the rain cleared and the wind changed direction "time to go". We shut the hatches, unplugged the electrics, turned off the gas, prepared the fenders and mooring lines…engine on – bow thruster on – slip the lines – this time we *are* going… As we passed Lynn and David our friends on Yacht Scarlett and Andrew on S/Y Andromeda they all waved and wished us fair winds – then as we passed out of the Marina into the river we saw Pam and Roger our new friends – how lovely our friends old and new came out to say good bye – and we thought we were making a sneaky subtle exit ….we will miss Lagos.

We travelled safely under the bridge.
May wasn't at all sure this was a good idea.

Chapter Nine

LAGOS TO MADEIRA

Following a quick stop on the visitor's pontoon to pay for our extra nights – and to enjoy a few surprise extra farewells from friends – we were away into the afternoon light, direction 240degrees – towards Madeira.

We decided to motor as the night was fast approaching, and with the wind on our nose (again) for a few hours we were unsure how quickly the weather conditions would change and we wanted to make a good start.

All went well and we soon were into a watch pattern – Mark and our crew make a fantastic team and I am first mate, chief cook and bottle washer. May is on lookout for dolphins and head of morale. We negotiated the enormous freight ships in the shipping channel for most of the night. There is a huge shipping 'motorway' for 25 miles that runs around the Southernmost tip of Portugal. One of the ships we passed was a third of a mile long – he radioed us and asked if we could pass him to his stern – strangely enough that was an idea we had already had!!

Sunday 11th October
The sea was bumpy and it was very difficult to get any sleep. By morning we were all weary. Except May, she had a fantastic night's sleep. At 6.00am I came back on watch and enjoyed watching the sun come slowly up. After a long bumpy night, it is lovely to greet the sun – there is some truth in the saying that the darkest hour comes before the dawn.

It's Sunday morning – our crew get up first and have several strong coffees and I have had some tea. Mark is still asleep as he did the last watch before I came on at 06.30. All seems well in the world. The sun is shining and the wind is a brisk 15kn from the SW (not what we wanted, the forecast had shown it moving around, we wanted a NW but we will be fine) The Atlantic is at play with 4-5metre waves and swell (it was forecast at 3m). It is tricky to do much when you are rolling around. The boat is twisting and bumping so we are doing only what must be done and not what perhaps we would like to do. Food is going to be 'easy to do food' – I am glad I cooked some meals in advance that I can just microwave and serve with rice or pasta. And of course, thanks to Jackie I now know where all the supplies are – the snack cupboard is working particularly well! With the engine having been running all night we decide it was time to sail – all sailors love that magical moment when you turn the engine off and all you hear is the water whooshing under the hull and the wind in the sails.

We check the lines – first issue of the day – I look up and notice that the main halyard has managed to flap itself around the mast and catch on the steaming light. In this swell and with the foredeck often covered in waves it is not ideal to have to go up there and muck about with lines. But our crew member bounds into action, as Mark is still asleep. He puts on his safety harness and moves forward to try to flip and flick it free – but it is stuck fast. My heart sinks as I know the only way to release the halyard is the Boson's chair. Someone is going to have to go up the mast and in this swell it will be horrible. By now, Mark is up and before he has even had breakfast he is up on deck with our crew discussing the issue – they both agree – someone must go up the Mast – Mark gets the boson's chair and our crew preps the lines on the winch – I take the helm to position us down wind in an attempt to keep us steadier. May looks on with interest.

Expertly our crew hoists Mark – I can't look – the forces are big and Mark although safety harnessed to the Mast and gripping with his legs – is still being bashed. He is being pulled away from the mast with one wave and then with the next hurled towards it. He says he is fine so, our crew continue to work the halyard lifting Mark up to the first spreaders. Mark reaches out and can free the Halyard, which I then pull in so it is tight and won't tangle again. Coming down the mast proves even trickier than going up as the swell makes the boat strongly sway. Mark is tethered to the Mast but just for the last few metres down he must un-tie the safety harness that keeps him close to the mast, and just at a vulnerable moment a wave crashes into our side he loses his grip on the mast and swings out, way beyond the rigging and over the sea!

I was on the helm watching open mouthed, I shouted out as I was so afraid – he was in the Boson's chair and held tight by the halyard and he swung back in thankfully with no bumps or bruises – it was all over in 30 seconds but I never want that to happen again and we certainly would not do that if we were just sailing with the two of us even if it meant we had to motor all the way. To see one of your crew actually flying outside of the rig and over the ocean is terrifying. May could pick up on my fear and snuggled in around my feet.

But the boys just continued with the task of hoisting the Mainsail and then the Genoa. I sat quietly reflecting on this sport – this adventure. Were we mad? – we were putting ourselves and May at such risk.

Finally, Mark had some breakfast and we were all able to enjoy that moment when the engine is turned off.

The sun was out and although the sea was much friskier than I would like we were taking a moment to just be at sea with the sails perfectly set … but just then:

Bang!

What now? – What was that?

Our crew member saw it first as he was sitting on the Port side on watch.

The Genoa halyard had come away from the head of the sail and the sail was falling towards the deck and the sea. He went on deck and quickly and expertly brought the sail onto the deck. I was on the helm and brought us around into the wind to take any stress off the sail. I turned the engine on.

Mark helped our crew member stow the Genoa on the foredeck. It's a huge sail and it was a battle.

The tapes at the head of the sail that the Halyard clips to had both come away from the sail – with the sun the stitching on sails can become frail and we think that this is what had happened.

How disappointing, just as we had all the sails set perfectly.

As you might imagine nobody was up for a ride in the Boson's chair to the top of the mast – the waves were still 5m. So that's it no Genoa until Madeira where we hope we can find a sail maker who can do the work.

It is so disappointing to have to motor/sail but without the engine on and just the mainsail – we would be out here much longer than expected.

We have enough fuel as we have full tanks and extra tanks too. We will get to Madeira but it is disappointing. To add to the anxiety May has not enjoyed the trip – she is very anxious about all the creaking and slamming and doesn't like the movement in this big swell. May finally had a wee but hasn't eaten or drunk a thing for 20 hours. I sit with her and drop water into her mouth but she just wants to snuggle in her bed with her bear. I think she is seasick.

Poor May.

I do have moments when I think – "*what the hell are we doing!?*" but I continue to hope that these moments balance out with a higher number of moments where I think "*this is the best time of our life*" and then…..

We turned to our watches – we can do 2 hours 'on' and 4 'off' and it works well. We are motor/sailing so the noise and heat of the engine isn't great but we are all tired so we each do our duties and sleep soundly.

Monday 12th October

My watch is 24.00 – 02.00 a pleasant one with stars – we are all very diligent on watch – checking the radar, the visual and doing the log – 2 hours soon goes fast. Our crew comes after me from 02.00-04.00 then Mark from 04.00 to 06.00 – I think the boys gave me the lovely watch times. I get the bright stars and the beautiful sunrises.

One of our crew came on deck at 07.00 looking rested – he tucked into his double coffee. Our inexperience shows – I think we would have left the sail on the foredeck until we had a rigger fix it. Not our crew, he goes up onto the Port foredeck where the Genoa is stowed – I watch feeling a bit helpless as the waves splash over us. Our crew is so competent on deck and so sure-footed. He retrieves the head of the Genoa and I gingerly step out onto the deck to reach him and pull the sail.

Mark is sleeping and the crew and I inspect the sail. The stitching has come away from the head of the sail. The sail was only in the sail loft a few months ago and so this wear should have been seen and repaired, but it wasn't. Our crew member gets out some pliers and the Sail-Makers' needle and waxed thread. He chooses not to use the 'palm' (a leather thingy that is put over your palm and works like a heavy-duty thimble) He knows that with the pressure needed – if the needle slips from the 'palm' it can go into your actual palm and that hurts – a lot. He works expertly, quietly threading the head of the sail. He is hurting his hand with the friction and pressure but he keeps going as if not to notice – Our crew is super tough and it makes me feel like a city girl out of my depth. I ask if I can help and he smiles at me –"no, you couldn't do it!" he says. I know he is right and it makes me feel helpless and a little incompetent. As he finishes the job on the sail Mark arrives. We are both so glad we have professional crew with us and we are learning a lot from his experience.

I offer a cooked breakfast – I hate the thought of 'pink' jobs and 'blue' jobs to describe jobs for women and jobs for men on the boat but it is true – so I go with it and do what I can do which is to feed them well.

There is a massive swell and I am grateful that I do not get seasick – so I cook sausages and Swiss potato rosti (sounds more impressive than it was as the rosti was Waitrose from a bag!) It is yummy and our crew are hungry and enjoys it.

May has recovered fully – she has eaten and drunk water and been for a wee – I am delighted. It has taken all of us a couple of days to get steady and orientated.

Mark is not so taken with his cooked breakfast – he takes one look at it and is immediately sick – Mark has felt queasy before and on this trip a bit but he has never been sick, ever. He looks – not sorry for himself but frustrated. Our crew and I finish our breakfast – poor Mark.

After breakfast, we are on a mission to hoist our repaired sail. We take the sail forward. I then take the helm. May watches. We take the boat 30 Degrees to the wind and reduce the engine speed. Our crew attaches the spare Genoa halyard to the head of the sail. Mark returns to the winch. Our crew threads the Genoa into the track on the forestay as Mark carefully raises the halyard from the winch. It looks like it is working. We raise the sail successfully and set a course for Madeira and then we do that Magical thing…we turn the engine off.

Bliss – we are sailing – the sky is blue with some small fluffy clouds; the sea is sparkling and we have a full Genoa and the main sail has two reefs in. The wind speed is 12kn from the North West – finally – perfect wind from the right direction with a good sea state. This is what we came for!!!

Mark and I thank our crew for his work and reflect on how much we have learned and how much we must learn.

Pleased with our morning's work, "206 nautical miles to Porto Santo" That means we should arrive by teatime on Tuesday – we can do 180 nm in one day at 7kn ish.

So, all is going well and we are happy and relaxed. Then after lunch we notice the sound of sloshing water under our feet the saloon. Not good. The two golden rules of sailing are – 'keep the people in' and 'keep the water out'

We opened the floor panels and our fears are confirmed. There was quite a bit of water in the bilges – we test it - salt water.

Now I am sure you will agree when you are in the middle of an ocean voyage this is not a scenario you would enjoy. We all set to work, even though we were all quietly anxious. There was a determined and focused effort. First, we use all bilge pumps to extract the water – the nightmare would be that the water would rise and the electrics would be damaged. Secondly, we had to find the source of the salt-water ingress – could it be the new seacocks we had fitted in Gib? There was a fizz of fear but we were all doing not talking.

We finally got all the water out of the boat and then methodically worked though checking each area – every seacock. The front area was all dry, the Port and Starboard Cabins were dry – we lifted every panel. So now we focus in on the Lazarette (the locker at the stern of the yacht) The locker is full of supplies for the ARC – bottles of water and tools and spares…it is stuffed full so that makes it really challenging to find out where the water is coming in.

This area is also where the water maker and generator were fitted – each requiring new seacocks. Also, this is where there is a large hydraulic door that drops down and becomes a swimming platform. This door has been repaired, twice – once in Holland by the previous owner and again in Lagos, Portugal. I was sure that the issue was due to more sloppy, careless work in Portugal. It makes me so angry to think of the work we have had done – the hours of time and thousands of pounds. And still there were problems.

We inspected the door and found a small amount of water was coming in through the lower port side of the door. It may be the seal or the brackets but either way it is the door that had been – 'fixed' twice — So we set up our bailing system to pump out any water every hour. The water was only coming in when we were heeling (leaning) on our Port side – which unfortunately for us was all the time on this trip.

It was very stressful but we worked fast and well as a team to resolve the issue and we know what needs to be done to make the repair.

Mark and I felt very, very low, first the sail and then the ingress of water. The issues seem endless and we wonder when the part where you can relax and enjoy the sailing begins. Our crew member says that '**this is sailing**'....urmm

We left instructions in the log book for the 'pump outs' through the day and night. Mark and I are feeling very glum. May is looking at us as if to say

"I told you this sailing lark was a bad idea!" Nothing worse when you are in a bind than a righteous dog!

Tuesday 13th

As we predicted we will arrive in Porto Santo around 16.30. It is lovely to look at the plotter and see Porto Santo and Madeira near us. Just now it is 12.15 the clouds are breaking and the sun is coming out. We have 30 miles to go. Mark and I are feeling a little better.

Watches went well again last night with each of us doing our 2 hours on and 4 off. May is also settled into the routine and is eating and drinking normally. Mark and I shared the first half an hour of my midnight watch under the stars. We both feel it is important to grab the beautiful moments when you can.

We reflect on why nothing is working as it should:
> The Genoa we had serviced, ripped
> The New Generator doesn't seem to charge the batteries
> The New Water Maker fills with air and stops – so the water maker doesn't make water
> The Hydraulic Door that was 'fixed' leaks
> The Yanmar engine that was fully serviced and coolant leak repaired – leaks coolant.
> The Iridium Satellite System for collecting weather reports doesn't connect to get weather

> It is sooooooo frustrating
> (Small diva ranting fit including stamping the ground and saying 'Grrrrr'-

To chill out we could always listen to music – but…..

Then the speakers that were set up in Gib now have a feedback hum so they don't work either...

Ah well, what do you expect from £50 000 of equipment, repairs and maintenance?

The issue seems to be that by the time you are properly testing stuff you are hundreds of miles out at sea and heading away from the supplier who did the work and on to a new country. The people that fix stuff don't have to care – their clients will be long gone if any further issue arrives.

We will have the Genoa repaired in Porto Santo and the rest will have to wait until we are in Las Palmas. It really is maddening to have to have repairs done to stuff that you just paid to have repaired or that is newly fitted. Grrrrrrrr

Food

We have eaten well. I have done all the catering but I don't mind, as I don't get sea sick even down in the galley in a swell. The issue is more one of stability. It is tricky moving about when the boat is at 40 degrees one way and then to 40 degrees the other in seconds. You must wear boat shoes to get traction and make sure the floor has no spills on it and you should keep your feet apart and bend your knees – like a sort of surfing position. Then you must use one hand to steady yourself – leaving one had to do everything else. The cooker is on a gimbal which means it stays flat and the boat moves around it so that makes a great surface to put hot things on. The microwave is another issue! I had cooked meals before we left and they were frozen. This is a great idea as you can have delicious hot, homemade meals following a long day – good for morale. However. There is a tricky manoeuvre where you must first open the freezer – meaning that everything frozen flies out and skids across the floor and second you then must open the microwave door and slam in the dish shutting the door fast so it doesn't fly out.

So far so good.

Then the problem arises when the now very hot food must be taken out of the microwave. The solution – open the door, put in a wooden spoon to secure the dish, secure foot position then carefully open the door and take the hot food out of the microwave to the top of the cooker where it can be flat. It is a major work out for your whole-body cooking and doing anything on a boat whilst in a heavy sea. We managed to have the following – cooked breakfast of sausages and Swiss Potato Rosti and scrambled eggs with smoked salmon and fresh thyme, Spaghetti with Picante Bolognese, Sweet and Sour Pork with Peppers and Rice, Brie and Pastrami wraps, Tri Colore Salad – and lots and lots of butterscotch sweets!! Nice.

I do take a moment to think that I have understood the Galley well and have prepared well – I love feeding people (and animals)

Arrival

13.45 Land Ahoy! As they say – whoever 'they' are.

We can see the misty rocky shape of Porto Santo 21nm ahead of us. Feels good. Put the Moet on Ice!

Our crew says, "let's have a 'land in sight' Whisky" I said, "good idea I will have a 'land in sight' Bacardi!" Our crew replies "no, you can't have a 'land in site Bacardi – that's totally wrong!" We all laugh – we are a great team.

May looks on, not so sure.

"Humans are weird" May says

Everything hurts. After 3 nights and 3 days at sea just the everyday effort of staying up right works every muscle – especially your core. You also eat a lot less and drink way less alcohol – Mark and I feel we have lost pounds. Then there are the bruises – my newly discovered hipbones were a joy to find and then ouch – they are now blue. Toes and fingers get bashed, heads bumped and skin torn – Mark chaffed his thighs clinging onto the Mast.

We will be in soon calling Ch9 and asking for a berth for the night in Porto Santo then tomorrow morning we will sail on to Quinta do Loarde where we will have to stay for a week to wait for the next weather window.

So – stuff is broken, we are tired, bashed, bruised and stressed – but as always, we are learning a lot!

Isn't sailing fun?

......Now, where is there a sail maker in Madeira?

Chapter Ten

MADEIRA

Sleeping on Soup and Fishing for Ladders
OCTOBER

Arriving into Quinta Do Lorde was such a pleasant surprise – what a pretty harbour – the sweetness of it seemed in such contrast to the brutality of our crossing.

As soon as we had moored up we were surprised to be greeted warmly by two lovely sailors who had been reading our blog. It is weird and wonderful when strangers greet you like a long-lost friend and of course because they have been reading the blog they know a lot about us but we know nothing about them. They gave us a hug and a lovely bottle of wine and said they were sorry we had had such a difficult crossing. How unexpected. How lovely.

Now we find we are stuck in Quinta do Lorde. The weather is too bad to sail to Las Palmas.

At first, we were not too unhappy to be pinned down by heavy weather in Quinta do Lorde. We thought it would only be a few days and we could rest and clean the boat.

Cleaning the boat was to include wiping up soup.

We had decided that the best place for some of the ships stores was the compartment under our bed. It is not only very large but also accessible. One of the cartons of soup was in a Tetra-pak carton and it had been laid on top of some cans – just too high so that when the heavy bed lid was laid down on it – Squish,

Squash – the carton burst and the soup smushed out – we didn't know until we opened the bed – urghh – soup over everything – This was not a job we wanted to add to the list – slippery, slimy, cold, vegetable soup all over most of the other cans.

Having poured over the weather data it soon became clear we would be in Quinta do Lorde for a week or more.

Plenty of time to clean up soup.

Being stuck in Madeira not so bad, you may think – but the weather was so appalling with torrential rain and electric storms that it was impossible to do any of the normal tourist things. Except for one trip to a stunning botanical Garden.

Fishing for ladders?

One night we had our lovely metal steps outside Magic – they are the perfect height to enable us to get on board easily. On waking we noticed that they were gone. Where?

In the sea, of course…we had a look and gave up on them – however for the price of a Magic Polo Shirt the Marina guys were happy to spend hours fishing with a large rusty hook for our steps and they caught them and brought them ashore – we were delighted …

As always, we made the most of what we could – we hired a car for a few days and toured the Island, we visited some of the property for sale in Quinta do Lorde and we made some new friends – we didn't do Madeira the way that most tourists would (of course!)

We decided to drive to Porto Moniz on the far side of the Island –(reflective note …I wonder what it is that makes me want to leave where I am and go to the extreme opposite side!)

On the drive, we thought we would see a lot of the incredible lush country but disappointingly that only came in glimpses, as the Madeira road network is mostly though chains of long dark concrete tunnels. These tunnels do burst out into incredible and beautiful vistas of breathtaking coastal drops or lush steep hills with exotic plants and flowers – Bananas and those Orange Dragon flower thingy's …and cows!

The Madeira people seem to love their cows. Madeira looked to me like the Island in the Jurassic Park movies and I would have not been surprised to see a T Rex thundering behind our car as we fled, just in time escaping into the next tunnel.

The rain had created that low hanging warm wet mist that movie directors would love for the tension and drama.

On our drive, we were stopped half way to Porto Moniz. The town we stopped in was not a town you would have stopped in.

The police at a roadblock stopped us. They informed us that today there was a car rally and that this town was the end of a time trial. So, as we were stopped we decided we would watch the cars arrive and have lunch in the town. Wow... the cars were fantastic – straight out of my teenage years in Northern Ireland – Ford Escorts and Cortina's and Lancia's – all adapted for rally driving. The atmosphere was great and it seemed that all the locals – all 12 of them had come out to watch. There was one old man who liked looking at May he was very friendly and seemed to be yellow and have a shrunken head. His face was so wrinkly that I couldn't see his eyes but he was warm – he smiled and, I think – winked. We thought we would have lunch and approached a building that had the optimistic sign – "Restaurant"

On entering it was clear that, although there were tables and chairs – food had not been served here for many years. The 'not' restaurant was linked though to a 'not' shop that was like walking into a time machine. It was well stocked with plastic dolls and toys and ornaments and kitchen ware and everything was neatly wrapped in polythene sheets, which had yellowed and gone hard over the years. The dusty, wrapped things stared out at me – They seemed to have been incarnated in the shop c1974 –

extraordinary 'not' shop

As we left the 'not' shop and 'not' restaurant a man appeared to see if there was anything we wanted – we thanked him and I was a little disappointed we didn't buy anything – Mark said that was ridiculous but – you know the purchase of an apple peeler or classic 1970s plastic doll may well help this small rural economy.

We decided to invest our attention in the bar opposite. Several locals were sitting on the wall outside and there was a party atmosphere. It reminded me a lot of the hill climbs and car rallies in the '70s in Northern Ireland – the locals in the small towns loving the excitement.

We entered the bar and watched what the locals were having. So, cheese sandwich and two Ponches it is then! Now Ponche is a Madeira thing and it is great if it is made fresh. Freshly squeezed juice of something – usually Mandarin Orange or Passion Fruit or both – with a, 'burn your throat out' 70% proof white rum and honey (the latter ingredient is – I think, for the throat pain) It smells like Mandarin Orange and tastes like fire.

One small glass of this is a great way to set you up for an afternoon of driving around pin head bends – Mark – who was driving, took one small sip and handed his glass to me – I thoroughly enjoyed both!

I am so happy Mark is such a grown-up.

We set off happy to Porto Moniz where we were going to swim in the natural pools – they looked stunning in the photos – natural pools of warm sea water created by the lava flow. But when we arrived the gale force winds and sea spray made them look cold and miserable so we drove on. We were stopped for an hour on the way back though the center of the Island as there was a large boulder in the middle of the road – there had been a landslide. The rain had caused serious landslides on many roads. As we drove back into Quinta do Lorde we noticed the sea had a band of brown around the island. The rain had washed the terracotta Madeira earth into the sea and the effect was a weird scene like something out of Charlie and the Chocolate Factory.

The days melted too and soon we had been there for 9 days – we were starting to feel trapped and Quinta do Lorde is a weird little place in which to be trapped. It is a 'resort' built by an American company for £100milion. It has a hotel, a church, a shop and a small restaurant/bar. There is a light house (that isn't a light house) and a marina (that is a marina) When you first arrive it is charming – like something straight out of a picture book – you can see the architect's vision. But it is a little claustrophobic for us and lacks authentic charm.

We viewed several properties there which are on the market for – around 1.5M Euro for a house and between 400-600Euro for an apartment. Not for us. But we did wish them well and really hope that this little place will fill up with people who will fall in love with it.

We have enjoyed Madeira – it is lush and green and awesome but it is ….
Time to Go!!!

Finally, we left on Friday 23rd – not as early as we would like because we were checking our electrics!! Ho hum – it's too dull to tell about it but it is all ok now. We left and then we stopped and pulled into the harbour wall and then we left again!

We left at 2.30pm and sailed away into the Atlantic, just the two of us – and you know what – we had a relaxing and wonderful sail – for two days and two nights – nothing broke and nothing was scary – just gentle waves, stunning sunsets, some rain and lightning and a clear and silvery moon that lit our way.

This trip is the longest we have done without crew to support us and we were pleased that it all went well – we ate well – slept well and sailed well.

We arrived in Las Palmas just as the sun was rising and we were amazed to be greeted by Liam and Liz whom we had met in Gibraltar – they were on the harbour wall shouting a warm welcome and they had a bottle of Bacardi for me!!

They followed us in and helped the Marina staff with our lines. The marina is packed full of boats and we were squeezed into a narrow space on T pontoon.

Another warm welcome in a strange port – it is so unexpected and so lovely.

One of the many special things we have been privileged to experience is fond farewells and warm welcomes.

We were shattered and did some cleaning and then went to bed to rest.

The ARC experience now begins. We have four weeks in Las Palmas – planning, people, parties and preparations.

There are some beautiful boats here and Magic has disappeared in a cloud of 50ft+ yachts – we get the feeling we are going to learn a lot

– again!

Chapter Eleven

DONKEY BELLY SKY

Rats and Roaches

There is a 'Donkey Belly' Sky today – that's what the locals call the sky in Las Palmas in November. It is a perfect description as the sky often looks like it is heavy and drooping and it is a soft powdery grey. It has been raining and very windy but now the weather is improving and is due to get better every day over the next week.

Today is Sunday and it is the 1st November. I am feeling rather like we are strapped into the car of a rollercoaster, which is cranking its way up and up, and we are not sure what's coming on the other side. I think that everyone is feeling a mixture of anxiety and excitement. The ARC+ (that is the boats who are doing the ARC – Atlantic Rally for Cruisers but they are stopping at Cape Verde before they cross to Saint Lucia) boats are all here and some of the ARC boats – the marina is literally crammed full. The ARC boats don't leave until the 22nd November so there is still lots of time. It feels as if we should have an ARCvent Calendar with a window for each of the next 22 days.

The list of things to do is finally getting shorter and we are now adding things for fun or comfort – I bought a bread maker and we are delighted to have the smell of freshly baked bread on board. Also, I have been testing the oven with things – I cooked a pie from Marks and Spencer and made delicious Apple Roses (they are yummy – find them on the internet just Google Apple Roses).

We are settling into Las Palmas and are pleasantly surprised. We had heard about rats and roaches and that it was unpleasant – we have found the opposite. The marina staff could not be more helpful and warm, the pontoons are well maintained, there are all the services you could need in the Marina and community life in the 'village' of yachts is building fast.

All the boats have flags – signal flags – dressed overall and flags from the countries that the sailors are from. There is a party atmosphere and a sense that everyone is checking each other out. Conversation with neighbours is easy as there are common questions like – "Where have you been cruising?" and "Where are you going once you get to the Caribbean?" and of course "What needs fixing or adding on your yacht?" There are also and lots of thoughts about the crossing itself.

The ARC office doesn't open until the 6th and then we will get a time for our safety check. The ARC does an excellent job ensuring that all the yachts that cross the Atlantic have all the safety equipment on board. A lot of the things on their list are mandatory and if you don't have it you don't get to go. As a result, everyone is anxious about their safety check. We will also get our race number and a pack with information on all the seminars and parties that are laid on.

We have wasted no time however and have already been to several parties and invited people to one of our own. We are on Pontoon 'T' so we have decided to have a 'T' party – with Long Island Iced Tea as the centerpiece. We have been with a crowd to watch the New Zealand v Australia Rugby World cup in an Irish bar and we have been to an Irish Whiskey Party – we are also planning a JAM session next week for musicians – so not a bad start!

I do seem to be constantly in one of two states – either hung over or drunk

The big surprise for us is Las Palmas – the new area of town which is 15 minute's walk from the Marina has everything you could want, but in a practical format. The streets are in a grid and on the main street there are large European stores – El Corte Ingles, and Zara and Carre Four. There is even a Marks and Spencer – everything is easy to get to and if you feel tired the Taxis are everywhere, trustworthy and cheap, you just flag one down, it's good.

There are two beaches, one on the Marina side which is odd with dark brown sand and Palm Trees looking onto an industrial port and then on the other side black sand and waves which delight the surfers. Walking around the town feels safe and fun. Then there is the old town, we didn't go there until several days in and it was such a wonderful treat, we wandered the cobble streets under the yellow street lamps and enjoyed the warm night, huge swaying palms, sounds of Spanish Guitar and delicious smells from the Tapas Bars. We had a special treat as we stumbled upon a tiny bar called La Otilia.

It looked like a 1930s-living room – softly lit and tiny with armchairs and side lamps. We were served the most delicious local wines and we had a snack with was totally unexpected. It was a 'light as air' crispy filo pastry with goats' cheese and spinach, sprinkled with rose petals and palm syrup – well as if the combination of the welcoming, cosy room, the wine and the delicious pastry wasn't enough then, the musician who was to play later started rehearsing in the next room. Contemporary Spanish Guitar, Mark and I just looked at each other in disbelief, it was one of those sensory moments that don't need words. Moments like that sear into your brain more than any photo can. The musician was Luis Quintana he was so expressive both with his playing and his wonderful singing. We bought his CD and hoped we could hear more of his playing later in the evening.

On our way to the old town we had gone to see the vet with May to get all her papers sorted out for arrival in Saint Lucia. The vet was a wonderful woman who couldn't wait to tell us all her top tips for a great time in Las Palmas. She recommended a small restaurant that specialised in Mushrooms – a Mushroom Tapas restaurant! We found it from her description and directions and it was amazing, quiet and quaint, and occupying a corner so the bar and walls were curved. The menu was divine and very fungal, deep fried mushrooms with a garlic sauce, mushrooms stuffed with chicken and smothered in a creamy curry sauce …wow, we will be going back to 'mushroom heaven' soon.

A Drag Queen Angel, Painted Boobs and Great Sax…. NOVEMBER 11

Las Palmas is becoming something of a strange dream. Time is behaving in a really weird way. On the one hand, it feels as if we have been here forever, having never lived or been anywhere else. It feels as if we have all the time in the world to prepare. On the other hand, it seems as if there is no time left at all and a rather large and invisible clock is ticking loudly to constantly remind us that we are about to leave this gentle place to cross the Atlantic Ocean. From time to time I get a 'pop' and 'fizz' feeling, something like a mix of excitement and terror! Then the feeling is gone again and it's back to this 'not normal' place and the things that are happening.

We are loving getting to know new friends, but it is almost overwhelming, there are so many people and we all have so much in common. Lots of people seem to know us from having read our blog and that is humbling and lovely. We are tired all the time as we never seem to stop rushing about!

Friends have asked us to explain what it is like in Las Palmas in the run up to the ARC and I must confess it is a challenge to explain. When I write, it is great to write what is happening as close to it having happened so it is more immediate and has the reality and feelings in it, but there is so much crammed in here, it is so intense almost every day that it is a task to unpack it. I will have a go.

In the past 11 days, we have met hundreds of new people and we have had friends and family on board. Our friends Rachael and Jim came to stay and we had a lovely time relaxing and laughing, walking, eating and drinking. I have discovered the local Rum in GC is delicious – oh no!!! We have done some great touristy things like a visit to the villages

We have had our safety check and passed – phew (general dancing about and relief) We have been to about 9 parties! We have shopped and planned and made more lists. Anyone not on the ARC reading this should be exhausted by now.

I never managed to stay in school to do my A Levels having run away with the circus at 16 so I didn't experience the first few weeks at University, fresher's week and all that stuff. However, this experience is what I imagine that would have been like, except that the average age is probably 60 and not 20.

Where to begin? There are hundreds of boats here and we are all squished in beside each other. The fenders (the squishy things we put on the outside of our yachts to keep them from bumping into harbour walls or other yachts) are constantly under strain and every day the marina staff seem to be on the lookout for any spare space as more boats arrive. We are glad we got here early. The boats are moored up in size order from A-T and then along 'The Wall' are lots of beautiful 60ft + Oysters etc. – The Catamarans are mostly a bit further away.

The atmosphere is intense, a community all gathered here for the same purpose all experiencing the same anxiety, it is like some surreal watery waiting room.

As always, we have dived in. Missing live music, we invited anyone who plays an instrument on board Magic for a Jam session. We managed one Saxophone player and a Guitar player, we did a few songs and it was fun but perhaps it would have been less pressure on Simon the Sax player had there been more musicians. Although there seems to be a lot of time, there is also a lot going on so not much time for the repeat sessions you would ideally need for musicians to jam. Music really helps to ease the tension. Fixing things continues of course, our Genoa will be returned next week, we had to wait for special tapes to arrive from the UK. A new seal will arrive from Germany for our stern door, when that is fixed we do hope that the water ingress will STOP!

Rules of the Boat
Keep the Water OUT - Keep the People IN

We are learning a lot about fixing things on Magic but we are still very reluctant learners. One great tip we got was this:
If it doesn't move but it is supposed to use WD40
If it does move and it isn't supposed to use DUCK tape
Perfect!! …. My kind of maintenance.

Not having 'always on' and fast Wi-Fi is very good for teaching patience and resilience. I saw a Maslow Pyramid drawn the other day with Wi-Fi at the bottom and I get that totally – it really has become a necessity not a treat.

While Mark and I are a generation that remembers no Internet, we are now so used to having it available to us that we get really frustrated being "off grid".

The ARC organisation has been fantastic, the office help with every question, the handbook is excellent, the lectures start tomorrow and we have heard from the ARC+ guys who left a few days ago that they are all worth doing. There was a Welcome/Farewell Party for all the crews of ARC+ and ARC, it really was a spectacular event. We were greeted by a Drag Queen angel and then given as much Sangria, beer and wine as you could drink, then there were the half-naked painted people and feather clad women, all from the Las Palmas Carnival, the entertainment was world class and the drinks were generous, a good combination

The conversations with sailors is inducing a deeper anxiety in me. One team I spoke to who were Russian and doing the ARC+ they said that they thought (having done the ARC before) that the most important thing was to have a spare water maker and spare autopilot!!! And we thought we were ready! Perhaps you should also carry a spare yacht!

It seems no matter what you do or how much you spend you will never be ready. As with a lot of things in life, you just must decide what is 'enough' for you. The sundowners have now begun, free drinks from 16.30 – 20.00 each night, sponsored by various people like the people you can bulk buy drinks from and the butcher you can order your meat from. For anyone anxious about planning the food for the ARC (as I was) don't worry, once you get to Las Palmas it is all made as easy as possible by the suppliers who know exactly what you need, how much and how it should be packed. The fruit and veg even arrive onboard in various stages of ripeness to account for the 20 are days at sea.

There are a lot of ARC prizes for things, best photo, best blog, best time to cross (the average is c21days), biggest fish caught, and more. But the prize Mark would like to win is the one for the best Wall Painting. All the boats taking part are invited to paint on a wall or a rock something that represents their boat. Being an artist who also loves food, Mark is taking this very seriously as there is a whole Ham, Large local cheeses and Wine to be won!! He has designed ours and had already picked his spot on the wall and invested hours, he loves doing it! There are a few more hours of work to do on it and he loves to paint. It was great to see him doing what he loves.

…. But then. OH NO!

(just found out that Mark should be painting on a ROCK to win the prize NOT the wall – whoops I will tell him tonight and see what he says about the hours he has already invested on the wall, yikes)

I told Mark about our error and he is so resilient and persistent that he decided he would begin again putting our yachth's painting on a rock and here it is.

Mark is tenacious and finally produces award winning artwork on a rock

We have decided that it is not good enough to have an old plotter and radar so we are investing in a new Zeus 7 B&G navigation system, sounds good eh! It arrives next week, so we are cutting it fine to have it fitted and tested but we know it will give us more peace of mind to be able to see more clearly who is around us at night. Also, some of our crew have worked with this system before so we can learn as we go.

Anxiety making moments seem to pop up during the day, and events or people can trigger them. We went to see a demonstration of a rescue helicopter taking a casualty off a boat, 'Pop! Fizz! ' rather than just observing and feeling "oh how very interesting' I was thinking, what if that was Mark and May and I are on the boat and I am watching him being lifted off. What if? What if?

Mark and I looked at each other and felt the same.

We said that we didn't want to ever see that in a real-life situation.

Then there was a demonstration of the proper use of flares Pop! Fizz! ' stomach turning and churning again, we just don't want to be ever in a situation where we have to use our flares.

Then we watched as our friends prepared to leave their berth for the ARC+ start.

Pop! Fizz!

We watched as 70 yachts left the harbour one following the other close behind. They were heading for the start of the 'not' race, the 'not' race has a handicap, a starting line, trackers on all the boats with a 'leader board' and prizes for the best times, but it is not a race.

There is a great deal of testosterone about and lots of talk of tactics and tuning. I have been watching the ARC+ boats on the tracker App, it is a fantastic App and it is wonderful to see them on their way and then read their related LOGs on the ARC website. We watch as the track of four boats have turned back, we know now that some were mechanical issues, one was severe sea sickness and one was taking on water, Pop! Fizz! that stress feeling just rushes though me, adrenaline pump on full.

Of course, it is not only Magic that has to be ready, May does too. May has been to the vet 3 times now for tests for things that we know she does not have, but now we have the papers to prove that she doesn't have what we knew she didn't! Her hair is going yellow in the sun which is weird looking so we have some blue shampoo for white hair, we will see if that works for her and we have some new anxiety meds for her, Zylkene, which are supposed to be like a natural 'chill out' hormones of lactating mother dog or something, we will see. May and I enjoyed the Bach Rescue Remedy stuff together so perhaps I will try her Zylkene. I don't get sea sick but I do get scared and I hate to be scared because it gets in the way of having fun.

Today we have James, Mark's son with us as well as Geoff and Beryl Mark's Mum and Dad. We love having family time and this is one of the things we have missed the most living aboard and travelling. Tomorrow John arrives and next week the rest of the crew, then, more prep and parties, we have a party on Magic on the 16th, we have the Fancy Dress Party on the 18th, then there is the Hat Party, the Owners Dinner, the Parade in Town, the Crew Dinner, the Farewell Party, the food and drink to order, the repairs to complete, the new Navigation instruments to test, more sundowners and 10 lectures, I think that the next 11 days are going to be a blur.

Chapter Twelve

SETTING OFF ACROSS THE ATLANTIC

Dog-n Chips
NOVEMBER 22

Well here we are on Pontoon T. The anxiety surrounding our adventure seems to swell up every so often, collywobbles! I am hoping that this is only natural. I am now avoiding talking to other sailors as their questions are making me feel worse.

"Are you ready?" should be a banned question!!

Well this is it, I am sitting in a manic Sailors Bar having breakfast, it's good to be off the boat but then again, the anxiety is palpable. We have been so busy this last week as the crew all arrived and we prepared the boat. We feel that we are ready (but as we have learned you can never be 100% ready).

It has been a rollercoaster of emotions. The highs of the parties and the fun of meeting new people, the lows are there too. We have spent so much money on equipment and food and drink and it never ends of course. I think the food and drink and stores alone have cost us over £2k now. It seems Bonkers.

One of the highs is that Mark has come second in the Rock Painting competition so that is wonderful, wine and cheese, great! Of course, he is not happy at coming second but we think he is great. One of the lows was a massive one. It has taken me months to apply for and organise all May's papers, she now has a file with about 20 essential blood test certificates, export and import permits and letters from vets, it is crazy, mad. Of course, these papers relate to her specific microchip number. That number is on all the papers so the authorities know that these papers are for this specific dog. The final thing we needed was a 'fit to travel' certificate from the vet a simple procedure including a health check and the vet checks her papers. We were confident and ready.

First the vet scanned May's neck. Guess what – no chip!
　　She scanned her whole body and scanned her neck again and again.

I went cold, if we have no chip then the papers are all redundant, I cannot get them done again as there is no time and some of them had to be done 3 months ago the one to prove she doesn't have Rabies for example. The reality hit me. If I arrive in Saint Lucia with May and no chip they will send us home or kill her (really!) or I will have to return home to the UK and not be part of the Magic crew, I will have to fly home from Las Palmas with May, leave her behind in the UK somehow and then meet them in Saint Lucia. All the exhaustion and the stress just washed over me and I just stood in the vet's office and wept. It was one of those tipping point moments, the vet was lovely and she said that everything would be ok. I wasn't sure.

She said that I was to leave May with her for the morning and she would keep searching for the chip. The vet explained that it is impossible for the microchip to leave May's body, the vet said she would find it. I wanted to feel reassured but I didn't.

What a morning, the boat seemed to be in chaos and there was a lot of tension, the crew were saying we were 'nowhere near ready' and that 'we would not be leaving on Sunday', how could it all be going so well and then take a twist to this.

I must admit to feeling low. We are all tired and anxious and it doesn't help that hundreds of other people in the Marina are feeling the same, 'behaviour breeds behaviour' a contagion: the thousands of missing parts and broken things adding pressure and concern. Then the vet called:

The chip could not be found.
　　Right, I thought, I am going home.
　　Then she said she would authorise all the papers and send us a letter to say that the previous chip number and the new one were still May, I hope it works.

So, I will be going on the ARC but if May is not allowed into Saint Lucia when we arrive then I will be looking for a flight home with her, that is if we are allowed in to get a flight. This is not an anxiety I need on the crossing but we are going. I have enough of those.

It is impossible to describe what a pressure cooker it is here in Las Palmas, everyone is checking each other's preparations, how much veg have you ordered? How have you stowed things properly? What equipment have you got? What place are you in the handicap? Are you going to wrap your carrots? Magic has been placed as the 6th fastest boat in the fleet by handicap so that means it will be a big challenge to win a place (in the 'not' race).

To be honest we just want to get there, safe and happy and with no damage to the boat, ok, ok I know there could be damage to the boat, but we are all doing everything we know how to ensure against it.

Onboard Magic Mark is waiting for a diver to arrive to take off the lazy line that is wrapped tightly around the bow thruster following yesterday's parking incident (don't ask) we really didn't need that this morning. We must hope they get it freed and that the bow thruster is not damaged. We don't need a bow thruster to cross the Atlantic but we cannot have it extended and wrapped with chord so we need the diver to help us.

I would love to say that this is fun and we are having a ball but the reality is more like we are well and happy but tired and anxious. Looking around me I seem more grim focus on faces than laughter, everyone is checking the weather and talking nervously, it is grey and raining and the wind is picking up - a lot.

We are excited and anxious.

We have been planning this for years and now we are going, it seems strange.

We have had a special tracker fitted, as have the whole fleet. Our friends and family can look for us as we cross.

More soon, from the Atlantic

Chapter Thirteen

THE ATLANTIC CROSSING

May's point of view

May took over the writing the whole way across the Atlantic
These next chapters are from May (with a couple of comments from Tina
and Mark)

Tuesday 24rd November The B'ARC – Day 3

I have been sailing for 12 months now and it still confuses me - a lot. When I lived at home in North Yorkshire life was so good, running in the fields chasing butterflies and looking at cows, now life is significantly weirder.

It all began when we arrived in our tiny new home, a boat, apparently. I couldn't understand why we had downsized. Then things got really strange. The floor in this new home moved and I couldn't figure out what was outside and what was inside, in other words where should I go to the toilet? I am a Maltese Terrier called May. Such matters are delicate and having fully understood the rules of our house this 'boat' situation was completely different. But eventually I learned where to go and I learned a lot more. I learned that living on board is fun – I get to see dolphins and I especially enjoy being with my owners all the time. In our house, they went out more but here they can't so I get to sit on laps all the time; that is if they are not rushing about pulling bits of string and raising flappy things up the big pole.

My humans are very odd. Having sailed for a year we then arrived somewhere really warm and I found that there were other dogs living on boats. We chatted by pee mail along the docks and I discovered that we are a select pack. We are going to be going on something I think is called the B'ARC which sounds perfect. My owners and their friends have been rushing about a lot and doing some strange things, like dressing up in mad outfits and buying a crazy amount of fruit and vegetables, I don't like those but the meat order looked inviting.

One not so good thing is that I have suddenly had to go to the vet a lot, I hate the vets but apparently, we must have a lot of paperwork for me because I am special and my passport alone is just not enough.

The B'ARC started well for my humans, there was a marching band and lots of excitement. They looked happy but I could tell they were all anxious too. I didn't like the first day, there were a lot of other boats close to ours and that made my owner Tina very anxious which makes me upset but then my other owner Mark was happy so it was confusing.

There was a lot of wind and some very big waves and I didn't like that so I hid in my bed and looked after Tina.

A view from a friends yacht as Magic powers into the lead at the start of the ARC 'not' Race – Reefed and Ready

Now we have been at sea for two days, things are more settled and we are having fun. Today I met a squid that seems to have flown onto the deck. We have also seen whales and dolphins a big brown turtle calmly swam by and a small bird came on board for a rest. It said hello to me as I looked at it but I only speak human and dog, perhaps someday I will learn 'Bird' as you never know when a third language will come in handy. Our home seems to be rolling a lot but we are all getting used to it now. I quite enjoy sliding down the floors. We are apparently 'sailing well', whatever that means. The humans are talking a lot about 'Jammin', I do hope they are talking about Parties in the warm place we are going to, but I think that perhaps from the way they keep looking up at the flappy white things, they are talking about something else. There is a weird dance they do around the boat whilst putting on boots and jackets, and why are they up at odd times? One human I do enjoy talking to is Chris Tibbs. We are sailing near him and today we talked on the radio thingy – I met Chris in Las Palmas and told him I can tell the weather forecast - "rough!" I said, in dog- He liked that.

I hope tomorrow we see more animals as people are, frankly - just weird.

It's a dog's life.

Magic on the B'ARC
Day four Wednesday 25th November Dog Blog
from May the Maltese on Magic

Being a dog at sea there are certain delicate subjects we don't discuss but just so you are not concerned for me I must report that all systems are working well. It has taken me four days to settle and I think the people are the same. It is odd at sea as our address keeps changing, apparently just now we are at 26.17.2N 25 09.31 W

There is an endless amount of entertainment for me on the yacht watching the feeders working. They are a good pack and work together well, but I have noticed that sometimes they are tired and stressed, that's where I come in to make them smile or give them a hug. They call it 'May Watch' when they must pick me up and cuddle me, but of course really, I am looking after them.

It is 2.30pm and all is calm. Mark is on watch with Tina. I love all the food they are making, spaghetti carbonara (that has Bacon!) Chicken Casserole (I love chicken) Scrambled Eggs and Smoked Salmon (my favorite). They are also eating a lot of fresh fruit, which is frankly weird. I love my owner Tina cooking on board as it is funny, she must dance about and hold things as the boat is rolling about like a barrel in a stream. I like it but it makes the feeder's tasks seem harder.

I must tell you though, I am tired this afternoon because I have had a lot of looking after to do during the last 24 hours. Things have been very busy on Magic.

I will tell you what was happening.

During the night, there were squalls and heavy rain. The people were wearing their funny suits again and looking very serious. Everyone has been rushing about so much I think they are tired.

Then I heard something I don't understand – a concerned voice shouted:

"the steering and auto pilot seems to be failing"

The feeders all looked very worried and they were talking about having to divert South to somewhere called Cape Verde. They were saying that the steering wouldn't last the whole trip to St Lucia. They had to do something called "hand steer" whatever that is they didn't look very happy about it.

They worked as a team all night and when the dawn came they focused on the problem they had. In the morning, they went into the bedrooms at the back of the boat (I think they said the Port and Starboard bunks at the stern) they took the roof down and saw that there was a wire thingy that had jumped out of a disk thingy and there was a chain thing that had come out of the cogs. I felt worried because all the people were worried. They got out the Emergency Tiller (I thought, good thing that nice lady, Anna, from the ARC safety check team made the feeders find it and check that it fitted). Then they worked on taking down the biggest white flappy thingy that they had been tending so carefully it made me jealous.

There was a lot of noise, creaking and banging and whistling wind. Then the "fix everything" feeders, focused and worked together to fix the problem, meanwhile outside, the on-deck team with the "emergency tiller" in place sailed the boat very carefully whilst handing tools and grease to the "fix everything" feeders.

Soon it was all over. I felt that they were all relived. They were all very quiet for a long time. I know they were not happy.

Then things sort of got back to normal – whatever normal is anymore!!

They tidied away their tools and the "emergency tiller" and declared that the now repaired, tightened and greased, steering was 'better than new', then there was a hesitant moment when they said, "let's put the auto pilot on" not sure what that is but when the button was pressed they were all looking at the button and the round wheels.

They seemed happy that all was well and when they are happy I am happy.

Then on to more serious matters – breakfast! I was delighted when they decided to have scrambled eggs and smoked salmon, did I tell you that's my favourite? It was raining and windy and grey so to cheer themselves up they then had chips for lunch. My main feeder is Tina and she has a thing called an 'Actifry' on the boat and it makes everyone very happy to have chips safely whilst at sea. I don't really like chips that much so I don't get it, but I love it when the feeders are all smiling. Tina likes that too, that is something she is very concerned with. I think she is like me, she feels it if people are not happy and it makes her unhappy.

So now everyone was happy, chips for lunch and there was even sun in the sky, then there was a loud bang and the big flappy thingy seemed to fall. Poor feeders they had just relaxed and now they all looked very worried again. It was very windy and I heard one of them say that "the Main Halyard had slipped dropping the main part way" They all looked stressed and Tina looked like she was going to breakdown and cry. They pulled on string and made that grinding noise that I hate with the big silver drums and then all seemed to be well.

Now dinner is made, it smells delicious and is one of my favourites; Chicken Casserole. Everyone is resting apart from me as I am writing.

This sailing life is great for me. I love the fresh air, all the strange animals to see and delicious food but I am not sure that the feeders are having a good time. In fact, I know that my feeders, Tina and Mark are very stressed. They are upset that the crew are not happy. I hope that they don't have any more stress now and that we can all enjoy ourselves.

Tina got the following email from an old friend just now and it made her very happy, so she had a little cry – I love my feeder, Tina so I am off now to give her a cuddle.

Thursday and Friday 27 and 28ᵗʰ November

The days are beginning to blur, but I am happy, I love looking out to sea and I spend my time watching for Dolphins. The feeders keep asking me about the weather; Tina even radioed Chris Tibbs on his boat Taistealai (I like Chris & Helen they were nice to me in Las Palmas) I wanted to ask him if he needed my help with the weather! When they ask me what the weather is going to be – I stop and think and sometimes I say 'rough' and that makes them all laugh! Funny feeders.

I have been talking to some of the animals I have met, Storm Petrels, Turtles, Dolphins and whales, they seem very interested in me too. A very tiny bird landed on deck for a rest it was lovely to share the boat.

The feeders had a crew meeting and ran through all the hazards and equipment in detail and everyone looked very serious, routines for fire and man over board were discussed at length, but no one mentioned DOB (Dog over Board) and that worried me a little.

The feeders are all working hard and every day they are up and happy one moment and then stressed and down the next. Today was a good example, we began the day with everyone having a happy breakfast of pancakes with maple syrup and Mango and then it all got very challenging quite fast. It seems that we have a faulty flux gate compass (get me with the technical language – not bad for a dog!) this means the feeders have had to hand steer on certain headings, that makes their watches very tiring. Now they notice two holes in the very big flappy white thing. The holes were caused because we are apparently sailing down wind and the ends of the things they call spreaders have rubbed holes in the big white thing. Mark and Tina are sad because they bought sail repair gear but the crew says it was the wrong sail repair gear and the sticky tape they have is not strong enough. This has caused a lot of stress and anxiety in the team and I hate that my feeders feel they have let the team down, they did the best they could, I have watched them preparing and shopping and doing lists for more than a year.

It turns out the big flappy thingy is called a Main Sail – I am learning a lot!

Two of them took the Main Sail down and did what they could to repair the holes. From one of them there was anger that the sail repair was poor due to of a lack of proper materials to do the job. Some thought the repair would hold. Some thought it wouldn't hold and they were very frustrated. Some thought we should divert to Cape Verdes. Mark and Simon discussed what to do. Simon was our most experienced crew member and Mark trusted him and his advice. Simon's opinion was that, although the repair had not been made with the correct materials, it should hold. So, Simon and Mark decided that the best plan would be to sail on to Saint Lucia. A couple of the crew were very unhappy with this decision and of course this caused a lot of tension. It doesn't feel good on board Magic and it makes my feeder Tina very upset. There is a really bad atmosphere and in a small space with six people that is very unpleasant even for me.

Now they are sailing by hand until we change course again tomorrow. I hope that everyone will not be too tired, I will do my best to support them.

Gybing, banging and squeaking makes me nervous I don't like it at all and the feeders don't like it now either as they are trying not to cause the damaged sail any more harm.

So, the flux gate compass is not functioning which means that the auto pilot is not working, there are holes in the Mainsail, the head of the furler on the Genoa is not functioning, a baton is missing, the water maker not making water, the Chart table is broken because John fell on it and the team are cracking up!

They are all talking about the issues and trying to work together but anxiety and tension is high. From two of the crew my feeders Tina and Mark are getting accusations of poor preparation of the boat and that is hard for them to bear. Especially as the crew onboard had all helped prepare the boat over the past year. Tina and Mark had spent a small fortune with specialists to ensure Magic had everything for an Atlantic crossing. They had all anticipated that many things could go wrong but none of them anticipated quite how many.

On the positive side the wind has dropped and the weather is great.

Information on weather and routing from my friend Andrew in Lagos is helping us a lot and it is lovely to know that friends and family are supporting us from a far.

My main concern currently is that someone spilled coffee all over me, and the deck, and then I got juice on my coat from a rotting pepper. That didn't smell good at all.

We all look a bit bedraggled!

One of the crew hasn't been very well. But is cheered up at the end of the day by catching a very big Dorado and we are all having that for supper. I love eating fresh fish.

I hope everyone is happier and supports each other more tomorrow.

Tina says that the sailing is the easy part. It is the repairs and the teamwork that are the greatest challenges.
She says what helps her is thinking, "The only way out is through"

My poor feeders are battling

Saturday 28th November

Current Status, Morale of the Crew is not good, things still breaking and being fixed - water maker not loving the swell.

Tina and Mark must get up every night at midnight and are on deck until 03.00 they like it sailing under the stars. I like being with them, everyone is sleeping and my feeders are relaxed and happy. Every hour they go and write some things in a book, that is a log, odd. Also, they don't look at me as much as usual as they are always looking out.

The halyard in just going around and around inside the foil at the head of the Genoa and so it will not furl and unfurl as it should, that's todays problem, everyday there is something and just as the people seem to stop and settle they seem to have another plan. This morning's big idea was to use the Big Black scary sail, the wind had dropped and they thought it was a good idea to get out the cruising shoot – there was a lot of mucking about with more bits of string and then the flapping and banging, I don't like it. All that gave them only 2 knots extra speed and then the wind got up so 15 minutes later the sail was down again.

Humans are really, strange and I don't think in my whole dog's life I will ever fully understand them.

They are having fun fixing things, the block on the first reef at the mast, which exploded and must be replaced. The team are concerned about the furler on the head of the Genoa which now seems to be stuck fast and the only suggestion seems to be for one of them to go up the mast to have a look and cut it down. I don't like the sound of that as Tina gets very anxious when people are going up the mast. It is especially dangerous in a rolling sea as the mast swings a lot.

Mark has been working all morning on deck. He has been putting up sails and taking them down again.

Tina has been on deck and is now watching me write my notes, normally I don't let anyone see me as it is a bit odd watching a dog type, I am a touch typist and can use all 20 toes which makes it fast.

As I sign off it is 14.00 and it is a beautiful afternoon mid Atlantic, everyone is happier today and even though we are all being tested in different ways we are all focused on the challenge of getting to Rodney Bay, Saint Lucia. I have enjoyed some of the Parma Ham the feeders had with their water melon.

Just off to chat to one of those flying fish thingies, I like them they tell great jokes! – but the feeders cannot hear them.

Our current address is 24.33.14N 33.31.92W (weird)

Saturday 28th/ Sunday 29 November

Well this has certainly not been the sort of Sunday we are used to at home.

We have been going a bit more slowly but that means we are making water, which is great for the feeders, as they seem to like showers. Some of them had a lovely evening listening to opera and hand steering and some of them were a bit frustrated that we were not going faster – we had the slowest 24-hour period yet.

Tina says it is more important to arrive safely than fast, some of the boys don't agree!! They have been mucking around with the clock again with is more feeder oddness, why are they doing that – isn't the time, the time? Dinnertime and Poo time and cuddle time – I don't understand what is going on but we are now GMT minus 2 whatever that means!

As they worked together in the afternoon and evening of yesterday things were calm, like the weather. There were flying fish and birds and everyone was on deck chatting and playing games and just having a relaxed time. It was lovely to see the feeders having some time out. They are happy that they are making water – more weirdness. How can they MAKE water?

They had Spag Bol for dinner, no chicken, what a shame. I am thinking that this is my new forever, I have learned to relax and I can even lean and bend while we are rolling about, the feeders think it is funny that I am good at it but that is crazy as of course I am good at it, four legs are much better than two.

As they got ready to have their dinner they turned on the Navigation lights, the Genoa was part furled out (remember it is not working well) and the Main Sail was full. There was a gentle roll to the sea and the air was warm.

I can remember lots of lovely relaxed Sundays with all my family and friends around and lots of delicious bits of roast meat that would come my way.

Today I did get looked after well and had some treats, I also had a lovely walk at the pointy end this morning. It was sunny and warm and there were some more of my favorites, the flying fish skimming along – some going our way and a lot were going the other way, I wonder what they eat or where they sleep or where they are going? The water seems to be getting bluer and bluer and the people say it looks like thick, molten blue glass and they think it is very beautiful.

Like other days, this day was a rollercoaster too – more incidents and issues.

The first thing was that the wind had dropped too much and there was no speed. We are apparently heading South (whatever that is?) so that we can find more wind. The people said they thought they would put up the 'scary black sail' but then the Genoa is stuck and they cannot get it down. What I heard was that 'the halyard is wrapped around the forestay and the top furler unit is damaged beyond repair' This means that they cannot furl in the Genoa (not sure what one of those is but I think it is the smaller white flappy thing at the pointy end). The feeders are concerned about this because if there is a squall then they will need to take that sail down fast and they can't.

I hate it when they are concerned – I can't relax.

The repair to the hole in the main sail seems to be holding with the tape that they put on. So that is good and they have "made water" how amazing is that!! Perhaps they are gods?

They didn't put up the scary black sail, which is good because following lunch the most fierce, dark squall seemed to be hunting us down. It looked dangerous and angry. Then...Mark – (that is my other owner) said *"right we need to sort this Genoa issue out, so I will go up the mast"* my other owner, Tina was upset and said she wasn't happy about it at all.

Mark is very brave, Tina is not. I will look after her.

The guys stood at the big silver stick for a long time looking up and discussing what to do. Then Mark got into a big blue nappy (I told you people are weird) and put something strange on his head, he also put on his life jacket and tether and the others attached a piece of strong string to him. The boat was rolling and the big silver stick thingy was moving – a LOT. I heard it was 27 metres high. His friends pulled Mark up the mast and Tina was so scared that she stayed in the galley and washed and cleaned everything, she sang songs and then cleaned the floor. I looked after Tina, as she was scared when she heard Mark shouting, "stop" or "go".
 She especially didn't like it at all when she heard the others say, "get him down *now* – a squall is coming"

Mark was very, very brave and went right to the top of the mast and cut the halyard. The mast was swaying wildly and he would swing out and back towards the mast. When he came down again we found that he had hurt his arm but he is tough and after he had some ice on it he was ok. I love Mark.

I said that Tina is not brave but forgot to tell you that she is sometimes brave - as she has broken a toe and is managing well with it even though it is a very funny colour.

My feeders are also all covered in dark marks and Tina says she looks like she is turning into a Dalmatian. I think they said they were bruises, but I don't have any. Mark had a cup of tea and a rest when he was safely down, he looked like he needed it. Trouble is that he may have to go to the top of the mast again tomorrow as what he did didn't entirely work.

Tina will be cleaning the floor again!

Then it was calm sailing for a while until they decided to mess about with the Genoa again.

Next thing that happened was one of the feeders pulled a big piece of string around one of the silver domes, a winch (they are very expensive and shiny – made by Lewmar and Tina says they are Carbon on the top (which is good apparently??) There was a loud "twang and crack" in that horrible way that makes all the feeders stop and look stressed – the line had broken the top of the "Starboard Electric Winch".

The list of broken things is growing but that was a very expensive one.

Tina says that at the parties in Las Palmas the people talk was all about what had been fitted to boats and what preparations had been done – she thinks that at the Rodney Bay parties in St Lucia the talk will be all about what was broken on the way.

It does seem that the poor feeders have some drama every single day, but I am just enjoying the movement of the boat, the treats and cuddles, the stars and warm winds and talking to the flying fish. I get the feeling that I am enjoying the Atlantic crossing the most.

The feeders are about to have a lovely supper of Chili Con Carne with Rice and earlier they had cake and tea, they are talking about how the only engine time since we left last week has been 90 minutes and that was today – apparently, they are happy about that, don't know why. Only 90 minutes of engine time in 7 days is apparently good but they are saying that during the next day or two there may have light winds and so must put the engine on.

Some of them watched a movie after dinner, some of them hand steered as on the current bearing (get me learning sailing talk) the auto helm doesn't work -the flux gate compass is stuck at 225 – yes, another thing on the list of repairs.

I must go as it is almost 1am. Tina and Mark are on watch while I write. I think they find it odd to watch me typing and Tina is about to come down below to write the Log entry which they do every hour.

She will write that we are sailing at 7.5knots, our course is 240, the wind speed is 13kn and that our new address is
> 21.40.68 N
> 35.55.45 W

I like sailing.

I think the feeders are planning a party for half way – which is tomorrow. That will be good and some time for them to think about the good things and not just all the expensive bits that are breaking.

List of broken things

Starboard Electric Winch
Furler at the head of the Genoa
(Foil) for the Geona which is now twisted
2 bowls that flew in the galley
2 lines that are chafed – they were brand new
3 blocks that exploded
Flux Gate Compass that is stuck on 225
2 holes in the Main Sail – currently stuck together with tape
Bow Thruster (got fouled on the start day and now doesn't work)

Injuries

1x Broken Toe – Tina from the deck
1x bashed left fore arm – Mark from the Mast
multiple bruises – everyone

They are all minor things and Tina is the ship's doctor and she has a lot of 'stuff' to make everyone better – I just cuddle them.

Aboard Magic – Mid Atlantic May is having a rest
01 December 2015

May is having a rest on deck in the sun so I am writing today… Tina…

We all woke up early following a night of beautiful watches, some of us had more wind than others but everyone had a fair wind, stunning stars and warmth as soft as cashmere. We are enjoying hand sailing as the watches go faster and our helm skills grow. We are glad we don't have to hand steer all the way but for this stretch it is enjoyable. We had a cracking start to our ARC 'not' race– crossing the start line on a Starboard tack and making good time. But now we have all had to let go of any thoughts of a place in the 'not' race – we have had a lot of issues with equipment and we are now focusing on morale and teamwork to ensure that the problems we are having get resolved quickly and safely. The frustration and anxiety has been palpable at times. There is a lot of tension and that is not fun.

It is incredible how many things have gone wrong – breaking – twisting – chafing or bursting. There is enormous strain on the boat and the constant downwind position makes specific points weak. There are a lot of things that were 'professionally' fitted or fixed that have failed – it is frustrating that the Marine industry maintenance industry is so 'hit and miss'. Especially when the 'miss' can mean putting people in danger.

I was reflecting today on the things that have gone right rather than the things that have gone wrong and that helped – our generator and engine are great – our stern door with its new seal is holding perfectly, the water maker is excellent and makes water – shame that it was fitted badly and we can only make water in certain conditions. The repair to the Main sail is holding well too – despite our not having the correct sail repair materials. We had purchased an Iridium and a Mail-a-Sail package so we can keep in touch by phone and email whilst at sea. The system works well but we seem to have used up all our credit which is odd as we had a lot of credit… something must have up or down loaded that shouldn't - ho hum. So, there are more things going right than going wrong – but that is easier to see now we are more rested and the sailing is less aggressive. Initially the issues with equipment caused a lot of stress and divisions in the team. We have had questions over decision making and leadership and about the preparation of the boat but we have all worked hard together – we have talked over everything and resolved the questions and concerns - the saying "we are all in the same boat" will never be truer than when things are going wrong in the middle of the Atlantic. You really get to know yourself and others when you are sailing for weeks on an ocean. In the Yachting press you read a lot about preparation and equipment and less about the human dynamics – but they are connected. Mark and I have been through a buffet of emotions from – "we are selling Magic and never sailing again" to "We love Magic and want to sail forever" and everywhere in between. Certainly, we feel we are not going to sail Oceans anymore and that we would like to cruise in the Caribbean and the Med. We are happy we can stay in the Caribbean for a few months to take time to cruise the islands.

Now, it is noon on Monday 30th – we are hoping to call Half Way at some point today and have a glass of Pink Moet. It really has been the most incredible challenge in so many ways. Everyone is dealing with it differently but fundamentally we are all supporting each other. Marking the success of half way is incredibly important for everyone. The weather now is sunny and there is only very little wind. We are doing only 5knots but we are heading South in the hope of more wind. We are still concerned that we cannot get the Genoa down.

Despite Mark's heroic efforts yesterday – going up to the very top of the mast when it was swinging like a pendulum – the Genoa Halyard is still stuck. Mark cut the halyard but what we think is that the foil (a piece of metal with a track in it) has twisted and torn and the halyard is jammed inside – so we cannot get the Genoa down.

This is a problem as, if a squall comes, we need to get the sail down or reefed fast. This morning we got up and had breakfast then Mark put on his oilies and harness and the crew rigged lines from the Genaker Sheets up the Mast so that Mark could abseil up (if that makes sense) the Main sail – he got beyond the first spreaders – which is about half way up. Yesterday when he went up I couldn't watch but today I watched – one of the more experience crew said Mark was safe and I should watch so that I knew he was safe – I still hate it. It makes me feel sick watching the man I love be tossed and twirled and smacked against the mast. He is very brave and doing this because he knows it is our yacht and we are responsible for the safety of the crew.

There seemed to be lines everywhere – he had two lines – one on either side of him and he had the halyard above – he had his life jacket on and his safety harness. The crew attached a Go Pro camera to his helmet and switched it on. I watched Mark going higher and higher holding the mast with his left hand and using his feet to climb the sail. Then, suddenly the boat twisted on top of a large wave and Mark's left hand was pulled from the mast – his body twisted and turned on the mainsail like a rag doll and I was terrified. He was safe from falling into the sea or onto the deck but not safe from crashing into the mast and breaking bones. He had his crash helmet on and all the safety lines and he was sitting in the new boson's chair – but I still felt helpless and all I could do was watch in fear as he was tossed around. Then he lurched towards the mast – I couldn't breath and everyone else was watching with concern.

It was very quiet on deck and all eyes were on Mark. He grabbed the mast and stopped himself twisting. "Up" he shouted bravely – but then no – the lines were so twisted around and around each other that he could not go up - "Down" he said "slowly".

I thought, let's get him down – but then he shouted "STOP", he couldn't go up or down.

What will happen now? The dark and angry squall is moving towards us at alarming speed and Mark is stuck up the mast. He is trapped in his safety tether as it is tied around twisted halyards – he is holding on to the mast with his left hand and using his feet to steady himself. For some time, he worked on the tangled mess of lines. Mark then shouted to us that he was going to have to cut one of the lines. I just kept thinking this was like some sort of hideous drama about bombs – which line to cut! The red one ? The blue one?

But this was real and this was my husband up the Mast in the middle of the Atlantic Ocean – he was stuck and a storm was coming. I wanted to be sick, or to cry or to run – but instead I was just still and quiet and completely focused on helping where I could – working the lines as the crew helped Mark with suggestions. Then Mark cut one of the lines and spent 10 minutes untangling the rest – finally he shouted "Down" I looked away. Soon he was sitting on the Boom – he looked exhausted. I felt so relieved and proud and happy.

When you are at sea things can go wrong very quickly and then smart thinking and calm, focused teamwork are critical. All that work and stress and he hadn't even been able to get to the top to solve the Genoa problem.

"That's it" – I said – "no more going up the mast we will have to find another way". When he got down and recovered he had a cup of tea (how very British) and said – "well that didn't work!" …

I have learned that I hate to be scared for my own safety but I hate it even more to be scared for others. We have it all on video and Mark had a GoPro on his helmet – he is very brave and strong and his motivation was to ensure we were all safe and could take the Genoa down in the Squall. He is our Hero today.

The squall seemed to go, just like the threat to Mark. Then everything settled down on Magic– we tidied the boat and had lunch. It is so strange at sea– one minute it feels like peril and then calm, and the mundane kicks in - cleaning, eating, sunbathing, sailing, relaxing …it defies explanation really.

Perhaps I could say – imagine being on holiday – you are happy and relaxed, then suddenly you must go up a mountain and jump off with a parachute that might be faulty and you are terrified but you must do it. Then when you land and you can go back and relax by the pool with a cocktail. That doesn't really describe it but it is shocking the HIGH highs and the LOW lows. Now writing it is 01.28 – Mark and I went on watch to relieve the crew and we brought the M&S Advent Calendar with us. Simon was on deck and he happily opened Window number 1 and got a chocolate Donkey! We don't know how many more days we have at sea but we are all happy and apart from a few bruises we are all well. Oh, yes and the Genoa – we found a way to furl the Genoa manually, so Mark does not have to go up the Mast again, is seems that having cut the halyard it has worked its way free to turn (furl). That means tomorrow morning with these light winds we can furl the Genoa away and hoist our 'scary' black Geneker. Perhaps we will pick up time again and make up for the time we have lost messing about with broken bits and ripped sails.

The ARC certainly tests all the parts of your boat and sailing skills that other sailing doesn't reach.

Today is the 1st of December, advent calendar opened and Christmas decorations up. We have had bacon and eggs for breakfast and we are flying our Genaker and doing 8-11kn. We are chasing an Irish man, Des Cummins in ALPAIRE in his Halberg Rassey 48, he's doing cracking speed and it is motivational to chase his tail. What a beautiful sunny day with perfect wind.

P.S. The Genoa furled away perfectly.

Magic
02 December 2015
May writes:

Hi, I'm back after a break, I have been enjoying the beautiful blue skies with little fluffy clouds and the sunshine. Mostly I have been sunbathing on deck or having short walks (I don't need or even like long ones!) At night from midnight until 3am I sit on deck and watch the moon and the stars and listen to the waves bubbling under the boat as we speed along. When I am not on watch, I sleep in Tina and Mark's cabin (on their bed!)

Today was the 2nd December, the people have an advent calendar they seem to be enjoying and they have put up some Christmas Decorations. They are relaxed and enjoying the sailing. Early this morning they put up the big black sail at the front of the boat and I didn't like it at all, it banged and rustled and made us go a lot faster.

My feeders loved it.

They had to work hard with the big black sail as they hand-steered for 11 hours. Tina says she enjoyed her watch hand-sailing from 11am until 4pm, she said that when the sun was going down she had a 'silver road' on the sea to follow.

They had fun watching their speed and monitoring how far they are going. They have an aim of around 200 nm per day. (I find all this stuff really dull and am more interested in the food).

Food is great on board, this morning they had Bacon and Eggs for breakfast, then for lunch a Spanish omelet with salsa and for supper they had Sweet and Sour Chicken with rice. Everyone agrees that we are all eating better on the boat than we do at home – Pasta Carbonara, Moroccan Lamb Tagine, Chicken Casserole, Fish 'n' Chips, Hand Made Burgers, Home Made Bread, Melon and Parma Ham, Scrambled Eggs and Smoked Salmon, Pancakes with Mango and Maple Syrup, and Cinnamon Toast. I love it because I get lots and lots of treats.

Today the feeders have been talking about arriving in St Lucia and they are excited about it but they all agree that the journey is just as important and there are quite a few days left. They have all had a guess at the arrival date and time and there is a bet on. The winner gets to be king or queen for a day and will get pampered!!

I get pampered every day and I don't mind when we get there, wherever 'there' is. I just think that home is where my friends and family are.

May
Current Address 19.04.31N 40.40.99W

Thursday 3rd December 2015
Address 17.35.05N 43.07.19W
May writes:

I still can't quite get used to having to get up at midnight and work looking after
Mark and Tina for three hours. Why on earth do they want to do this every night?
It is odd, they meet Simon and John who say hello from outside and then they go to
bed, why can't we just stay in bed? We are staying positive about everything Tina
says, so I will too even though I am a bit tired. I am also quite scruffy now and need
a spa day, but I have been promised that when we get to the warm other place I can
have a bath and a haircut.

We have had a quiet day but still a lot has happened. The generator, which is
the whirry thing that makes the feeders happy – stopped working. They had to
rummage around for a special box of things and found in the box a small black
wheelie wotsit they called an impellor. Then the crew (who fixes everything!)
jumped in the hole at the back and after a while the Generator was working again.
Tina and Mark thanked him. He is a valuable crewmember. But he does get moody
and quite grumpy.

I think some of the feeders were thinking "oh no! not another thing going wrong",
but Tina and Mark just accept that things go wrong and the key is to have a positive,
'can do' – 'can fix' attitude, that and, of course, the spare parts, the manuals and the
ability to fix things.

There is a new hole in the mainsail, the feeders say it was caused by a split pin that
had been fitted in reverse puncturing the sail when it rests there. They sigh and add
it to the list of things to buy or fix.

"All is well that ends well", Tina says.

Tina and Mark have their daytime watch that is from 11am until 4pm. Today the
people messed with time again and the extra hour was added to Tina and Mark's
watch (again!). They didn't mind really but it looked hard work. Everyone wants
to make the boat go as fast as possible and often that means more focus and more
work. So up went the Big Black Sail, the one I don't like at all, and Tina and Mark
manually steered so that it didn't go all bangy and crashy.

There is more wind today and we were going 9-10 knots, which is good apparently.
Seems slow to me.

There has been news from other boats of things happening, one dismasting, other people have had serious injuries on board. When my feeders read these things, they are very sad for their fellow sailors and wish them well. They also reflect on what a dangerous place a yacht can be and it makes them renew their safety procedures and respect for the equipment.

Mark needs no reminder of being safe as he is nursing two enormous bruises on his inner thighs, Tina says she will look after them, well she is the ship's Doctor and that is why – she says!

My people are careful and watch out for each other all the time.

Food was good again and I got some great stuff, they had Parma Ham at lunchtime with Melon and then for supper they were excited because they had homemade burgers with chips and homemade bread followed by Apple Crumble with Cinnamon and Marzipan topped with Brandy Cream (only a teaspoon of brandy!)

I got some of the burger and it was divine, Tina is great in the Galley but she made the boys clear up the pots and wash the dishes.

As the evening drew in the crew that were on watch under the night sky, noticed that it seemed to have grown bigger. There is also something very strange going on as the Moon has twisted. At home when there is a half moon the slice is vertical but here the half slice is horizontal, it just looks wrong and I wonder what is happening in my dog world.

There is always something not good about your watch and something better about someone else's. Some of the crew say the other boats have, as they put it "everything we don't have!" I would love one of those so Tina and Mark feel they have everything, I wonder how much an "everything we don't have" is, and where the feeders would store it.

Some of the crew were down below and decided to watch a movie together. Tina says it is lovely to take time out to watch a movie but it really feels weird being in the mid-Atlantic and watching 'Hangover'. I do love to hear my feeders laughing, that's a great sound. The crew who were on deck felt left out that they were not watching the movie. Even these small irritations seem huge when you are at sea.

Into the night and Tina and I go to bed at 9pm before our watch at midnight. We are being chased by two Norwegian boats. In Las Palmas, we were next door neighbours with one of them – Vitesse, the owner – Hakon wanted to beat Magic we now have a Magic v Vitesse contest.

We are also watching our Swedish friends on Sandvita and Thindra and wishing them well. My feeders have decided they just want to arrive safely into Rodney Bay. The times are only a bit of fun. This is a 'not'race.

One of the many unique pleasures of sailing in the Atlantic hundreds of miles out to sea is that I meet some extraordinary new friends, today there are two beautiful birds who are white like me. They are singing and I cannot quite make out the lyrics but I think it is something to do with fish. On the subject of fish, one crew member caught an enormous fish yesterday and he battled with it. Tina hates the thought of killing a fish so she couldn't watch. I heard the fish laughing as it bit down hard on the expensive lure, spat it out and swam deep down away from us. The flying fish that tell the good jokes have an odd and fatal sense of direction, they fly right out of the ocean and hit the feeders and land on the deck – it's so sad.

I love watching fish fly. But I don't like it when they kill themselves by landing on the deck.

Now our ever-changing address is 17.01.41N 44.13.35W - it is sunny, everyone is up and has had breakfast, I had egg and cheese – yum I love sailing!
     We have Gybed (I don't know what that is but I don't like the noises at all when we do it) I do love to slide across the floor, that is fun and the feeders think it is great too. I have just had a bath and I feel fantastic.

The mood on board is good even though the feeders had hoped to see that there was less than 1000 nm to go, this is a long journey. The sun is shining, there is 23kn of wind and a big blue swell is pushing us towards Saint Lucia.

I wonder who we will meet there?

Weather Forecast from me – 'Rough'

Magic -
Friday 4th December
Address
16.40.7N 46.17.62

Well my weather forecasting was right – it *is* rough. The boat is twisting and turning like a cork. It is funny to watch the feeders try to get their balance as they only have two feet. I am doing well with my balance, it is simple you just lean into the movement and stay grounded. I had a shower today; I think I am the only one who did. Mark and Tina are disappointed that the new water maker that they had fitted for the ARC doesn't work when Magic is rolling, which is pretty much always! The 'experts' who fitted the water maker and the Generator in Gibraltar didn't fit either properly so it sucks up air. That's why the Generator needed a new black wheelie thingy fitted. Mark and Tina are disappointed because they had the Water maker fitted for the ARC crossing so that that everyone could shower when they wanted, they like everyone to be happy and comfortable.

But it is only a few days to go now so everyone can cope. One of the crew is still unwell and as a result he sleeps most of the day and night – it is a real shame that he is missing out as the rest of us are really appreciating every moment. We are all worried about him.

Today was the first 'nothing' day the feeders have had. The autopilot – called 'Merlin' was on duty all day and now all night. So, all the feeders had to do was some cleaning and tidying, rig checks and be on watch. Our 'fix anything' crew are bored as they like to be busy and fix things. The guys had the fishing rod out but only caught some weed. There was a lot of weed floating by and it looked very strange in the blue, blue ocean.

The waves are incredible – about 5-6metres high and cobalt blue. If you look at them you can see the sunlight shining right through their tops and then the colour is pale turquoise. I am glad that Tina and Mark are telling me the colours as dogs are colour blind. I cannot fully appreciate it but it makes all the feeders very happy and I love that.

They have all been talking about wanting to go for a run or a long walk, I don't mind a short walk to the pointy end but I think the feeders are getting restless. They are fine when it is busy on the boat but today they have had a lot of time to think.

Magic is whooshing along and I love the sound of the water passing underneath us. It bubbles and gurgles – whooshes and slides. When the boat twists and slides down a large wave we are all glad that one of our crew had fitted all the door restraints and bungees in cupboards.

It is dark now and the sky is full of stars. The air is warm and in the boat, it is 31 Degrees. There are 23 knots of wind at our back and our heading of 276 is taking us straight to Saint Lucia. Tina and Mark are loving the thought of our friends and family watching our progress and reading my notes and they like it that we have friends in yachts near us, Eupraxia with friends – John and Sandra Pickles, are only a few nm behind us and Vitesse – Hakon (the Norwegians) are a few nm to our Starboard side. I know that Vitesse would like to beat Magic and the crew are a bit disappointed that we cannot optimise Magic's speed but Tina doesn't care at all about racing. The Doyle Gennaker (dogs can't spell) does not work as well as a Spinnaker or Para sail and the Genoa does not have a pole to keep it flying right. Tina says we are doing well enough and that we should be happy with our progress.

The food is going well and there are lots of stores left which is great for me. Tonight, the feeders fed themselves home-made meatballs with pesto and spicy tomato sauce served on fusilli with fresh garlic bread. They seemed very happy and I was happy as they left me one meatball.

Life doesn't get much better than this!

We don't know exactly when we will get to Rodney Bay but we think it might be Tuesday which is only 4 days away.

May Blog
Saturday 5th December 2015

We woke up this morning to no water. With the roly-poly sea, we cannot make water. Tina is so disappointed because she spent months researching and specifying the right water maker so that the crew on Magic could enjoy showers every day. The reality is that they have had to ration water and now it has run out completely. We have enough drinking water but they will have to do the dishes, cook and wash themselves with a combination of salt water and baby wipes. I don't mind because I hate to be washed anyway.

I am very sensitive to mood and this morning the feeders were tired and irritated. Tina said you could cut the atmosphere with a knife. This is a tough enough challenge for the feeders without the list of challenges they have had. It seems too difficult for some of them to remain positive and moaning and negativity has set in. It is hard for them because they can see other boats passing us, none of them have had much sleep due to the 5m waves and swell rolling them about in bed and just moving around the boat is like a work-out in a gym they say – whatever that is. I feel bad because we are 'hove to' (stop the boat completely) at the moment as they try and sort out the water maker, I don't know what to do to make them feel better, I can't fix things, there are too many of them to hug at once and it is too rolly on deck to move around them. So, I am doing my writing.

It is 10am on Saturday morning, the feeders have been talking about how many miles and days and hours to go. I know they are all wanting to get there now.

Each one of them is coping with the challenges in different ways but it is critical that they work together and support each other. Relationships are straining with the fatigue and the challenges and that is sad. I can feel the stretch on them like the strain on the rigging and the tears in the sails.

The flying fish have been laughing, I am not sure if they are laughing at us or if one of them has told another good joke. I suppose they must have a good sense of humour as they are being chased by something scary most of their lives. Poor fish.

I hope that the next few days are kind on my feeders. They have had to manage so many things.

They have done a water audit and they have 111 Litres for four days for six of them and me and they think that is ok. There is a lot of food left and plenty of treats and sweets too. So that is good. Tina is going to make Marzipan and Chocolate sweets for everyone as a treat and morale boost!! Then sausages for tea. On the morale front it has been fantastic to get the weather reports from Andrew in Lagos and the messages from friends and family are precious and poured over –

Now it is 11am Tina and Mark are going on their 11 - 4pm watch. When they are on watch, it means that the rest of the crew can rest. They read or sleep or sunbathe and listen to music. Five hours when they can relax. The sun is shining and we are doing 7kn which is ok even if some of the boats in the fleet are passing us. The important thing now is to get my feeders to Rodney Bay, safe, happy and still friends. Although I do suspect that the latter will be the most challenging objective.

I think they are all fantastic and I am proud to be part of Team Magic.

Current weather - "Rough"

Current strange Address 15.58.5N 50.30.3W

Sunday 6th December

Hello from the Atlantic Ocean with only 421nm to Saint Lucia:

Another day of sun and rolling begins! It is 10am and we are doing 7 knots (but I can't see any knots – weird!)

Last night the feeders had a delicious meal of sausages with fried potatoes followed by a homemade apple cake. That made them all very happy.

I had to work hard last night as I had to cuddle Tina, she went to bed early and she couldn't eat supper as she was feeling very low. That was the first time in 2 weeks. In my blog, it is difficult to write about the emotions on board but they are as complex as the boat's systems. Tina said I shouldn't write about all the crews' emotions as they are private but she said I could write about hers.

Tina said all the things that have gone wrong on the boat dis-heartened her. (Did I mention that the VHF radio has now gone on the blink, outside and inside, good thing that Tina and Mark have a spare hand-held one)

Mark and Tina have worked so hard to do everything during the last 12 months to ensure that the Atlantic crossing would be safe and fun and fast and yet so many things have gone wrong or were not up to the standards that the crew would have liked. The crew said that doing the ARC is like putting 10 years of wear and tear on your boat so I suppose things may wear and tear on the crossing. What Tina didn't realize was that it would also be like 10 years of wear and tear on your relationships with friends.

Some of the feeders have been very critical of Magic and its preparation and it is hard for Tina and Mark as they did their best. They also know that everything can all be fixed or replaced. And they know that the intensity of the journey and the small space amplifies each issue and that is all that is happening.

This morning Simon had an idea. The water maker has made everyone cross and 24 hours ago we ran out of water. Simon's idea was born out of need, and Tina says there is a saying that "need is the mother of invention" and the feeders 'need' is for showers. Simon is a genius when it comes to anything regarding making or fixing stuff. His idea was simple but clever. The feeders say that the water maker is simple – it sucks in salt water – filters it into fresh water and gets rid of any dirty stuff. Our problem is that because it was fitted badly the water maker cannot suck up water. Genius idea – use a bucket over the side to fill up a larger bucket on the aft deck and put the inlet hose into the larger bucket.

It worked perfectly, they are making water even though the boat is rolling.

The feeders have been talking about managing resources and all of them are used to having plenty, plenty of water, plenty of food and plenty of energy. Managing with scarcity is a good experience they are saying. And there is plenty of plastic packaging…. so much that it is shocking.

Try this experiment. Do your normal shopping and cooking and for a whole 7 days keep a large black plastic bag tied up somewhere in the kitchen. Put anything that is plastic in this bag. If you do this you will notice how much plastic is used in packaging and it is so shocking.

Yesterday we saw a beautiful pod of silver grey dolphins. I love to hear the dolphins, they are very eloquent but they are best when they are saying "come on let's play". I wish I could play with them as their games look so much fun. They speed forward and then suddenly chase each other around with sharp fast turns. I could see one of them break away from the pod, it was racing alongside us just under the water. He was so close and the ocean so clear that we could see the bubbles racing down his skin, I bet that feels lovely. Then, with impeccable judgment, the beautiful dolphin twisted backwards and around the back of a large blue wave. I watched the wave build with a bloom of foam on the top and then suddenly I could see the dolphin positioning himself with accuracy right in the middle of it, just under the foam. Then, with a muscular surge he pushed himself forward, his speed calculated to be just fast enough to punch his whole body out into the air ahead of the wave. His lean, strong muscles flexed into a perfect aerobatic arc and then – splash! nose first back into the warm, blue Atlantic Ocean. For a long time, we were all quite staring at the space where he had re-entered the water, mesmerised by the skill and beauty of this wild creature. Tina says she will never forget that sight for the rest of her life. I am happy that she has this movie in her mind to sustain her in the tough days.

Meanwhile it takes hundreds of buckets of salt water – each one hauled out of the sea at the stern (to fill the tanks with filtered water), the boys are enjoying it, in a way, as it is a form of physical exercise and that is something they have missed on the boat. It isn't possible to do any exercise when you are swinging around; the rolling around is hard to explain. Lottie and Tina have been talking about what an amazing experiential gym it would be to have a yacht simulator. Even though you are not doing 'exercise' just staying upright uses all your core strength. Sailing Pilates.

As I am writing this I am watching Mark take bucket after bucket out of the sea, it will take about 180 buckets out of the sea to fill the tank. One of the guys has now had a creative idea – take the emergency bilge pump hose from under the galley floor and use it and its electric pump to pump seawater into the bucket. Bilge pump into the sea from the stern, electric pump up water into the big bucket on the stern deck – pipe from that bucket to the water maker, it is funny to watch my feeders all running about working together and solving the problem. They must really want water a lot!

There should be an ARC prize for ingenuity at sea – our crew would win it!

"Saint Lucia is going to Love Magic". Tina says, "We will be good for the local economy – all the work that needs to be done!"

P.S. Bilge pump solution didn't work so the boys are back with the manual 'lifting the bucket', solution, "Something to do", they say bravely.

May is sleeping

Sunday 6th December
15.23.4 N 53.51.7W

Monday 7th December

Weird Address

15.19.08N 55.58.20

Now it is 9am and this morning's issues are: The Lewmar hatch in Tina and Mark's Cabin has been pulled off by the sheets (ropes on deck) and the hatch has gone overboard and the autopilot has decided to keep cutting out again so we can't rely on it.

Tina and Mark are now just resigned to the issues and just sigh and add things to the now, very long, list they are keeping.

'Good thing we have only 273 nautical miles to go', they are saying.

Today was a good day for the feeders, they had great fun playing with ideas to make the water maker work and it did work. They had all manner of tubes and pumps and buckets and tubs on deck. It looked funny but the result was that they could all have showers and that made them very happy. They have been so inventive.

They had a good day sailing and as the sun was going down they opened a bottle of something fizzy, the brown top went pop loudly and scared me. They were celebrating only 300 nautical miles to go to Saint Lucia. Then they had some pasta and sauce and then fell into the watches for the night.

Everyone says there are good and bad things about their watch times. Some say that they always get rain and squalls and Tina and Mark say they have been lucky and not had rain or high winds. Until tonight that is!

As Tina, Mark and I got up we could hear the wind picking up. We took over the watch from Simon just as the squall hit us, the rain flooded though an open hatch in a torrent and Tina was soaked as she battled to shut it. The wind was 30knots and there was a very black cloud right above us. We had to alter course to deal with the strength of the wind.

Good news, we are doing 8-10 knots of speed, bad news, we are heading for Boston!

Now the leech of the Main sail is trapped and they will have to wait for the wind to ease before letting the preventer loose and playing the mainsheet to release the sail – at least that is what I think I heard them say – I don't really understand when they talk 'sailing'

We are surrounded by ARC boats, which is great – Hot Stuff, the boat with the all-girl only crew passed us. Poor Simon was gutted to have Magic passed by so easily! He is a competitive sailor and Magic should be faster.

Tina and Mark are not bothered and just enjoy sailing safely and having company. Hot Stuff were on a Port tack and Magic was on a Starboard tack so they should have moved as they were close, half a mile and gaining, Simon spoke to them on the VHF and agreed that Magic would move – what a gentleman! We also have with us several other ARC yachts – Toothless, El Mundo, Tapatl, and Zheliko. I think we are all going to arrive around the same time. It is odd as Magic is a fast boat. We all try and consider the too long list of reasons for our slow progress. Could it be that the bow thruster that was damaged as we left Las Palmas is down and covered in weed? Is there fouling on the hull? Perhaps it is the holes in the sails .... did we take the wrong route? ...wrong wind? Or perhaps the gods are wanting us to stay longer???

Tina is still just happy to arrive happy and healthy. She is a positive thinker and even said that perhaps our role is to make all those who have passed us feel great! (she did think that sort of comment would not please the rest of Team Magic).

The welcome party for the ARC is on the same night as the ARC+ prize giving - Wednesday 9th December and we are hoping we will get into Rodney Bay, Saint Lucia for that. It will be great to see friends like Liam and Liz from Odyssey and find out how their ARC+ adventure has been. It will be so strange to be in a Marina again and not rolling about all the time.

I just snuggle up and stay dry. I wonder if the vet in Saint Lucia will be as kind as the vet in Las Palmas

I wonder if Tina and Mark have all the right papers for me, we will soon see.
     I wonder what jerk chicken is like.

I wonder when we will get there

8th December
Wednesday 9th December 00:39
14.65.07N 57.55.85W

The feeders have loved the sailing today, the wind has been perfect for them and Mark was manually steering for the sheer joy of it, sometimes we were doing 12-13 knots which is more like the speeds Magic should do in these conditions – apparently. Tina doesn't mind what position in the fleet we arrive she is just proud of our achievement as a team and happy that no one was injured. It has been an incredible journey for my feeders.

It has been sad for the crew member that has been unwell since the start, but as he says at least he is now thin and tanned!

Sailing seems to challenge everyone in different ways and this trip has been a significant challenge. I really miss running about on grass or on the beach and I know the feeders really would love to get off the boat for a walk or a run too.

When you will ask us "So, how was the trip?" I am sure there will be lots of people who say that the ARC was all just great fun. But my notes are always very honest.

My feeders *have* had fun and laughs and played, they have seen Dolphins, Jelly fish, Flying fish and a Turtle they have seen a LOT of floating seaweed, they have caught a fish and caught up on reading, they have watched movies in the evenings and had delicious freshly cooked meals every night, often with a sundowner beforehand. They have had showers on deck, done laundry and played board games too. But there have been a lot of challenges and although I have been fine with four legs the poor feeders have been bashed around for weeks with the continuous pitching and rolling.

They have been baked in the sun and soaked in torrential downpours.

They have been cut by knives and bits of metal and burned by the oven and the sun.

They have felt sick and tired

They have been bashed and bruised on the rigging

They have bashed and broken toes

They have had to do with only one shower per week each

They have dealt with continual broken sleep from watches and the rolling sea

They have been hot and bothered

They have cooked and cleaned and fixed and sailed and sailed and sailed

So - cut, burnt, bruised, tired and dirty they have dealt with all the Atlantic could throw at them.

They have worked hard as a team and supported each other (mostly).

They have been creative and innovative making things and fixing things – the "Heath Robinson way" of ensuring the water maker worked using two black gorilla tubs and four pipes was genius – people are clever.

But most of all

They have had an incredible journey.

Sailing gives you time to think about the future, time to reflect on the past (neither of which dogs do by the way – we live in the now).

They have laughed a lot together and they will never ever forget crossing the Atlantic Ocean, out of sight of land for 16 days.

Tina keeps thinking how amazing it is to have been under sail the whole way, only using the engine for a few hours! It is the most continual sailing most of the feeders have ever done. It has been wonderful to do the ARC, to have had all the support and help from this amazing organization and to be sailing in the fleet. Everyone has enjoyed the fact that friends and family have been supporting by watching the tracker and reading my blog.

Andrew in Lagos has been a superstar sending us world-class weather and routing information, what a good friend – we miss Andrew and Susan. The feeders have loved having emails from home.

Now we are nearly there, just one more day and night to go.

We may arrive at breakfast time on the 9th. If we do then it will be check in and do all the paperwork and I must see the vet, then the feeders hope they can get an afternoon nap because at 7pm there is a welcome party!

Tina thinks it is funny that Magic will arrive into Saint Lucia just in time for the welcome party!!

Must go now as we are on watch and I need to give Mark a cuddle under the stars.

May
At Sea

- The Last Day
09 December 2015
115 miles, 18 hours to go

Sometimes the time seems to have gone on and on and on – minutes seem like years. Then time goes faster – like when I am busy looking after the feeders or playing 'catch the cheese' in the galley. This morning's issues include a frayed main halyard, which could 'snap' at any moment meaning the main sail will fall down. The feeders don't seem too worried as they are prepared for it, they have been watching the blue string thingy at the top of the mast for a few days now, they can see it as they are using special 'come-to-me' glasses. Another Block has exploded, the one that was being used on the Genoa. They just took it off and put 'new block' in their notebook. They are just used to things popping and breaking.

There is a relaxed feeling this morning, it is the last day, we think we will get to our 'way point' on the North of the island of Saint Lucia at around 05.00 and that means we will cross the finish line around 06.00 into the marina at around 07.00 The plan is then to 'clear in' which means doing the official paperwork and all that, clean the boat and then begin the jobs and repairs, then I have to see the vet so they can see that I didn't bring any horrible things with me like fleas and ticks and they will check that I am well – which I am.

9th December at 03.11

I am just standing down from watch

It has been a very odd day today; mostly the feeders were making water and talking, reading books and standing watch. There is still a palpable, negative tension around and it seems like an analogy with the rig, strained and tired and chafed but, hopefully, holding together until we cross the finish line and moor up in Rodney Bay.

When we came on watch we could see the lights of Martinique and Mark and Tina talked about how they were going to have Christmas with Mark's son Gareth there. I think we will all enjoy being with our families again, we have missed them.

Tina says that she had wondered if having 3 skippers on board would have created issues. One person's decision on course or trimming or the preparation of the boat v's another's. I knew we would all have to work together and as ship's dog I think it is my job to go to whoever needs a cuddle the most.

Tina was saying that it is like when you go on a long-haul flight, at the start of the flight you don't even notice what later becomes a mild irritation and by the time you arrive the smallest noise is hard to bear. The boat is like that and we have travelled a long, long way in a very small space and coped with many challenges.

Everyone approaches things so differently and believes that their way is the best way, there must be support and flexibility but that seems to wear thin, like the sails. So, in the end, everyone must deal with this in his or her own way.

Everyone finds a way to cope. Perhaps taking some time out – listening to music or reading a book or just moving to a different space.

When the feeders reflect on this journey I hope it will be good thoughts and memories and I hope they will be proud of their achievements.

Yes – things broke and needed repair – yes, things were done differently sometimes than some people preferred – some people love to hand steer and it didn't matter a jot that the auto pilot didn't function on certain headings and for others this was a major source of irritation. Tina is certainly very interested in crew dynamics and it could well be something to study in the future and perhaps something the ARC could consider having some guide notes on.

The best thing now is that we can see the lights of Saint Lucia shining in the distance, there is the most beautiful flashing phosphorescence in our wake like molten stars have fallen under the front of the boat and are being washed under us. There is the gentle whooshing sound of the warm Caribbean Sea gently supporting us and we are almost there. Only a few more hours to go now, then we will all be up to cross the finish line together and take the boat into Rodney Bay to moor up.

Well Done Team Magic.

Now – can I go for a walk please?

I watched May sleeping on the deck as Mark and I sailed towards the lights of Rodney Bay. We woke the crew as we approached the shadow of Pigeon Island. This marked the entrance to Rodney Bay and the finish line of the ARC. It was 3am and dark. The land mass looked as if it was joined with the sea and it was a challenge to pick the right line into the Bay. We were all on deck. As we approached the boat that was moored up to mark the finishing line we were all feeling different emotions. I was tired and overwhelmed by a trio of powerful emotions, I was relieved, we had done it and we were all safe, I was happy – it was such a huge adventure and I was deeply sad that we had fallen out with each other. There was still a toxic atmosphere on board. I asked the crew if we should put the negativity to one side and just celebrate – their answer … "No"

So that was the last straw for me. We decided to drop anchor in the Bay and wait until dawn to go into the Marina. As soon as we were safely anchored, I sat on deck alone and wept under the stars.

Chapter Fourteen

CARIBBEAN BEGINNINGS

Ho Ho Ho – Breadfruit Roasting on an Open Fire
DECEMBER 16,

We should have been proud and happy – it had only taken us 16 days and 8 hours to cross the Atlantic. But we were all so tired and emotionally battered. Three of the crew all left Magic and it was very unpleasant and very sad. Things improved as Simon, Mark and I dusted off the intense atmosphere. Now we should move forward "Hello beautiful Caribbean".

It really is stunning here as Quincy from 'Ride the Tide' is showing you (photograph below) – this is part of the beautiful coastline of Saint Lucia

This morning our water maker is being refitted. This process will then continue tomorrow when Magic must be lifted out of the water for a new skin fitting (hole in the hull) as it was so badly done in Gibraltar that it didn't work the whole way across the Atlantic. It is too dull to moan about but having to pay twice to have such an expensive job done is not ok.

There is always something going on, for example in about 20 minutes the last boat on the ARC rally arrives into the Bay – she is being towed in as she has engine failure.

The Rodney Bay experience is odd – in many ways. First, it is as if we are still in Las Palmas as the ARC fleet are all here and everyone is talking about boats and fixing boats. But then there is Caribbean culture, the local people we have met are so lovely, warm like the weather and joyous, they sing and dance and laugh often – we love that. May is a big hit as it turns out the Caribbean people don't have pet dogs so she is a real novelty. Everyone smiles when they see her and they all want to talk to her and us about her.

We have just welcomed in Sea Symphony – our friends from Sail Ionian. They are the last ARC boat to arrive and they had a heroes' welcome. Their engine had failed but they managed that and many another issues they had with a positive attitude. They took the slower southern route across the Atlantic and they said it was slow but lovely, a 'relaxed cruise' which they described as fun, they ate well, sang sea shanty's and wrote poetry – how different their crew dynamics were from ours.

They said it was possibly because they didn't know any of the crew beforehand – this is contrary to all the advice but it has certainly worked for them and that is wonderful. It was lovely to see them all in their crew shirts, smiling and relaxed as they were towed in.

We wanted to explore beautiful Saint Lucia so Simon, Mark and I went on a wonderful adventure down the coast – we sped in a speed boat, in and out of some of the exotic bays, swam in crystal clear water, ate in a local restaurant and bathed in a warm waterfall. For one day, we felt like we were on holiday rather than working.

Happy in beautiful Saint Lucia. With the Pitons as our backdrop May, Mark, Simon and Tina are relaxing after the crossing. May is a bit hot!

There are many strange things about Rodney Bay and one of them is the relaxed and open way that drugs are sold and prostitutes and pimps hang around the bars. Simon is so funny – he said it is a new spin on Christmas

"Ho Ho Ho"

Brilliant.

We are loving the music and tomorrow night we are gathering on a friend's yacht with musicians to sing and laugh – I am learning the reggae versions of some Christmas carols – "Breadfruit Roasting on an Open fire – mongrels nipping at your toes" ....fantastic!!"

So – we are relaxing into the Caribbean way – we have reggae music on, whilst we rock gently in our new hammocks sipping rum and coke. Mark is thinking of growing dread locks and turning Rasta (just imagine)

There is a big party on Saturday night to end the ARC experience and then on Sunday most of the boats are leaving to go their separate ways around the Caribbean. We will be going to Fort de France in Martinique to collect Gareth – Mark's eldest son who flies in from Boston on Sunday night. Then our Caribbean cruise will really begin.

Reflections on the crew dynamics of our crossing.

Six sides
DECEMBER 17

When six people are on a yacht for a long time with different strains on them all there is a lot of anxiety and behaviours change dramatically. Discussing this seems to be a taboo but if we discuss it then we can learn.

There are six sides to our story of Magic's Atlantic Crossing and we can only honestly tell our own.

We got safely across the Atlantic because we had an experienced crew on board – many of them more experienced than us – and that is why we were happy to have them on board. We had sailed with them all before and they were our friends.

Many of the ARC crews have talked to us about their crossing and we have found that many had issues with crew dynamics. Sometimes around money or sometimes division of labour, even disagreements about food and drink or in some cases there was just a bad attitude on board. On some of the boats this was so serious that it could have been dangerous. Some crews had their bags packed and jumped off their yachts as soon as they arrived on the dock in Rodney Bay. Most of the boats had things that went wrong – some serious and some not. In all cases, it was *how* issues were dealt with that was the key to everyone enjoying the trip or not. Many boats had terrible trouble with serious things breaking – but if they pulled together and remained calm and positive then the outcome was good. Just like the shining example of the crew of Sea Symphony.

It is sad that so many crews have had serious behavioural issues aboard. Crew dynamics on the ARC and on other ocean passages is something that is not aired enough. It is obviously difficult for people to discuss. I think it would help people who are preparing for the ARC or any long passage to think about how they will deal with difficult behavior on board – from managing negative moods to what to do when there is a massive differing of opinion. If this subject was given more emphasis it would help other yacht owners to understand the pressures and dynamics that can build up. It would help to know what is best to do. We did discuss attitude and behaviour in our first crew meeting on board Magic but it wasn't enough to help.

The tension and frustration that built up for all of us on board was expressed in six individual ways and when people are feeling so much they do not hear each other and resentment builds. Sitting down to talk just doesn't seem to be an option.

On Magic the vibe became so unpleasant that when we crossed the line and there was a suggestion to put our issues to one side for a moment and celebrate our shared achievement – the answer was "No!" That I think gives you the indication of how tetchy and difficult things had become between some – not all, of the crew.

Perhaps something good can some of this debate for others in future years.

For the record, we have and are saying here as we said along the way – thank you to our crew – we did and are saying "thank you".

We have all certainly learned a lot.

One of the key lessons is that May and I are not sailing an ocean ever again. Mark might! Some suggestions we have had from more experienced sailors may help you if you ever decide you are going to do a long passage on a yacht:

1. Do bring experts but also ensure that they respect the skipper
2. Make sure your crew are genuine team players – if they have been used to skippering their own yacht they may find that they cannot take directions.
3. There is only one skipper
4. Consider carefully before having different cultures aboard – foods, cultural differences, language etc. – all can bring conflict and tension
5. One very experienced skipper, after hearing about our on-board issues gave us this advice about selecting crew –
   Ask them this question "Do you have any opinion about how this yacht should be run?" If the answer is something like "No, you are the skipper but I have lots of skills you can call on" take them if they go into a long list of how they would manage the yacht – don't take them.

"Were shall we meet tonight?"–
"The bar near the palm tree"
"Which Palm Tree?"
DECEMBER 22,

We finally left Rodney Bay on Sunday 20th. We were on our way to collect Gareth from Fort de France in Martinique and we were so looking forward to seeing him. To have family with us is something we have really missed. I felt the usual departure anxiety – getting lines ready and thinking about the wind direction and weather for our crossing. It is only 4 hours North from Saint Lucia to Martinique but we have been tucked away in our cosy berth for over a week and now we are off again. Like a lot of things, you always want what you don't have. When you are out on a rolling sea with squalls and rain you long for the safety of a marina but when you have been in a marina for more than a few days you are desperate to leave, and be on the ocean again. We were ready to go – The ARC has been an incredible experience with highs and lows. We were so glad we left on a high with a Prize for innovation – May's Blog was a hit during the crossing. We could see so many happy crews and talk with other teams about the positive things that happened during their time crossing the Atlantic – the achievement, the fact that we are in the Caribbean…these are all good things – very good things

We were longing for that Caribbean experience that we had had in our minds for a long time – white beaches fringed with Palm Trees and children playing in the warm sea…

So, we set off – we got out of the marina without a hitch – well apart from the fact that we couldn't pay for our laundry, as the laundry guy didn't come and we left all my diet cokes in the ARC office! We will be going back to Saint Lucia in the New Year and will pay Sparkle laundry then. It is an excellent service run by a lovely guy who comes to your boat in his boat to collect the laundry. We love that!

Out on the sea again and it was blowing hard with 25kts of wind gusting 30kts – the gusts are alarming at first and they make setting the sail correctly, a challenge. We put up the mainsail and decided that a mainsail with two reefs in would be enough. We sail like cowards! Then, our new friend Tim Aitken on his beautiful yacht Braveheart of Sark came up behind us with full sails – urm we thought …perhaps we should put up our Genoa (the sail at the front) It was a bit rolly and we knew the Genoa would stabalise the movement.

In Rodney Bay, we had someone came to look at the Genoa. As you may remember we had had issues with it on the crossing. It needed some repairs (I refuse to go into what as it is so dull!) but he said it was stable for now and we could sail.

We unfurled the Genoa and at first it slipped out perfectly then – and I know that you know what is coming – BANG – the sail completely collapsed and fell in the ocean over the side of the boat. Bloody hell – we are so sick of things breaking – we are resilient but this is getting beyond a challenge.

We would love to 'just sail'

I took the helm and Mark went forward to try to retrieve the sail. We had been told that if the sail went into the water it would be unlikely that it could be retrieved. But we have learned not to trust all that we have been told so we were determined to get our sail back on board. We needed to de-power the main so we decided to take it down. I turned Magic into the wind and dropped the main. That went well. I needed to help Mark with the sail – it was a two-person job and we struggled in the mid-day sun for over an hour until finally it was all back on board and safely tied on the deck. Mark thinks his little finger on his left hand is broken (an injury from previously going up the mast at sea) it didn't help the injury much hauling in a huge wet sail from the sea – We had to pull it up and across the guard rail and then tie it onto the deck.

Once again, we find ourselves wet, bruised, burned and broken and the sail was looking like it had seen better days too. Now we will have to get a rigger to repair the head of the furler unit and a sail maker to repair this sail or make us a new one. Ho Hum.

We were tired but happy that we had managed to get the sail back on board.

We thought "Enough of sailing" – we would motor the rest of the way to Fort de France.

It was gusting over 30knts – so we put on some music – a fantastic selection of Reggae tracks given to us by Quincy in Rodney Bay and we enjoyed the moment. The air was warm, the sky was blue and there were Boobies flying and fishing around the boat. We were going to get Gareth and that was all that mattered.

We arrived into the bay at Fort de France later than we had hoped and we took a while anchoring – but it all went fine.

Being in the Caribbean brings a whole new set of things we must learn to do every day like – take the anchor up and set it down, dinghy on board and back in the water, outboard for the dinghy on the dinghy and then back on Magic. It can be tricky with just two of us but you learn to think differently and good teamwork is important. To be honest it is wonderful being on the boat just the two of us – The ghosts of the toxic atmosphere on our Atlantic Crossing have left. May is happy too – she loves just sunning herself on deck and watching the sea birds.

There are a lot of things that are different when you live aboard. We don't eat as much and we don't watch any TV – we have limited access to the Internet so we are almost on a digital detox permanently. We have NO 'normallys' – every day is completely different with new – sometimes exciting and sometimes serious challenges.

We do love it but after 14 months living aboard Magic we are starting to think of a life in a house with a garden. Strange how much I miss a garden.

So back to collecting Gareth. After we had anchored we got the dinghy off the deck and into the sea, then we got the outboard on the back and got the security line to lock it ashore
(theft of dinghys' is common and we don't want to lose ours) we got the dead man switch, the fuel can, the head torch and a dry bag. Mark started the engine (it worked! – amazing) and he went ashore. Gareth and Mark had to rely on old school communications to meet up – one email had got to Gareth regarding a time and rendezvous (well we are in France!)

Of course, Gareth's flight was delayed an hour and then both of them missed each other as they walked around trying to find where to meet. Then, eventually, they bumped into each other in a park – funny.

I was on board Magic making her feel warm and homely – turning on lights, making up Gareth's room, plumping cushions and making supper. I love nesting!

So, Gareth came on board and we had a lovely evening. It is strange being on Anchor and where we were there was some 'ferry wash' that makes it roly from the small ferries that leave too frequently from Fort de France to some of the other bays. None of us slept too well but we didn't care as we were happy to be together.

In the morning, we decided to go into the town and we had all imagined a small French café with excellent croissants and great coffee. Reality hit immediately as we discovered the small and grubby town with boarded up shops and a lot of noisy, dusty road works – it was a disappointment and we didn't find our lovely French café – We were hungry as it was late morning so we dropped our ideals and went for what we could find.

Then we 'cleared in' this is how you complete the entry papers for our arrival into any new country and as we had left Saint Lucia and we were now in Martinique we had to "Clear In" this was something we would become very familiar with.

It was a funny experience – just a grubby computer in a corner of a remote ship's chandlers – fill in the form – print it – hand it to the owner of the store who stamps it and then that's it you are in!

Nothing for May as we are in 'France' and so doesn't have to see the vet. Clearing in was just us. We were told that 'no one will check it anyway' – but we were glad to have done the official paperwork properly as we don't want to get in trouble so early in our Caribbean adventure.

Then, it was off to the mobile phone store to buy a data sim (we are always on the hunt for internet and we thought we would try again) we got one and it seems to be working – amazing!

As so many things are a struggle we are always so elated when something works – we celebrate it like giddy children. I know we will always be grateful for things working!

Back on the boat – we took the dinghy on deck and then hoisted the outboard and stowed it. Then we were off – we lifted the anchor with ease – good team working again. We were thinking of staying in Fort de France to get work done on the Genoa but it was not great there and we wanted to leave.

I had been researching where we should go and we set off to Grande Anise D'Arlet 'a little village set on a white sand beach fringed with palm trees' as the guide book said. Perfect! That is what we were looking for.

We arrived only an hour later than we had planned and as we entered this perfect little bay we were delighted to see Liam and Liz whizzing up to us in their dinghy. They were smiling and waving – this is the second time they have been warmly met by Liam and Liz as we entered an unfamiliar port. (Remember we met them in Gibraltar and they found us in Las Palmas and again in Rodney Bay).

Liam is from Tipperary in Ireland and Liz is from Wales – they are so fantastic – young and fun and great sailors. They had been in the bay for a few days and knew where we could get a mooring buoy. So, they went ahead of us and we followed them to a buoy.

Liam and Liz did the ARC+ (ARC PLUS) and had a lot of adventures on their trip. They are the sort of people who make fun happen. They are always positive and optimistic and laughing – whatever challenges they have. They came alongside to tell us all the tips for the area – swimming with turtles is a must in this beautiful bay and which bars are best.

They have arranged for Christmas lunch and there are now nearly 40 people who are meeting to celebrate Christmas together – here in tiny Grande Anise D'Artlet. This is the sort of thing that Liam and Liz make happen – a sort of happiness alchemy. It's Magic what they do.

Last night we met with them and their friends ashore for food and drinks. It was quite an adventure getting ashore as the dock is way too high and the ladders do not reach to the dinghy – it was tricky – I felt very Lara croft! (in my fantasy version!) climbing up on the wooden plank then across to the ladder and then finally to the dock.

When we came to leave the dock we all went in convoy – Liam gave us a tow behind his dinghy – our outboard engine would have started (I think) but it was quicker to get a tow.

Today we woke up late and had a big breakfast on board. We were slowly taking in how stunning this bay is. Soft wind, crystal clear waters and turtles slowly swimming by. We are just going to read and sleep and lie in hammocks and swim with turtles today – now this *is* what we came for!

T'was the day before Christmas when all through the
boat – not a creature was stirring not even a goat!
DECEMBER 24,

Sitting on deck watching the sun rise over the warm Caribbean Sea I am reflecting
on how amazing this adventure is. We have had so many challenges and we have
learned so much. We have been supported by many people and let down by others.

Today it is Christmas Eve, Mark and I have been on deck checking things and
drying out our Geona. We are going to stow it and have it repaired in Saint Lucia.
The plan now is to stay here for our Christmas Eve BBQ on the beach and our
Lobster Lunch tomorrow and then leave to go to Saint Anne or Marin and then on
to Saint Lucia for New Year. There is a ferry from Rodney Bay to Martinique and
Gareth may take that when he goes home. It is interesting how close all the islands
are to each other and a big Aha! moment for anyone coming to the Caribbean on
holiday – you don't have to be stuck in one place you can so easily island hop.

May loved being on the beach. She adores sand and was snuffling around and
skipping about. Everyone loves to see May and they comment on what a good
traveler she is. I sometimes think – poor dog she wasn't given the choice!

Last night we watched 'About Time' – which was the perfect Richard Curtis film
for the Christmas holidays – who doesn't love a Richard Curtis movie during
Christmas? We were delighted that none of us had seen this one and it was a funny
and sentimental and perfect. It did make us reflect on a lot of things, which is good.

This year has been so tricky. We are so fortunate and so happy so we have decided
to donate to a Caribbean children's charity instead of sending cards and gifts to
friends and family. We have chosen the Jermain Defoe foundation in Saint Lucia.

Don't judge me but I am going to have another Banana Colada!
DECEMBER 29

We are living in a sort of gentle, warm blur – which is rather lovely.
The Caribbean temperature and lush surroundings are very soporific. We stayed
days in the picture-perfect bay of Anse D'Arlet. Some days were rough and splashy
on Magic with the wind funneling down through the hills towards us and some
were gentler. We have heard stories of the yachts that sailed south and they have
had a lot of wind. It is the 'Christmas Winds' apparently and it will settle later in
January and into February. We are not going to rush – we are going to see if we
can spend New Year in Marigot Bay in Saint Lucia and then after Gareth leaves we
are meeting friends – Sara and John Templeton who are coming to Saint Lucia on

holiday. We might see if we can leave Magic in Rodney Bay Marina and join them in their resort for a few days on land.

We are really enjoying Martinique. What could be better than snorkeling with turtles in crystal clear, warm water, a cobalt blue sky overhead and green hills and palm trees fringing the white beach just ahead?

Well actually there is something better than that… it is being in that situation with family and friends. Friends from the ARC and the ARC+ surround us –Lovely Liz and Liam are here and they have been telling everyone to come and join in the fun.. That is what some magical people do – they are like magnets for fun. Liz and Liam have become great friends – they have welcomed us into four ports – Gibraltar, Las Palmas, Rodney Bay and now D'Anse Darlet. How extraordinary to see friendly faces in strange places? Thanks to them there were 57 of us for Christmas lunch!

On Christmas Eve, most of us gathered on the beach for a BBQ – everyone brought food and drink and it was a lot of fun – we all beached our dinghy's and helped each other unload. It was fantastic fun and there were a lot of Christmas hats and stories of Atlantic Crossings. The subject of conversation is typically – 'where are you from?' and 'where are you going next?'…peppered with – 'what broke?' and 'where are you getting that fixed!?' Sometimes I notice how natural the conversations are about hopping around exotic places – then I pinch myself – wait! We just said, "we are going to stay in Martinique for a while and then we are sailing to Saint Lucia and then on to Bequai and Tobago Cays" – that, is a very normal sentence in this group of friends but an out of this world conversation in any more 'normal' context.

I remind myself often that we are so fortunate to be living this way.

And, as we plan towards booking our fights home in early May we will appreciate the time even more.

I must admit to being a total lightweight on Christmas Eve – Mark brought me home to Magic in the Dinghy and then he returned to the Party. I think I have just let the whole ARC and Crew thing hit me at once and I have ended up with a very bad cold sore on my bottom lip which hurts like hell and I am feeling quite a bit under par. Sleep is what is needed – batteries need a re-charge. If I don't feel well I am always comforted by having May with me. She curls up beside me and her little warm body is so soft. May makes an excellent nurse.

Christmas Day and Gareth, Mark, and I are up and sharing Bucks Fizz and gifts. May is happy as we have given her a Christmas sausage. Gareth has brought us the most fantastic gifts – a captain's hat for Mark and an inflatable chair for me – perfect for floating in the ocean (tied on to Magic!) We gave Gareth some Marks and Spencer Brandy Snaps – which we know he loves – we got them in M&S in Las Palmas and have nursed them all the way across the Atlantic

It feels more like Christmas Day than we all thought it would.

The Christmas supper with 57 yachties was a hoot – Lobster and Rum – the perfect Caribbean treat. One of the highlights was Father Christmas. Liam and Liz had asked a wonderful white bearded sailor to be Santa and for his crew member to be the elf – a sail bag was filled with secret Santa gifts that everyone had brought – it was special – everyone came up one by one and sat on Santa's knee! The Elf pulled out a gift and gave it to Santa who handed the gift to the person on his lap – laughter everywhere – of course there were some actual children too and they were not allowed to sit on Santa's knee!! –The modern world rather sadly creeping into our fun.

We sang Christmas songs, ate Lobster and drank (a lot of) Rum
On Boxing Day, we were going to leave for Marin for repairs – but having checked the weather we decided it will be too windy so we will stay for one more day. We have learned to view a 'delay day' with joy and not frustration we see it as a bonus and look for something special to do. Sailing changes the way you think about planning.

We had a relaxed morning and then decided we would walk to the nearby town to get some exercise and cash. Just as we were leaving the bay I saw what looked like a potentially lovely restaurant. So…being naughty, I suggested that instead of setting off at a pace for our walk – that we go for cocktails and lunch instead!!

What a surprise – it was the most perfect place. Gentle swaying palms, white-washed washboard roof and a delicious homemade fully French menu. They even made May feel welcome – which is rare. I often must smuggle her in to places in a large handbag.

The place is called Restaurant L'Escale and if you are ever fortunate enough to find yourself in D'Anse Darlet on Martinique then please do not miss this special place – the décor, the service and the elegant freshly prepared French food all divine – the three of us could not resist having 3 courses with cocktails and wine and the bill – 100 Euro Amazing – it was one of those meals that stays in your memory and you have foodie flash backs – bliss

The following morning, we set off to Marin early – with the rigging repairs we needed doing we decided to motor around the corner. Gareth took the helm and it was great fun to see him enjoying Magic. The wind was on our nose the whole way so it was a bit splashy but it was only a very short trip. We moored up to the fuel dock and filled up – I still get very anxious when we moor up. We are so much better than we were but when you are mooring up anything can go wrong. This time was no exception I saw the bow of Magic round up to the pontoon on a spot that had no fender so I moved forward too fast with a fender in hand and 'bash' 'Smash' the little toe on my right foot crunched into something hard on the deck – oh I hate that feeling – it jangles through your body and the pain reverberates for hours. Ouch! I had ignored my own 'wear shoes on deck' rule. So, no one to blame but me. I need not have been so concerned as Mark is great at parking… and he put Magic in a perfect spot. The guy on the fuel dock was looking very concerned at my pain and I was feeling sorry for myself too as I watched my toe going blue and swelling up. Ho hum – sailing eh! Time to cuddle 'nurse' May again.

Today – while Magic was at the rigger's hospital we went to Saint Ann on the local bus – it was a sleepy seaside town and we had lunch by the beach – then we tried to get back – no bus….well not for 3 hours, very Caribbean!

When we eventually arrived back to Magic we had no forestay – the riggers had removed it and it needs to be replaced… not sure we are going anywhere tomorrow!

Some friends have arrived in to Marin so that is good and we will meet them for drinks tonight. The rigger whose name is Mr. Rivet (no really it is) says that he will have four guys on Magic from 8am as he needs us to leave at noon.

We are having

- Our third reef put back in – following Mark cutting it when he was stuck up the mast
- Our Vang (kicker) repaired
- Our forestay replaced and the foil repaired
- Our furler repaired

Wonder what that bill will be?

Oh yes, and the Banana colada? – when we arrived in Marin we had a lovely meal and Gareth spied the cocktail menu – Banana Colada made with ice cream – just had to be done. So, he had two. He made me laugh when he said, "don't judge me but I am having another Banana Colada"

Happy New Year
JANUARY 2

As you do early in a fresh new year, we have been reflecting.

We have been talking about how it has been living aboard Magic for14 months. It has certainly been an adventure. We have learned a lot, been hurt a lot (physically and mentally), been scared a lot, spent a lot but most of all we have enjoyed a lot.

Living aboard is not for everyone – there are significant challenges. But, for us, the advantages have outweighed the disadvantages.

Now we have booked our flights home – We will fly home on Friday 15th April from Antiqua. It feels very weird to have an end but it also feels good.

Honestly, we are looking forward to moving off the boat. Having an end is making us appreciate the time we have left as of course now we now only have three and a bit months. I keep having thoughts and conversations that don't seem real, like – "three and a half months cruising the Caribbean in our yacht" – really? is that our life?

The plan is shaping up for our next steps. Currently we are in Rodney Bay, Saint Lucia again. We sailed here from Saint Ann in Martinique and it was a great sail. We needed one of those – 'sailing when the weather is fine and everything works' days and those seem to be rare.

The only challenge was that we didn't arrive into Rodney Bay until after dark – never a great idea. May was on deck with Mark at the helm and Gareth and I were on the foredeck keeping watch. There are a lot of yachts moored in the bay at the entrance to the Marina in Rodney Bay and many of them do not have lights so it can be tricky to navigate. We were later than planned to leave the rigger's dock in Marin and we knew we would arrive in the dark. It was tricky to find the entrance to the Marina but once we did we were in familiar territory. We called in on Ch9 and were given a berth and then to our delight we were greeted by lots of ARC friends who shouted to us "Hello Magic" then they took our lines and helped us settle in. I think lots of ARC people have made Rodney Bay their base in the Caribbean. The ARC really has been fantastic – it is wonderful to be traveling in strange places and meeting up with familiar people.

On New Year's Day, we took a cab to Marigot Bay (yes, we could have taken Magic but we were – frankly, way too hung over!) we had a delicious lunch and cocktails at the Dr. Doolittle Bar and Restaurant and once again met some ARC participants that we had met in Las Palmas. Marigot Bay is beautiful but one whole side of it is owned by a resort hotel and they said May was not allowed in!! Once we showed she could be stowed in a basket they were happier and let us in – it is odd in Marigot Bay – pretty but commercialised – so mixed feelings.

It has been wonderful having Mark's son, Gareth stay with us but now we have just dropped him off at the ferry which will take him from Castries (capital of Saint Lucia) to Fort de France (capital of Martinique). He has been with us for Christmas and New Year and it has been a lovely relaxed time. It is Saturday and our plan for the weekend is to try to relax and recover! Fixing the Mainsail, the Genoa, the Fluxgate compass and the VHF can wait until Monday....on Tuesday Sara and John Templeton – our friends from Northern Ireland are arriving for a holiday to celebrate their 30th Wedding Anniversary. It is funny as they have booked a resort that is right beside where we are now. We are hoping we can sail Magic around to Morgan Bay and anchor – it would be fun to dinghy in to see them. We are looking forward to seeing friends and then we have no plans – how odd that is! No plans...

We are so used to having lots of plans.

We have noticed that there is a music festival in Bequai at the end of January and we would like to go to that and Yvonne a friend from Nun Monkton arrives into Grenada on the 1st February. We would like to see her and her partner Hans. Then there is, swimming with turtles in Tobago Quays and the adventure of making our way up to Antiqua for the beginning of March – what a life!

It feels like our Caribbean adventure is just beginning really!

When living in paradise becomes normal
JANUARY 12

It is odd living in the Caribbean, which for many people is a dream destination for very special occasions and holidays. For example, our friends Sara and John are here in Saint Lucia to celebrate their 25th Wedding Anniversary – but we are 'just here'. We were talking today about the concept of going on holiday – where would you want to go on holiday when you are already spending months in the Caribbean on your own yacht?!

We constantly remind ourselves that we are very lucky and we are doing what we can while we are here to use local services and buy fruit and veg from the guys who sell stuff to the boats. Our new normal is weird – we buy fresh in-season avocados from the boat boys and a singing guy on a paddleboard wearing a Santa Hat delivers our fresh bread. We are moored up beside Steve Job's super yacht – Venus and we have just met Rob and Jules from Lagos who are here with our friend, Han's yacht – Thindra. As always conversations that are common include enquiries as to where people have been or where they are going next – the most frequent is something like "we *are spending the whole season in the Caribbean– down to Grenada via Tobago Quays and Bequai and then up again to Antigua stopping in Martinique and lots of other places*" – and "*are you going to the Bequai music festival at the end of January?*"

We are becoming used to the soft warm winds and the views of mountains and palm trees. We love the Caribbean and feel very at home. In particular, we love the people – they are welcoming and interesting and warm and fun – reflecting their home.

We have been surprised by the lack of any threat – threat to our property and ourselves is something we were told we would feel. But we don't!

Making new friends in the Caribbean is easy

We were told about high levels of petty crime and how you should lock yourself into your boat at night. Perhaps we have been fortunate or perhaps it is our outlook and experience of global travel – but we have not felt any tension or threat here at all and we have certainly never locked ourselves in at night. Not that we could, as we have no air conditioning on Magic and it is around 35 Degrees aboard.

The weather is interesting too – after Christmas it was windy with gusts around 35 knots and very lumpy sea states – now it is beautiful with fluffy fair weather clouds, gentle sea state and winds of around 15knots – 20 knots – perfect for cruising about. I get a rush of adrenalin when we leave or arrive somewhere but not so much out of fear but out of the excitement of finding out about somewhere new. We have become accustomed to mooring Magic in any manner of ways – bows to, stern to, on a buoy, on anchor, along side…. We can lasso any manner of things to keep us steady and we are getting more confident by the day. Our repairs and maintenance skills are improving too and we have a go at fixing most things now ourselves before we get professional help. We still have a technical problem with our auto pilot and despite replacing the fluxgate compass it still isn't right and it may be the auto pilot computer – we will need professional advice for that and our main VHF radio which stopped working during the last days of the ARC was due to the transceiver failing so we have ordered a new one and will have that professionally fitted too. Our sails need some TLC and we are getting quotes to have new ones made. What is a transceiver?

All these things become part of the everyday – we tend to do jobs in the morning and then in the afternoon we play. Some friends of ours from the ARC – Les and Mike from Sea Symphony (you might remember that they were the guys who arrived into Rodney Bay last following their ARC crossing) They have big problems as their engine has ceased and must be taken apart and rebuilt with some new parts. They had a great crossing in that they had a lot of fun and a very happy crew and they were delighted to win the prize for coming last – they knew what mattered most. But now they are stranded in the Rodney Bay Marina and we know how that feels – as we can reflect on when we were stranded in Lagos. Yes, it is a lovely place but when you want to go and you can't it is frustrating. We took them out on Magic and cruised to Marigot Bay yesterday. We ate at the rainforest café and it was wonderful. We were moored close to the restaurant and we all got in the dinghy and just paddled across to the entrance – great fun. Surrounded by the Mangroves and the sounds of the frogs. Each time we go we learn more how to get the most out of our stay. The first time we sailed in to Marigot Bay we were met by a boat boy who helped us take a buoy but then we realized that the outer buoys are the local ones and not the ones belonging to the hotel – so the next time we arrived we went right into the Bay and took an official buoy – fantastic value at only $30 a night and you get to use the hotel gym and pool which are lovely. It feels like a holiday inside a holiday going to Marigot Bay.

We are excited about our time in the Caribbean. When we talk with friends who have done the trip before they tell us that there are so many more delightful surprises to come – swimming in crystal clear, warm water with turtles in Tobago Quays is one of the treats I am most looking forward to. And all the while we are also planning our return home. Currently we plan to leave Magic in Antiqua until mid-May and then she will be returned to the Med where we will keep her. We shall be home mid-April and we will live in our converted Chapel in North Yorkshire until we find our new home which we hope will be in our beloved Nun Monkton. It's fun to be here in the Caribbean knowing that we have 3 months to play but it makes it even sweeter knowing that we are shaping a plan to move forward with our businesses and home.

May is certainly looking forward to coming home and running in cool fields and we hope that we can find a way to be reunited with Bear our Bernese Mountain Dog who is living in Wales….we will see what happens next. It was certainly the right decision not to have Bear with us but we miss her a lot. May is a bit hot but Bear would have been ill in this heat.

But for now, it is back to some Genoa repairs. Then later we are going to see Mrs. Job's yacht Venus and take some photos – then perhaps a few rum and cokes and dinner with reggae on board Magic.

Chapter Fifteen

ON THE TRAIL OF THE GIANT

Snail and a very Dangerous lunch
JANUARY 16

It is 07.30am and I am sitting under the Bimini while some gentle rain falls, there is a soft, warm breeze and I am watching the sunrise over the Mangroves in Marigot Bay. The birds are singing and a graceful, grey egret has just flown past, its wings just kissing the glassy green water. Meanwhile the singing Santa on his paddleboard is delivering Bananas to boats his song is "I am your sole provider" how perfect and I am thinking – this is a magical moment. It's lovely when you notice one of those moments in amongst the rest of life.

Marigot Bay is where the original Rex Harrison version of Dr. Doolittle was filmed. I can see why, it is a perfect natural harbour and the light is incredible. I think it is a mini paradise. Yesterday we had lunch on the little beach, which is a natural spit of sand with very tall palm trees. The locals serve delicious lunch – in fact the little beach restaurant is the number 2 place to eat in Marigot Bay on Trip Advisor – even though there are about 30 other restaurants here including 5 star ones at the Capella Resort.

Lunch was delicious, but dangerous. As we approached we heard a loud crack above our heads and a large brown palm frond fell from its tree and landed heavily on an unsuspecting diner. She was only shocked and slightly grazed. Her family was upset and her husband was very cross with the owner of the restaurant.

We laughed when we got our lunch delivered to notice a note inside the basket.

The note said that the management could not be made responsible for falling coconuts and leaves!

Lunch was – plantain, breadfruit, lentils, rice and noodles – all carbs so far! With BBQ chicken and creole sauce – yummy.

Later today we are going back to Rodney Bay – we have some reality to meet up with.

Mark fell from the dinghy when getting on Magic two days ago at the time he had his iPhone in his pocket – so it is dead.

His fall was really nothing to do with the happy hour at the tiny thatched Hurricane Hole bar!

We shall add his phone to the list of Apple things lost or dead – my phone is lost and of course there were the two laptops that got soaked and died in Lagos.

We have 3 'reality' things to do – Mark's Phone, Our VHF and the import papers for May.

We need a phone so we will go to Rodney Bay Mall to buy one. We also must check if our new part has arrived to fix our VHF – we hope it has and that we can have it repaired on Monday.

I have been doing some research on how to take May to the Grenadines. We would like to go to Bequai and on down to Grenada – we have discovered two things

1. Her current permit for Saint Lucia has run out...."ahhhh nooo" – I thought it was longer than a few weeks – I have emailed the official vet and hope they can come to the boat and give us an extension and I hope we won't be in trouble??

2. The Grenadines rules seem to say that May must have been in one country prior to import to the Grenadines for 6 months – and she hasn't, so not sure what will happen there – The paperwork for May is so confusing and I do find it frustrating and overwhelming. But she is worth it and we love travelling with May. So, we will just fill out the forms and send them our papers and hope for a permit.

Mark is happy as he has found a sports bar in Rodney Bay. He is delighted that he will be able to go and watch his beloved Manchester United play football on Sunday – then on Sunday evening we are meeting up with Sara and John for supper as they are still in Saint Lucia. On Monday, we hope we will meet up with Hans – our friend from Lagos – his beautiful Swan yacht is here to collect passengers for a charter to Grenada. We can sort out the VHF and the papers for May and then we hope we can leave for Bequai on the 19th January for the Mount Gay Music festival, which starts on the 21st.

I am looking forward to the paperwork for May and the VHF stuff being behind us! I am anxious about going to new places because we don't know what the weather or sea state will be and we don't know what the mooring possibilities will be – it is strange – going to new and exotic places should be a dream – and it is once you are there and secure – but the unknown is not as comfortable for me as it once was – adventures are a little more challenging as you get older but I suppose that is why it is important to keep doing them – can't let that comfort zone shrink!!

A fish and two Chips
JANUARY 20, 2016

We don't have ordinary days any more, which I love.

I know I keep repeating this but despite the challenges that living aboard a boat brings – we know we are extremely lucky.

We have been giving a great deal of thought to purpose – what is next for us? and what for? It is good to have time to think.

An example of an extra ordinary day is this – 'A day in the life'

We were working on Magic – cleaning and tidying and sorting – these three things are in constant rotation when you live in a small space. Vincent, the excellent electrician here in Rodney Bay – was fitting our new transponder (whatever that is) So that our VHF will work again. (optimists!)

He suddenly came out on deck and looked out into the marina – "oh look over there, that is a friend of mine and his engine has just cut out" – we hadn't noticed it but when we looked a large blue steel boat was suspended in the lagoon, slowing drifting backwards towards the private pontoon of one of the large houses on the bank.

We have never used our dinghy to help move a boat before but we didn't think twice. We jumped into the dinghy – starting the outboard took a while (it always does when it matters!) A local man was skippering the blue boat and he had two passengers who, it turned out, were a lovely Scottish couple he had taken out on a fishing trip.

I was thinking that it was lucky that his engine had cut out while he was in the Marina rather than out at sea.

It didn't take us very long to reach them and we took his bowline. We drove the dinghy forward but we didn't have enough power with our small outboard to pull the heavy steel fishing boat. Our dinghy just struggled and went sideways.

Then we heard a friendly "Hello – what are you two up to? Messing about with boats?" …It was Simon the Saxophonist and Linda – we really like those guys – it is so lovely meeting up with people you know from the ARC– We had met them first in Las Palmas where Simon had played Sax on Magic – then we met them in Marigot Bay and now they were here in Rodney Bay. They were in their dinghy – on the way to the supermarket (yes, that probably seems strange but that is how it is done!)

We explained to them what we were attempting to do and Simon said, "You are going to need more horsepower" He had a larger outboard engine and suggested that he and Linda pull the boat and that we should stay alongside it to nudge and steer it. Together we managed to get the blue boat safely to its dock. The skipper shook our hands to say thank you and the lovely Scottish couple gave a beautiful, silver shining, 'just caught' Tuna to each of us.

Perfect! Simon and Linda took their fish and headed off to the Supermarket and we took ours and headed back to Magic.

May was delighted with the fish – she finds them fascinating. We took a picture of our prize and then ate it for lunch! It was delicious – there is nothing like the taste of very fresh tuna. It all felt very 'Island life'

We were still waiting for the vet to come on board Magic. I had been fretting about it, as I seem to get quite stressed and anxious about officialdom. I needn't have worried – the vets (three of them turned up!) were charming. Two of them came on board with a scanner to read Mays microchip. The scanner immediately found the chip – but then they said, "that's strange – what number is this?" Their scanner had found May's original microchip – I explained about what had happened in Las Palmas – you might remember that the vet there, not being able to find the chip had fitted a new one. I had a letter from the Las Palmas vet explaining about the fact that May's papers all had one microchip number on them but that microchip was lost and stating the number of the new one – what a muddle.

Then the scanner went ping again and the new number was displayed on the screen – I couldn't believe it, now May has <u>two</u> microchips! Well at least it is now clear that the papers I have do relate to this dog and there won't be any doubt.

It does seem strange to me that there are thousands of people moving about the islands, birds migrating and fish and things swimming about but May – she must have microchips, 50 tests and certificates and vets to come on board to check her before she can move from Island to Island. They don't care if people are moving around with all sorts of diseases but May – she is a biohazard.

But all is well that ends well and I am happy that we now have our new Saint Lucia Permit for May. May doesn't seem too bothered and just lies on the deck like a royal princess.

It was a day of two chips and a fish.

Today is Wednesday 20th January – we were due to leave this morning to, finally, head South to St Vincent and Bequai but we decided to have the mainsail repaired here in Saint Lucia where there is an excellent sail loft. The sail maker says the sail is in good condition and only needs minor work so it will be back on Magic tomorrow morning. That probably means tomorrow afternoon – Caribbean time – so our plan is to spend this morning sorting out Magic for our journey and this afternoon on the beach.

First, we must tidy up after our lovely evening with friends on board – we had a "chippy Tuesday" Lesley from Sea Symphony made delicious chip shop curry sauce and white bread and we made lots of chips – Val and Cliff from 'Why not' were with us too .it was fun!

Tomorrow is my daughter, Sara's Birthday – she is in Australia so the time zones and the technology make it hard for us to get in touch but I hope we can manage a Skype.
    I love and miss her very much.

Falling in love with the Delta Blues
JANUARY 29

As always, it takes longer to get Magic ready to go sailing than we think it is going to. Each time you have taken time out in a marina or anchorage the things you own creep out of the spaces to which they have been squirreled away. Glasses for wine, perfume bottles, an ornament or a bowl with some precious shells collected along the way – all find their place again which makes Magic feel homely.

When it is time to slip the lines again all these treasures become detritus as safety and sailing trump homeliness. (Writing that word makes me think of Donald Trump – the news only occasionally creeps through the cracks of our blissful world and it is horrible! What are Americans thinking! – I had to watch some Kevin Spacy interviews to calm myself! – He was at Davos and his thinking is beautiful) anyway, where was I? …oh yes, we are getting Magic ready. Rather than the usual two or three hours it took us around six hours to stow everything – we must have really nested in Saint Lucia!

We had done a passage plan – we had to get to Blue Lagoon in Saint Vincent to 'clear in' and get May's papers. Important, as if a dog without the right papers is identified, they say they will shoot it on sight. Poor May – that is why we do all the paperwork right.

We knew the entrance into Blue Lagoon was tricky so we decided to arrive late morning. This meant leaving Rodney Bay at midnight. We love night sailing so it was an easy decision.

We finished our prep and went to bed at around 7pm – it is hard to go to sleep that early but it was important to get some rest. At 11.30pm our alarm went off and blurry eyed we began to do the final preparations to sail. By midnight we were ready. It was almost a full moon and it was warm. We slipped the lines and quietly left the dock – bliss.

We motored into the bay and then raised our sails. We sailed for several hours before the wind dropped and then we motored sailed for a while. It was one of those perfect nights – warm gentle wind and a fair sea, millions of stars and a bright almost full moon. It is hard to describe just what an incredible feeling it is to sail under the stars.

Mark and I both stayed up on deck, each taking turns to be on watch. As we neared the Southern tip of Saint Lucia the sun rose and so did the wind. Around the tips of the Islands the wind is stronger. Our sails were reefed so we were fine and we sailed on to Saint Vincent. In the channel between the South of Saint Lucia and the

North of Saint Vincent it was choppy as there was a strong current running. It was a bit uncomfortable until we were in the Lee of Saint Vincent. We arrived at the South coast of Saint Vincent at around 11am – perfect! We got out our guidebooks and pilot books and nudged further in to the coast to have a look.

We were not happy – Magic's Draft (depth under us) is 2.8M and the cut through the coral reef to the bay was much less – there was no way in. There was another cut but the pilot book says it is not recommended. So, we called the Marina and they said – "no problem!" "They would send out a pilot!" That was new we hadn't experienced that before.

Out came Ras Mike on his tender whizzing through the waves – he came along side – tided up his tender and climbed aboard – that is not easy as Magic is very high sided – he introduced himself and said to Mark that he could take the helm and take us over the reef safely. Mark and I looked at each other nervously – that didn't feel right. Then at that moment I noticed Ras Mike's tender floating away from Magic – he had not tied it on securely.

Mark tried to round Magic up so we could get Ras Mike near his dinghy – we lowered our stern door for him to step out – but as we were doing these manoeuvers we realized that we were moving more towards the reef – so we had to say we couldn't do it – then another dinghy came along and retrieved Ras Mikes dinghy for us – this was NOT what we needed, it really is stressful enough coming into a new place without this.

We looked at each other and said – we are in a strange harbour, there are a lot of uncharted rocks and reefs, we have a pilot on board who cannot tie up his own dinghy, he is about to take Magic over a narrow entrance across a reef, it is low tide and it is Springs (meaning v low and v high tide) – what could possibly go wrong!

Ras Mike took the helm – reluctantly and nervously we let him take us across the reef. I have never seen anything like it – the cut in the reef was only 1 metre wide and we had to be right in the center if we were to avoid damaging our hull – the wind was blowing quite hard and Magic's high sides mean she can slip sideways – I held my breath.

Mark looked anxious. Ras Mike looked relaxed and happy. May just looked. The waves were breaking over the rocky reef on either side of us – it was incredible and terrible at the same time. Within moments we were across and safely into the deep Blue Lagoon – relief is a word that doesn't sum up how we felt. We were happy to pay Ras Mike his $20 for being our pilot. He then helped us take Magic alongside in the little Marina. We got a huge warm welcome and were given a delicious Rum Punch – how lovely. We needed it!

We like it here! We settled in – went to Customs Office and cleared in and then got to work finding the vet – we had been emailing them but there was no way of knowing if we had all the right papers or if we would get a permit – we were travelling optimistically as usual.

We passed a pleasant day in 'Blue Lagoon' but as time ticked on I was concerned the vet would not come – but in true Caribbean style she turned up at 6pm. She inspected May's papers and May and then gave us her Permit – what a relief. We are all getting used to how things work in the Caribbean.

"Don't worry 'bout a 'ting" as the song goes.

Today seems to have been filled with a weird mix of tension, trust and relief! We treated ourselves to a delicious lunch and met Nicki – a local lady who was great fun – she was talking about going to the Music Festival in Bequai and we mentioned we were going too – Nicki was going to get the ferry but instead we offered her a lift on Magic! Nicki was delighted and mentioned a friend of hers who was coming too – we said they were both welcome.

Bequai is only about an hour and a half from Blue Lagoon on St Vincent so it would be no problem. Later we had a few drinks in the local bar and then back to Magic for supper and an early night.

The next morning all the hours of preparing Magic for sea paid off, as we didn't have to do anything to get ready to leave. We had May's permit and all was well in the world – well except for the fact that we had to sail over the reef again!

Our guests arrived on time and so did Ras Mike – we all set off and crossed the reef without any issues. Ras Mike left Magic and we sailed to Bequai. It was a lovely sail and we were soon anchoring in Admiralty Bay. This is what sailing in the Caribbean is all about – island hopping! It is so lovely to navigate by sight – leaving one Island and heading to the one you can see not far away. Our guests loved the sail too and soon their friends came alongside in a motorboat and collected them.

We were excited to be in Bequai as we had heard so much about this special little Island. We made sure Magic was secure and then we got the dinghy and the outboard ready to go ashore. We found a perfect place to secure the dinghy and then got a cab to Friendship Bay where the music festival was that afternoon. At the festival, we met lots of people who we had sailed with and it was great fun – we love meeting up with people we know in strange places – its weird and wonderful. The rum punch flowed and the music was good – we were going to make the most of the festival – there was music that afternoon – then again in the evening (Saturday) and then on Sunday there was more – perfect!

I had a magical musical moment listening for the first time to a musician called Martin Harley – he was at the festival to do the Sunday afternoon slot – he is from the UK and touring. I had never heard anything like him – his slide guitar and delta blues drawl – I was totally transported to Louisiana in the heat – I stood transfixed as I watched him and let his music wrap around me like a hug – I have never experienced a musical moment like it. I bought his Album directly from him as he packed his gear away on stage and I felt like a teenage groupie! It was great.

Since the end of the festival we have just been enjoying beautiful peaceful Bequai – we went to the Firefly Plantation with friends and ate fresh fruits from trees and sipped cocktails whilst looking at the cheesy – 'too good to be true' Caribbean view of crystal waters and swaying palm trees – honestly most days we cannot believe we are here doing this. May is now famous on Bequai and we are often walking about with her and locals will shout out "Hello May" from across the street – it is so lovely.

We feel so happy here – more than safe – we feel welcome and cared for. It is strange as we, like so many people – were afraid of coming to the Caribbean because of the continual security scares. Bad things still happen but there are bad things that happen everywhere.

For example, we were at the Music festival on Saturday night – we were at DE Reef where the event was and this was on Princess Margaret's Beach – while we were there a bag was stolen from a woman getting into her dinghy – it was around her neck and the thief took the bag by cutting it off her with a machete – very scary. But that does not mean the whole of the Caribbean is dangerous – we have lived in London and if you go to the Notting Hill Carnival there will be things stolen and even violent crimes – it doesn't mean you don't go. It means you are aware. Perhaps it is just being aware or perhaps it is being fortunate but we love love love the Caribbean and feel we should defend it somehow. Nowhere is perfect or 100% safe and 99% of all the people we have met have made us feel welcome and safe.

This morning we are slipping our lines and making the short 1.5-hour trip from Bequai to Mustique. It is a bit blustery so we will just have small sails. We are looking forward to visiting Mustique – it is supposed to be one of the best-preserved Islands in the Grenadines – because it is a private island. The snorkeling is good and this weekend is the final weekend of their famous Blues Festival held at Basil's Bar. What a perfect combination.

Life is Good

Peacocks, Tortoises and silly Dancing with John Cleese
FEBRUARY 3,

I am scrunching my toes in the white sand and feeling the tiny grains rub on my skin. This is the world's best pedicure. I wonder at the millions and millions of granules that were once the stuff of sea creatures, glass and shells. The waves are gently lapping, each one curling neatly under the next. We are blissed out on Mustique. To my left is Basil's Bar – it is always great, when you are not too far from the nearest Rum Punch. But Basil's is special. Basils is a famous bar it is famous for its owner being a local celebrity and it is famous for its Blues Festival which is held every year. This year is Basil's Birthday and all the musicians are playing for free with the profits from the entry charge going to a children's home. Basil has created an incredible business on Mustique – he has a wine shop and a store with treasures from his travels in Indonesia and Bali – he has a boutique and of course his famous restaurant and bar. He lives opposite his bar in a quirky and creative home surrounded by the exotic treasures he has collected – vases hold flowering lilies floating on warm water and Buddhas patiently protect his door. Tropical plants hug every wall and it all looks much loved.

Basil is a slim, tall, silver-haired man who has a gentle smile and a little bounce in his walk. I admire the consistency, tenacity, focus and hard work it has taken him over the past 40 years to build his famous business. I was thinking that the song "Ain't nobody's business but my own" would be perfect for Basil.

This morning after cleaning the fridge (even in paradise there are mundane chores!) we went ashore and had a coffee and delicious, fresh pastries from the Sweetie Pie Bakery.
    The Bakery is nestled between two beautiful (but ridiculously expensive) boutiques. They are pink and blue and look so perfect in their place. After coffee, we went for a walk and were delighted to discover two large tortoises plodding around. I touched their warm hard shells and that feeling transported me to when I was a small child growing up in the '60s. Having a tortoise was all the rage – I am sure it was not a good idea for tortoises who would, like me, rather live in the Caribbean sunshine than Belfast's grey cold and rain.

Then we were disturbed by a strange nasal 'honk honk' we turned to see two Peacocks and two Peahens in a large enclosure – perhaps one of the wealthy residents on Mustique had become bored with them… it seemed a shame that they were not allowed to roam freely on the Island. We 'honked' back and headed back to the dinghy.

Back on board for a rest – or 'disco nap' as someone recently called it. Then back to Basil's at 5.30pm for more world class jazz. This is the last night of the Blues festival. We sat with Sandra and John – fellow cruisers who also crossed the Atlantic with the ARC. It was great to sit with them, not least because it meant I could go up and dance!

Having May with us all the time sometimes means we are a little bit restricted. There are a lot of places that do not welcome dogs but May is happy if she is in my bag. However, if I move away from the bag then she jumps out.

Sandra and I went up to dance and as we danced one of the musicians asked if we would clear the floor for his friend – Mr. John Cleese! I was excited to see John Cleese walking towards me – he was laughing and dancing. Then when he did the silly 'hands sliding over knees dance', (my dad had taught me that dance) I mirrored John (as I now call him) in the dance and we both laughed –

I was doing silly dancing with John Cleese in Basil's Bar, Mustique!!!

What a great evening. We had danced and laughed, listened to great live Jazz and drank a bit too much. We went back to the dinghy and Magic for supper.

We reflected on our day – it started with meeting Tim Henman in the supermarket, then tortoises and peacocks and silly dancing with John Cleese – what fun!

This morning is the 1st of February and we shout 'white rabbits' to each other. Not sure why we do that – we are not superstitious but we always think that saying 'White Rabbits' will deliver us a lucky month – I don't make the rules!

We are leaving today but first we must go ashore to get some cash, some groceries and a fish! We have seen the fishermen going out every day and we love a fresh fish. As we approached the fish market we spoke to a man who works on the Island. He said he was very proud of how safe the Island is and how nature thrives on Mustique. I was thinking that it is sad that the Island must be private for this to happen. Mustique is a nature reserve and due to the many millionaires, that live here it has so much security that it cannot be anything but safe! The guy told us the fish was fresh and that the Barracuda was excellent and safe – safe? – Well, it is sad but true that a lot of the fish in the Caribbean are poisoned.

"Fresh fish it's delicious, and one of the healthiest foods you can enjoy, right? Well, usually. But in some parts of the world, including a few areas of the Caribbean, a certain toxic organism travels up the food chain through reef fish, then predatory fish and eventually to man, causing the bizarre and uncomfortable set of symptoms known as ciguatera. In extreme cases, death can occur."

Death by a poisoned fish? I don't like the sound of that – and Barracuda is a predatory fish...

Oh well – you only live once (perhaps?) so we bought the fish. It looked fresh and we asked if they could prepare it. The answer was – "yes, the guy outside will prepare it!" So, our fish was handed through the window with no glass to 'the guy outside' and in an instant, he had filleted it for us. As we watched him we also noticed two guys carrying a large bucket of Lobsters – the Lobsters were twitching and sliding, their bodies clicking together – I think "how sad" and then I think "how yummy" – what have I become!

On the way, back to Magic we said good-bye to the peacocks and the tortoises. The tortoises ignored us because they were having a lunch of cucumbers and mangos supplied by Stanley who owns the fruit and veg stall. Then we noticed a stunning humming bird –its invisible wings whirling so it could stay parallel with its flowers – we like Mustique but it is a mystery – a private Island with millionaires and billionaires – safe but perhaps too perfect. A strange enigma.
     … A paradise or a paradox?

Back on Magic we slip our lines from our mooring buoy and set the sails – we are heading to Mayreau and we should be there by 4pm. The wind is due to lighten over the next few days and our aim is to be in Tobago Cays by Thursday, February 4th – for the lightest winds. Tobago Cays is a nature reserve with turquoise waters and turtles swimming about. It is a place I have always dreamed of going so we want it to be in the best conditions possible. Ahhhhhhh

A Deadman in the fridge and Banana Bread
FEBRUARY 3,

As we approached Mayreau it looked very crowded so we sailed on past and headed to Union Island. As we are travelling we are using a variety of sources to research where to go but Doyle's Guides are the best. Chris Doyle has sailed everywhere around these islands and his notes on where to go and what to do and see are invaluable. Union Island looked promising so we made our way into the harbour. We like Union Island so we decided to stay for 3 nights. Having done some passage planning we realize that we can take time in places we like. We don't have to be in Antigua until the middle of March and it is surprising how close all the Islands are. So, we can slow down and chill. How blissful this is.

Union Island is very special – each Island does have its own unique culture and Union seems to be friendly, relaxed and cosmopolitan. Some of the local business owners come from France and Belgium and the feeling is that every nationality is welcome. There is a delightful little dinghy dock – you must go under an arched bridge and then you can moor up your dinghy in a bespoke area. It is funny how soon, something like using your dinghy to go ashore, becomes normal. When we arrived in the Dinghy Dock the other day we were met by a charming local man who was holding a large, fresh Tuna in each hand – he was singing "this is my Island in the Sun" – I said to him that is not something you see every day – "I do love to see a man swinging fish and singing" – he laughed. We have met up with him several times since and he loves May. Everyone loves May – she causes quite a stir when she walks down the high street. She makes everyone smile and they shout to us "Hey, lovely Puppy!" in wonderful Caribbean accents.

There is a wonderful charity here on Union Island that is looking after stray dogs and runs a castration programme – offering local people castration for their dogs for free. There is an issue in the Caribbean with stray dogs as a lot of people fall for a puppy and then when the dog grows and costs money for food and care they cannot deal with it and just let the dog become a street dog – it is sad. May, Mark and I went to visit the charity and helped a little. We do try to think about our footprint as we travel.

This evening we went to Happy Island for a sundowner – Happy Island is a great story.

There is an intelligent and charismatic man called Janti. Janti had a bar that wasn't very busy and he also worked for the local tourism authority where his job was to clean up the town. So Janti had two problems – his bar wasn't busy because it was in the wrong place and the town had an issue with conch shells – a very large pile of them had accumulated from the fishermen discarding them (Conch is a much-loved food in the Caribbean)

So, Janti had an idea – he took the Conch shells and piled them in the sea at the end of reef – so creating his very own Island. He called it Happy Island – on it he built a bar, which has become very successful and his home. Problems solved – creative, enterprising – and fun. Now the shells are all cleared up and his bar is thriving – sipping rum and coke there listening to Reggae with Janti as the sun goes down is a pretty unique experience.

3rd February

This is going to be our last day and night in Union Island. The wind is dropping and we plan to go to Tobago Cays tomorrow. As the wind should be light we will be able to hire a buoy and stay for a few nights. Tobago Cays is a unique part of the world – turtles thrive there protected in their turquoise warm water by the largest crescent reef in the Caribbean.

We hope that we will meet up with Hans and Yvonne on Thindra – Yvonne is my dear friend from the village we lived in, in North Yorkshire – the beautiful village of Nun Monkton. It is a wonderful story – as we introduced Yvonne to Hans. Yvonne flew out of the UK to Lagos in Portugal where Magic was moored up beside Thindra – we introduced Hans to Yvonne and that was months ago. Now she is here in the Caribbean with Hans – it is always an unusual feeling when worlds collide – we are so happy for them both and are excited to meet them.

How funny to arrange to meet someone in the Tobago Cays!

As I write I am sitting on a sun lounger on soft powdery sand looking out at a perfect lagoon – there are only two motorboats and it is quiet apart from the gentle sound of waves lapping a metre from my sun bed. Mark is swimming and May is sleeping under my lounger. We are at Sparrows – a new bar and restaurant on the far (one mile!) side of Union Island from Clifton. We are relaxing following a bit of an incident this morning.

We are not happy with our anchor mechanism so we take a mooring buoy when we can. Friends of ours – Di and Neil from Sail Ionian own Sail Grenadines and the business here in Union is run by their daughter Katie. We called Katie as we arrived to see if we could use one of their mooring buoys as in Doyle's Guide he says they are the safest. Katie was unable to let us use one of theirs as they were taken. So, when a local approached us (as they often do) as we arrive into the harbour we followed him what he said was his mooring buoy. We moored up and tested the buoy and it seemed secure. He asked for 100EC, which is a lot so we said 80 and gave him a bottle of wine as well.

He pretended to be unhappy with the lower fee and said he would be back tomorrow to see if we wanted to stay. The following day we spoke with Katie and were surprised when she said we were on one of *her* mooring buoys. We explained what had happened and she said they had been having trouble with that guy. So, we paid Katie for the next two nights.

That should have been that – but this morning the same guy came aggressively towards Magic on his boat shouting that we owed him money. We explained that we had paid Sail Grenadines and that this mooring buoy was not his to sell. He was shouting and yelling and calling Mark a racist and a liar and told him to fuck off – whow …it was very stressful. I stepped in and said to him – "ok, so let's sort this out – let's all go and see Katie as we have paid her and she says that the mooring buoy is hers and not yours".

He then sped off – so we thought, let's go see Katie and ask her advice.

We don't know how things work here but if this guy is not happy he could cut our lines and Magic would be set free to crash or he could board the boat …. We felt uncomfortable. We took the dinghy into the dinghy dock and then went to see Katie. She advised us to go and see the Tobago Cays authority and she would come with us. As we walked along the dock the guy came along side us in his boat. He wasn't making any sense and was saying he was a Spirit and that we couldn't tell him what to do. We walked with Katie to the officials' offices and made a statement to them. They then called the police and we had to wait – so we went to The Snack

Shack nearby for a coffee and waited. About an hour later we were told that the officers wanted to see us. They had dressed in civvies so that they could go and find the man. They took us very seriously and apologized sincerely. They said that nothing would happen to our boat and we could be sure of that. So – rather than feel like victims and watch our yacht we have left her and gone to Sparrows on the other side of the Island and we will trust the police and luck. It is a real shame that these things happen in the Caribbean – the authorities are doing their best to regulate things but it is difficult. Yesterday a catamaran got into trouble on the sand – within minutes seven locals in their speedboats were racing out to help. Some pushed and others took lines and pushed. The cat was moved off the sand and freed. Then as they moored up all seven of the local boats attached themselves to the yacht and the guys got on board – I was concerned for the owners as following a stressful situation they then would have had another challenging situation trying to negotiate with seven different locals – I am sure they would have all wanted $100EC – Tomorrow we will leave this behind us as the only mooring buoys are official Tobago Park ones and going North we have not found any issues. Union Island is so very wonderful and friendly and the authorities' have said this will all be sorted out for next season. But for anyone sailing here – just be wary, anchor if you can and only take a buoy from someone who is officially from one of the companies like Sail Grenadines. It won't put us off – we have been in the Caribbean now for three months and this is the first incident that has directly affected us. We understand that the locals must make a living and we genuinely do what we can wherever we go – we eat local and buy stuff from boat boys. Yesterday we bought some delicious Banana Bread – they come to the boat and sell bread and cakes – lovely. In some islands, they have formed associations to protect their reputations from guys like the one we have encountered here and that is a great idea because we all want the Caribbean to remain safe and for cruisers to enjoy the islands and add to the local economies.

Oh yes, and the dead man in the fridge? For our dinghy, we have a dead man switch, it is a clever and simple chord that is attached to the engine and wrapped around the driver's wrist. This protects us by cutting out the engine should the driver fall over board. We need it to start the engine and yesterday morning we couldn't find it.

We looked in every cupboard and bag and pocket. I used to be bad at losing things (or good depending on how you look at it) and have been better recently – Mark started looking and knowing me he opened the fridge – and you guessed it – the dead man key was in the fridge – I had carried it in my hand along with the bag of fresh salad I had bought in the market – got on board and just put both in the fridge – a dead man is not supposed to be in our fridge.

Got to go as we are just about to have lunch at Sparrows under the palm tree – another rum and coke? Oh, I think we need to support this local business, don't you?

Tomorrow Tobago Cays then north to retrace our steps back up the islands – Mustique, Bequai, St Vincent, St Lucia, Martinique – then new places …Hee hee

Mark is such a Weirdo
FEBRUARY 7, 2016

It is surprising how close everything is – we slipped our lines from the buoy in Clifton Harbour, Union Island and crept out carefully. It is a little tricky around here when you don't know your way around – there are strong currents and lots of reefs – a bit of a challenging combination. We are avid readers of Chris Doyle's wonderful cruising guides and we were checking his notes on the passage. We made our way out of the harbour and across to the Tobago Cays. As we approached we noticed the water-changing colour from a dark blue to an almost outrageous turquoise – you could see right to the bottom and it was breath-taking. If you look at photographs of the Tobago Cays you will see one or two boats – the reality is that there are hundreds of yachts in the area and as the weather was calm the Cays are at their best – so busy. We went up to a buoy and I stood on the foredeck ready to lasso like a pro! I caught the buoy perfectly but then Mark reversed and the line slipped back over it – that's when 'Lovely' arrived on his boat and said – "can I help?" I really wanted to do it again ourselves but I can't resist the boat boys – I think they have all perfected their unique ways with persuasion – "Lovely" was – well, lovely. He looked at me with big brown, kind eyes and I couldn't help but say, "yes please" – he took our lines and secured Magic to one of the safe Tobago Cays Park buoys. He left saying he would be back soon – he didn't want a fee for his work, he wanted to sell us a fish…Well we must eat!

Our friends Yvonne and Hans are due to arrive later their beautiful Swan yacht – Thindra. It would be lovely to see them and a little weird – when worlds collide it is strange – when you meet people who really belong somewhere else in a new place where they don't belong – Hans belongs in Lagos and Yvonne belongs in Nun Monkton and yet they will both be here with us in Tobago Cays and our yachts will be moored up beside each other – odd and wonderful.

The first instinct on arriving in Tobago Cays is to strip off and jump into the water – it is so warm and so crystal clear and so very, very outrageously blue. How is it so blue? If we took a jar of it would be clear – just the same as if we took a jar of the water from mid-Atlantic where it looks dark. I still don't understand and think I will leave it as just Magic! So, swimming costume on – snorkel on – fins on Splash! Oh, yes this is incredible – the water is the same temperature as your skin and it feels like a hug. The visibility is astonishing you can see for metres and metres and then – as this wasn't cheesy enough, a turtle – just in front of me taking its time and gracefully paddling through the water. I watch as 'she' (I have decided she is a she as she is so beautiful) slowly flies over the starfish and the white sand to a patch of juicy sea grass. She gently grazes for a while and I just float above her in wonder. Tobago Cays is a special place – a protected place and I hope it remains so. I swim on to the small spit of white sand and trip up getting out of the water as a wave hits the back of my knees and knocks me over – I do wish I could perfect that, James Bond girl coming out of the sea, thing – but it never works for me. I do the clumsy, tripping, dripping mascara smudged look – it is so much more me. I flip my fins across the sand and just dive in the other side of the sand spit – wow this is different – lots of swell and coral and although there are some amazing fish to see – I remember what it feels like to be dashed on coral so I flipper fast back to the beach and then swim back to Magic.

Back on board I see – Mr. Quality coming up to us on his boat – he sells a lot of things including the T shirts by local artist – Felix – it is a fun graphic design and of course Mr. Quality is charming so I buy one. Next up are the guys collecting rubbish and next is "Lovely" again – he wants us to buy a Tuna but we ask if he will come back in the morning as we are going out for dinner. By going out for dinner what we really mean is going to the beach for a BBQ. Hans and Yvonne have phoned and asked us to 'book' dinner for 8 on the beach. So, we take our dinghy ashore to see 'Willy' his boat is "Free Willy' – Willy explains that his ex-girlfriend is cooking and she is a good cook – what is for supper? – Plantain and Salad and BBQ Lobster with Baked Potatoes – Oh yes! We book our table (very odd) and then walk up the beach to meet some of the locals – huge Iguanas who are hanging about waiting for Willy to throw them some lettuce. What a strange world – booking a table on a beach and then talking to Iguanas. We hopped back in our dinghy and headed back to Magic. More swimming and then we rigged our hammock – we hopped in it and it worked brilliantly – how perfect – just as we were gently swaying on the foredeck we noticed Thindra sailing in with Hans and Yvonne. They were waving – it was lovely to see them. I went to the stern of Magic and jumped in the water (any excuse) and swam towards them – they dived off the side of Thindra – impressive! And we swam to meet each other – now it is not every day your guests swim up to meet you – we met with a watery hug and swam together back to Magic. Beers and welcomes all round and a good catch up on adventures on the high seas and in low bars.

We all then had some time out before meeting for dinner.

At about 8pm Willy turned up on Free Willy to give us a lift a shore – it was pitch black and we couldn't see Thindra – they had been in front of us but they moved to our stern – Willy found them and we collected Hans, Yvonne and their guests.

Ashore we all hopped out of Free Willy and onto the beautiful beach. It was like being in a film set – low lighting, friends laughing, Lobsters on the BBQ,

Palms swaying gently and the ocean lapping at our feet...we were a world away from everything. The meal was delicious and we laughed and ate together. Then Willy gave us all a lift back – Hans and Yvonne came and stayed the night on Magic and we did an impressive job at trying to empty our stores of alcohol.

We all slept well – Tobago Cays is a beautiful, safe and welcoming place. Knowing you are on a safe mooring is bliss and sleep comes easily as you are gently rocked by the soft swell of the clear warm water under our hull.

The next morning, we had breakfast together and over breakfast Mr. Lovely returned and Mark negotiated with him for a very fine fresh Tuna. Is that not an odd thing to do during breakfast? Then Hans and Yvonne had to leave Magic and return to their guests on Thindra. Mark gave them a lift back in our dinghy. As we said goodbye we noticed that a lot of other boats were leaving – time to check the weather. We check the weather from several sources – Wind Guru and Passage Weather and Weather 4D Pro for Grib files on our iPad. All the sources said the same thing. They were predicting winds of 15 to 20 and although that is perfect for sailing along the Lee coast it is very exposed on the Cays so we decided to leave and sail to Mustique – the first stop on our reverse journey back up to Rodney Bay in Saint Lucia.

We prepared the boat – again, we are getting faster at this. Mark does his set of jobs and I do mine – stowing and locking everything, engine checks – we had done our passage plan and knew that, we would be sailing for about 4 hours. For this length of journey, we would hoist the dinghy onto the foredeck and keep the outboard on. We strapped the dinghy down and the outboard was bolted to its transom. We then had to slip the lines – I was on the foredeck and Mark on the helm – engine and bow thruster on. There were still quite a few yachts parked around us and as we come off the buoy we want to be sure we are in control of Magic. I slipped the first line with no problem but the second one was jammed in the ring on the top of the buoy. Tricky – we couldn't take the dinghy round and there were no boat boys in sight– so I had to flick and twist and twiddle the rope to try to dislodge it – Mark moved Magic forward and back and generally we messed around for about 20 minutes – it was all great fun for our neighbours to watch. At one point the line loosened and I moved my hand to shake it then suddenly Magic juddered back as a gust caught us – there is a lot of power when a 20 Ton boat pulls back with all her weight on one line – a rush of adrenaline ran though me as I realized how close my fingers had been to being crushed in the Cleat. Sailing is a dangerous sport and you can't be lulled by the weather and gentle sailing into thinking it is anything else.

Then we set off – very gingerly at first, as it was unfamiliar territory and 'reefy' as one sailor friend called it. Soon we had crept past the small islands and we were making our way North on the Lee side of Mayreau. The Southern Grenadines are so beautiful and all so close to each other – perfect for explorers.

The sun was shining and the wind had dropped to about 12knots – we were relaxed and happy. Mark was on the helm and I was on look out and brushing May. There were quite a few yachts around and it looked set to be a wonderful, relaxed sail to Mustique.

Then, very slowly we noticed the wind picking up and the sea state building. We thought it should rise from 12 to 20/25knots and that is fine. We hadn't put the main up yet but we had full Genoa – we decided to leave the sails at that and review them in half an hour. The wind and sea state were steadily increasing. I stopped brushing May and made sure she had her tether on. I looked at Mark – my rock, he looked happy and content – so all is well then. Magic started to pitch and roll more and more so I suggested it might be a good idea to get our life jackets on. I went down below and got them. We both put them on.

In another 10 minutes' things had got a lot worse – water was now coming over the deck and splashing us in the cockpit too. So, we got our oilskin jackets, life jackets and finally our tethers. Magic was now slamming and pitching into the ever-increasing waves. Mark still looked calm and in control. We were in deep water and the auto helm was working and keeping us on our course accurately. May wasn't happy and I wasn't feeling so relaxed either. I know we can sail Magic and I know Magic is a safe and seaworthy boat and I know that 30 knots of wind and 4 m waves are not much – but it still makes me anxious. As I have got older I tolerate anxiety less well. I suggested we reef the Genoa and as we did we were getting slapped on our side and shoved to Starboard. The crests of the waves were being blown off and soaking us as we worked – not pleasant. We were glad we had reefed the Genoa as now the wind was up to 35 and gusting 40 knots and there was foam on the waves – Magic was rising up the crests and pitching down into the troughs of waves which were now around 10 metres high. It was uncomfortable and we had to be aware of moving about so we wouldn't fall. I kept checking Navionics on my iPad – my quiet and adult equivalent of "are we nearly there?" This is not what was forecast I thought to myself.

Magic was coping with it all and Mark was actually enjoying himself – May and I were not. I sat under the spray hood, cuddling May and looking out at the roaring ocean. We were glad of the Spray hood as every few minutes a gallon or more of seawater crashed into it. Although we were on auto helm Mark was at the helm position – on look out. Then I noticed through the windows of the spray hood that the dinghy was levitating when Magic dived down into a wave. Two, three times I watched as one after another wave left the dinghy behind in the air as Magic dove down hard. Then the strain on the dinghy became too much – it wasn't the straps that broke but the rubber on the dinghy tore away and it was literally flying off the deck – one more violet pitch and twist and it was gone – it completely flew over the Port guard rail and into the sea – at it went it twisted in the air and landed upside down. Mark and I were shocked and thought for about 2 seconds about whether we could retrieve it. We decided that it was not safe to do that and we had to let it go.

We were gutted – our dinghy and outboard had become much loved and treasured since arriving in the Caribbean. What a blow. There was nothing we could do now but concentrate on the conditions and get to Mustique safely. We sailed on keeping a very careful watch for other yachts – and on the conditions and on the autopilot and our course.

With the high waves on our starboard side Magic was getting a slapping. There was blue water on the deck. I was holding on – I had braced with my feet on the cockpit table and I was comforting myself by cuddling May and chanting the little prayer I had made up when I got anxious parking in the Med – I find it really comforting but I am sure I do look like some crazy woman rocking and muttering.

"Neptune and Poseidon,
Gods' of the Sea,
Look after Magic –
Mark, May
and Me"
(repeat)

The waves are terrible and so beautiful. You see them cresting above your head – fluffy white foam on top of a clear, cobalt blue, a crystal glass ridge with a solid green base. It is Magic and then you think – *"oh shit, that is about to either slap our side hard or fall on our heads?"* Neither option is good. I must admit I was afraid – because I was winding myself up with thoughts of being knocked down (the boat being slapped on the side so hard she turns right over) and I was thinking about the grab bag (the bag we sailors keep with all our survival things should we need to abandon ship) I knew we were not in peril really but I was stressing myself. So, I turned to Mark and we talked about how amazing Magic is – we had to shout to be heard by each other. Sometimes the waves make eerie noises – rumbling and roaring – there is so much power in the waves – respect.

Finally, after 3 hours of horrible sailing filled with fear, we turned towards Mustique – now we were straight into the waves and wind. We still had 40 knots of wind but driving into the waves seemed so offer less jeopardy. Rising and Falling – up and down and slamming. May and I were longing for the sanctuary of the little horseshoe bay that is Britannia harbour on the Lee side of Mustique.

As we arrived into the bay the difference was instant – the relief!! Calm…

We called the Harbour Master and Berris Little came out to see us. As he helped us onto one of Mustique Moorings' safe mooring buoys, he told us they had had 60knots of wind come though just an hour before. "Yes", we said, "We sailed through that!"

Perhaps he was using the fisherman and sailor's allocated 10% exaggeration allowance but it was certainly blowy. On the Beaufort scale, it was a Force 8 and we don't like to sail in that – we like 4-5 that's our sort of cruising.

May was the most relieved we had arrived and like us she was cold and soaked. I was next happiest and Mark exclaimed that it was exhilarating – what a weirdo! We were so happy to be tied up and in calm waters and we thanked Magic for looking after us. We reviewed what we had done in our preparations and in our sailing and we were pleased with what we had done. We have certainly learned a lot since we bought Magic 15 months ago. It had only been a very short journey but it reminded us that the sea is a fickle lady and must be respected.

Mark had a cup of tea and I had large rum and coke and May had a cuddle. We were gutted at the loss of our dinghy and outboard – but as our friend in Rodney Bay, Mike from Sea Symphony said – *"each year you have to pay your dues to Neptune – usually a fender or two – so you have paid and are in credit!"* Good, positive sailor thinking. Thanks Mike.

Now, peacefully resting in Mustique cleaning the steel and washing the salt from the deck we take time to notice the gentle order of things here. Only one Seagull allowed per empty mooring buoy and every empty mooring buoy has its gull – if another gull approaches there is quite a fuss made of this uncouth behavior.

Tomorrow is Monday 8th February and we will be doing the one-hour sail to Bequai. We love it there and they have water taxis and we will use one of Daffodil's safe mooring buoys. The plan is to stay a couple of nights and then head to Blue Lagoon Marina on the Southern tip of Saint Vincent – we need to get a 'fit to travel' permit from Dr. Glasgow the vet in Kingston and we need to clear out of Saint Vincent and the Grenadines before our sail to Rodney Bay, Saint Lucia. The Sail from the South tip of Saint Vincent to the North of Saint Lucia will take around 9-10 hours and after our recent adventures we want light winds – those are due on Thursday. We will be watching the weather and planning carefully.

We should get back to Rodney Bay Thursday night or Friday and we hope we will be able to source a new dinghy and outboard by the weekend. We will stay a few days in Rodney Bay to 'clear in' and clean the boat and then we will be heading north to Martinique and onwards towards our final destination of Antiqua.

But for now, …

Picnic on Macaroni beach, Mustique to sit on the white sand in the sun, swim and lose ourselves in a book for a few hours? – I think that is a good plan.

Chapter Sixteen

STARING AT BOOBIES

...Reflections on the Water
FEBRUARY 15,

What do you think of when you think of the Caribbean?

It is interesting – lots of people have different views. We must admit that we were so focused on getting across the Atlantic that we almost forgot that we would then have five months cruising in the Caribbean. We hadn't met many people who had been to the Caribbean and those that had been had very different perspectives – one couple – Susan and Andrew from S/Y Andromeda in Lagos spent years there – cruising extensively and other friends had been for holidays, a two week, all-inclusive holiday at a resort or one week in a hotel in Barbados. We spoke to a lot of people who were anxious about security in the Caribbean and we had been told horror stories of yachts being boarded and tales of murders, machetes and theft. One person told us that we would have to lock ourselves in each night. We were told that we would have our dinghy and outboard stolen if we didn't always have it locked when went ashore. At night, it should be hoisted onto the deck when were out at anchor. There was also a lot of talk of boat boys being a nuisance and being threatening. So, all in all, not a very gleaming report. The reputation of the Caribbean being a vision of crystal clear ocean and gleaming white sands is so tarnished by these security fears. But, having grown up in Belfast in the '60s and '70s I know what it is to come from a place where people are afraid to visit and I know that the fears are not based on the reality. Northern Ireland is a stunning place and that fact was not changed by 'the troubles' – we found the same when we visited Iran – a beautiful place but their issues cloud this too much for many people to risk a visit. I think that I have an affinity with these places. It also seems to be the case that people who live in places with security fears welcome visitors with special care and warmth as they are aware of the fears their visitors may have.

We have found a different Caribbean from the one that the naysayers prepared us for. Everywhere we have visited we have been welcomed and respected. The people have been warm and friendly and fun. We have felt safe and not threatened in any way. We are not sure if it is the way we travel and how we interact with people or if it is just that the incidents of violence and theft are few but much publicised – the fear of crime is an issue in many places including the UK or perhaps we have been fortunate.

When we arrive in a new place we always take time to talk with the boat boys – warmly. We respect that they are there working. They are only making a living and they are always interesting. We always look at what they are selling. If we want something we do negotiate, they are good at persuasion and they do, of course want to get the highest price they can. We have bought – T-shirts, bread, wooden turtles, fruit, baskets, diet coke and fresh fish and we have used the water Taxis and the guys who own buoys (that sounds wrong doesn't it!) Then when we are ashore we always stop to talk to the people who want to see May. May is so popular here as many people have never seen a Maltese Terrier before. We keep her always well-groomed and so as she trots along on her lead her hair flowing resplendent in the breeze – she stops traffic – literally, people stop their cars and want to meet May. Children cluster around her and she has been known to turn a 7ft, 15 stone Rasta to mush. She is happy to be stroked and held and although she keeps her eyes firmly on us the whole time – I am sure she loves the attention. Local people in the Caribbean do not walk dogs on leads there are street dogs and dogs to guard property but no dogs on leads with their owners.

We went to the beautiful island of Bequai a few times and on our return visits – local people in the street would shout out "oh look, it's May" and "Hello May" it was so lovely – May is a star here!! Several people have said, "Oh, hey man you have a Rasta dog" I wonder what they would think if they saw a Puli or a Komondor – the dogs that really do have dread locks.

We have noticed that each place we visit – whilst having some similarities is unique. Each Island has its own, unique culture and we are fascinated to hear what the local people say about how things are for them – education, health, employment and infrastructure – roads and housing. Generally, things seem to be improving all the time for the people across the islands. Education is the key to all of it, of course and if they have well-travelled and well-educated people in power then it seems to be going particularly 'well. For example, the people in Saint Vincent are happy with their Governor as he is working on building secondary schools and focusing on health and education.

The Caribbean is a large and complex place – you cannot give an answer to "So, how was the Caribbean?" The Caribbean it is not *a* place of course – it is hundreds of places, there are hundreds of islands– some are independent and the UK, France, Holland and others govern some. In the south, there are the Netherland Antilles – Aruba, Curacao and Bonaire – the 'ABC' islands as they are known – they are Dutch. Then there is Martinique in the middle, which is French, and at the top there are the British Virgin Islands – there are also private islands like Mustique and there are independent Islands like Saint Lucia and Saint Vincent and the Grenadines. Some islands are tiny and some are large – some are flat and some have spectacular mountains and volcanoes. All these cultural influences and geographic differences make for a rich and varied experience for visitors.

Cruising sailors who have the privilege of being able to spend months visiting different islands will get a very different experience from those who only visit one island and stay at a resort. We are so very lucky to have time to get to know these wonderful people and spectacular places. There are many things that add up to a Caribbean Culture that the islands share. The positive, healthy and loving Rasta culture, the wonderful local food, the spirit of enterprise, creativity, the love of nature, the reggae music, dancing and singing, brightly coloured houses, smartly dressed children going to school, laughing a lot and Mum is the boss!

As we are travelling in and out of a lot of different countries we must check in and out of customs all the time. This is called 'clearing in' and 'clearing out'. The complexity of this is added to significantly because we are travelling with May. The ministries of agriculture, fisheries and food in each country vary in how they deal with the import of dogs so it is tricky. We must do our research on how each place deals with things and we then must get the paperwork, complete a lot of forms and visit vets and officials in offices in tucked away places. May is worth it, but you may like this description of a morning in Saint Vincent getting a 'fit to travel' certificate for May.

We arrived into Blue Lagoon on the South of Saint Vincent. The reef is too shallow for Magic to cross but there is one cut known to locals for which you need a pilot. We crossed the reef with Ras Mike – the pilot – we now trust him completely with Magic but we still held our breath as he took the helm and we watched breaking waves either side of our hull. Mark said, "Ras Mike, the instruments are saying the depth is 2.5 and we draw 2.8!" Ras Mike looked at Mark and just said "No problem Captain" and by the time it was said we were over the reef and into the Lagoon. As is often the case around the Caribbean we noticed friends we had met in another bay arriving and had a wonderful lunch with them. They travel with a dog to – a wonderful young couple (young that is in their 30s!) – Simon and Holly – Simon was a Royal Marine and lost most of his hearing in Afghanistan when an IUD went off near him. He is now retired and living on their boat with their fantastic Jack Russell – Scrumpy who May loves!

Scrumpy comes aboard Magic to visit May

The following morning, we had an appointment with the Vet at the Ministry for Agriculture in Kingston. We needed a certificate of health. This paper says that an official government vet has examined May and that she is healthy and that she has all the right paperwork – Rabies test, Heartworm test, and all the vaccinations in the world!

We had booked a taxi and he arrived in perfect time. He wanted to collect us at 07.30 because although it should only be a 20-minute journey the morning traffic is a problem – everyone going to school and work and not enough roads. He thought it might take an hour and our appointment was at 08.30. He drove like a professional through the winding back roads – whizzing past children and goats at an alarming speed. He explained he was taking the back roads through the villages to avoid the traffic and not to be concerned as he used to drive a truck in the USA and he was a professional driver. We did feel safe in his very shiny bright orange van. But I was concerned about the children and goats. As we sped past enormous breadfruit trees and lush dense overgrown fields with coconut palms and banana trees – we thought – it is so rich here – there is food everywhere. As in other islands we have noticed that there is a real mix of housing from very palatial, grand homes with lots of pillars and gates to more modest homes with scabby dogs hanging around in the yards. The houses are all brightly coloured – Blue and Orange and Yellow – our taxi driver show us his lovely blue house in one of the villages we flew though. Our windows were open and as it had just rained and was now getting warm you could smell the damp earth.

Just on the outskirts of town we passed a really unusual old man standing in the road taking notes. He caught my eye and I asked who he was and what he was doing. "Oh, he is writing down number plates – that is what he does – he has been standing there doing that for years! He is a bit mad of course but he is also quite useful. I needed to see if a particular number plate had been seen on the Island and he was able to tell me the exact date when it was last seen by him" – cool

Arriving to see Dr. Glasgow in Kingstown St Vincent – May often preferred to travel in my Bag. This was also how we took her to bars and restaurants.

We were dropped at the ministry for agriculture at 08.20 – perfect timing. We thanked our driver for the incredible journey and went off in search of Dr. Glasgow with whom we had our appointment. We soon found a peeling green door with a notice pinned to it "Knock&Enter Animal Health & Production Division" that must be it – we were met by several people – "Dr. Glasgow knows you are coming, please wait" As we waited we noticed a lot of things – the office looked as if someone was doing a rubbish job of propping a scene for a 1930s movie –this scene was set in an office – there were heavy wooden desks that were authentic 1930's but the chipped folding metal chairs seemed to be from the 70's and the filing cabinets were perhaps from the 50s and the large blotting paper holder thingy on one of the desks was definitely classic 80's. The walls were an institutional green – I wonder what Farrow and Ball would call that – dead toad probably. There were three desks and only one phone – that was certainly a classic Bakelite phone. Piled up on the floor along the back wall there were piles of bulging, yellowing and ripped files and on the notice board were curious cartoon pictures of how to ensure you notice the signs of your pigs catching a cold. We learned that we should boil swill before feeding it to the pigs and we now know all the signs we should be aware of to notice if our pigs are poorly. Outside the heavens had opened and it was thundery and grey. School children in their smart school uniforms were screeching and running – rain isn't something they prepare for like we do in England. It does rain here a lot but mostly at night and if it is in the day it is usually light and in short bursts. As we waited we met a lady who introduced herself as a new vet. She used to work in fisheries and food and this was a good career move. She stood awkwardly in front of her 1930s desk with the 1980s-blotter pad. No one welcomed her or helped her settle in. She had no chair, no computer, and no phone. How different with how new people are welcomed into our companies – flowers and a welcome card and lunch out and a well-prepared work space with the best of everything we can get for them. I went outside to see if there were any stores nearby as it would have been lovely to get a vase of flowers to cheer up her desk. Mark said I shouldn't as we don't want to cause offence and we don't know how things are done around here.

About 40 minutes late (that's ok, its Caribbean time) Dr. Glasgow introduced herself and showed us to her office. We had to walk through the surgery and she apologised that May could not be examined there as they had had a chemical spill and hadn't finished cleaning it. We walked past the chemical spill and past a two-headed lamb pickled in a large jar. We walked down a narrow dark corridor and into Dr. Glasgow's micro office. Dr. Glasgow, Mark, May and I filled the space completely and we were like one of those puzzles trying to move to get Dr. Glasgow and May together. The vet put May on her desk and examined her professionally and tenderly. May just rolled her eyes and looked at me. Poor May she doesn't really like the vet or sailing and she must do both almost every week! Then May was declared fit and healthy and it was time to pay our $45EC – that's about £12.00.

We were told to go and see the secretary. We handed her the money but she said "no, you have to take this piece of paper and take it to the accounts office which is out this door and around the building to the left" – incredible! So, off we went with our piece of paper to find the accounts building and hand our piece of paper to an official. We found the accounts office and when we entered there were 8 people at dark brown wooden desks – these people had phones and computers but didn't seem to be doing anything with them. There were two glass hatches and no signs so we just picked one and stood there. A lady shouted out "not that window!" – So, mad here! So, we moved 7 inches to our left to the other window and were met by a rather grumpy man who enquired what we wanted. We explained and handed over our paper. He looked at it for a long time. Then he showed it to two other people and then he went and got someone else to serve us. We were asked for our $45 EC but we only had a $100EC note. "We have no change," he said. Mark was losing it! "We don't have any either," He said. The official looked a bit put out and then went around his colleagues to change the $100 note. Finally, we had our change and we were given another piece of paper and told that we were to take that piece of paper back to the secretary in the vets' office. Feeling like we were in some sort of weird Monty Python sketch about the absurdity of bureaucracy we set off back to the vet's office. We handed the receipt to the secretary and she handed us our Certificate of Health for May. Process complete – it had only taken only 3 hours!

We decided then that we would have a walk around Kingston. It is a small town but busy. There are a lot of interesting shops that sell car batteries and knives alongside dresses and shoes. Street vendors sell vegetables and jewellery and it was a local place for local people. May was the center of attraction once again as she trotted along the high street. We stopped and bought a chicken and potato roti from a street vendor and talked with him for a while – it was delicious – a warm, mildly spiced, fruity chicken curry with potato wrapped in a delicate flour wrap. Then it was time to take a cab back to Blue Lagoon and prepare Magic for an early start the next day. Our friends – Holly and Simon and Mays new love interest Scrumpy came on board for a sailor's supper of Spag Bol and we all drank too much and stayed up too late.

The following morning, we had to be ready to leave at 06.30. As soon as it was light Ras Mike would be taking Magic over the reef again. We were sailing to Saint Lucia and the trip is about 10 hours. We had chosen a weather window and all fingers and toes were crossed that the weather forecast would be correct. We are not up for another 30-40 knots of wind. We want the 15-20 we have ordered.

As we leave Blue Lagoon at dawn we are accompanied by about 10 boobies who are fishing all around us and I find I have time to reflect while we are on the water – 10 hours to Rodney Bay.

Oxymoron – Caribbean Customer Service
MARCH 2, 2016

Now, I don't want to be negative or moan but. Let me .. please let me vent – just a little – Aghurghhhhhhhhhhhhhhhh – that feels better.

We have said many times about how positive we are about the Caribbean but ....

I need to talk about Customer Service in the Caribbean.

Yes, yes – I know it is a different culture in the Caribbean and I know we are still working through culture shock. But first let me say – as we mentioned in a previous blog we love the Caribbean mostly the people are fun, warm and friendly and the music goes into your bones and we have even got used to Caribbean time – where people turn up late, very late or not at all. And, yes, I realise we are living on a yacht in the Caribbean – living the dream. But sometimes there is a large void between the dream and the reality. I was thinking of taking a set of photos to show the dream v the reality. (Perhaps I will)

Some days are just bloody frustrating and some days your resilience is low. Living in the Caribbean is so different from anywhere and so it should be. Some days it is easy to understand that 'this is the way it is' and some days it is just "ARGHHHHHHHHHHHH get me out of here!"

Just indulge me with a few examples so you can judge for yourself if I am being a petulant, hormonal, middle-aged woman or if these incidents really are just annoying.

1.Diet Coke in Rodney Bay

We were in Rodney Bay, Saint Lucia and we needed to go to the supermarket. For some reason, low calorie soft drinks are not popular here and you have to hunt down places that sell them. So, an adventure to the supermarket to get Diet Coke is needed. This entails getting the dinghy and outboard ready – getting us and our bags and May into the dinghy – crossing the bay and getting out with the help of a local 'guard' on the dinghy dock. Then walking to the Supermarket.

Not so bad so far, but still significantly different from just popping to M&S in the car. There are two reasonable supermarkets in Rodney Bay Village – one has Waitrose stuff and the other has more American groceries. We opted for the Waitrose Supermarket as we were hunting Diet coke and thought the choice there was wider. We couldn't find it – no surprise – so we asked a rather surly (aka Caribbean attitude) woman who was bored with stacking shelves.

"*Excuse me, do you have any Diet Coke please*" I rather sheepishly enquired. Sometimes (especially the women) can be quite scary with their – "*and, you are?*" attitude! The "*go away*" aura they give out, in this matriarchal society, can reduce a once confident and assertive European woman to a quivering mess.

Her response to "*Excuse me, do you have any Diet Coke please*"
was clear
"*NO*"
Having lived here a while I persisted and went to the soft drinks aisle to look again anyway. There I found:
Waitrose Diet Cola, Cola Lite and Coke Zero – delighted I filled my trolley. As I passed the shop assistant again I said in as jolly a voice as I could muster "*I found*

some!" She said, *"That is NOT Diet Coke and Diet Coke is what you asked me for – we do not have Diet Coke"*

Firmly corrected, I slunk off to the check out.

2. Mooring Magic in Rodney Bay

We are good at mooring Magic now – over the past 15 months in approximately 30 Marinas we have learned a lot. We know how she moves in various wind conditions and we know her shape and length. We know the best routine for Mark and me to adopt to bring her in safely and calmly. So as usual we had prepared her fully – we knew we were coming in bow's too (pointy end first) and we had prepared fenders along her Port side with lines forward, aft and a breast line (the line in the middle). I have learned how to lasso the breast line so we are fully secure. That is the first line we get secured so Magic is held while we get the bow and stern lines on. We are often offered help and we have learned that unless the person really knows what they are doing we are best left alone to secure Magic. However, when the dock master of a Marina comes to your help we are grateful. Mark lined Magic up perfectly to gently come in on our Port side. I was mid-ships with the carefully coiled line in both hands. I throw the coils in my left hand over the cleat on the dock whilst holding on to the coil and end of the line in my right hand. In this way, I can pull the right coil in having looped the middle of the line around the cleat (perhaps that needs a diagram!). Anyway, suffice to say we know how to do it to secure Magic. But the dock master was there so as I threw the line he took it and rather than secure it around the cleat he walked to the stern of Magic. I pleaded with him to secure the mid ships line and give it back to me but he ignored me. Mark was urgently asking him to do it and he wouldn't. Then he asked Mark for the stern line. Mark was now shouting at him to take at least one line and secure it. Now he had the stern line in his hand and yet he was just standing there shouting at Mark. He was saying that he was in charge and that he was the dock master and that he knew best. Whist he debated this point with Mark Magic was drifting slowly but with the confidence of a two-ton lump – towards the boat next to us – yes, the side with no fenders on. Just as it was getting too close a fellow sailor saw what was happening and took our forward line to the dock cleat. Mark could then use that to spring back on to bring Magic back into control alongside. Then the dock master finally secured the mid line and the aft line and stormed off shouting that he was the expert on this dock. Mark was furious. He is the skipper and unless asked for advice his requests should be followed by anyone who is helping – especially 'expert' help. If there was damage to Magic or another boat it is us that would be liable not the dock master so he cannot take control. He does know his dock but he doesn't know how each boat handles and how each skipper likes to do things. I hate conflict and I hate a messy mooring it just makes me feel all screwed up and stressed. Sad face.

3. Internet in Grand D'Anse D'Arlet, Martinique

The Internet is a big deal and we are often deprived of it. So, when we get to a bar or restaurant that has Wi-Fi we indulge. As usual we ordered drinks and then we asked the assistant for the Wi-Fi name and code. She pointed to a chalkboard with the information on it. Like junkies we were straight on our computers tapping in the precious information. But no, whatever combination we tried – and that included: checking with the lady if we had typed it in right, shutting down and restarting our computers, running diagnostics, moving around in the bar to different spots. Then we asked her what might seem like an obvious question – *"is your Wi-Fi working?"*...

"*Oh no*" she said, "*It doesn't work!*"

Well, what do you think? Would these three scenarios drive you potty or am I being a grumpy old bag? I would love to hear from you.

And so, the adventure continues. This morning we are leaving the bay of Grand D'Anse D'Arlet – leaving the pretty, palm fringed beach and the gentle graceful turtles and setting out for St Pierre in the North of Martinique. Then on our way to Antiqua we will go to Dominica, Les Saints and Guadeloupe.

It sounds amazing and we are looking forward to seeing new places but we are also going a little crazy on the boat. I am sure anyone who has lived aboard will know the tension that comes and goes like waves. Mark and I are feeling it – perhaps we need some time at home.

Imagine if your home was always moving and you had to constantly check that it was safe. Imagine always not knowing where you are or how things work for basics like getting food and fuel. Imagine not being able to get Diet Coke – Imagine parking in your drive with a crazy person shouting at you how you should do it – Imagine having no Internet unless you beg for it from strangers – oops sorry lost it again...

Going for a lie down and I promise I will reflect on the fact that these are Middle Class Problems.

Must do better! But thanks for listening...

Wild Steaming Wilderness
MARCH 5

Dominica

We are in the Dominica channel. We are watching as the definition of Dominica ahead of us slowly takes shape. We had a restless night on anchor in St Pierre, Martinique. Perhaps it is because we never truly have a good night sleep when we are on anchor, as we don't trust it, or perhaps we were both thinking about all the people who died when the hot gasses rolled into town killing all but two people in the town and burning and sinking the ships in the Bay. When I did sleep, I had the weirdest dreams – one of which was my teeth falling out – what the hell does that mean I wonder!! Fear of toffee? Or of growing old? Must look that up.

I thought I would write something of how it feels to navigate from one Island, one country to another as although this has become 'just another day at sea' for us we are trying to remember how unique this is. How special this is and how fortunate we are.

We have spent a lot of time with charts and pilot books looking at the distance, the prevailing wind and any special notes on potential hazards. We love Chris Doyle as we have mentioned his guides are invaluable – our copies are well thumbed and I am sure he would love to see how much pleasure we get out of not just reading them but acting on them – from the navigation advice to the tours, the people to meet and the shops and restaurants and bars – his guides are unique and wonderful.

Having done our research, we are on our way to Roseau on the South West Coast of Dominica. Dominica is described as the only Island in the Caribbean that Christopher Columbus would still recognize. It is apparently wild and natural with waterfalls and exotic plants and birds. In the hills are Rasta farms and even – get this, Restaurants!! Fantastic. We are planning on calling 'Sea Cat' as soon as we get a phone signal. Sea Cat is a local entrepreneur who has run his business looking after yachties for many years. He has mooring buoys, Wi-Fi, helps with clearing into customs and he does the best tours on the Island. We are going to get all the above from him! It is 09.00 and Mark is on watch with May at his feet – we are doing one hour on and one hour off, as it is a 6-hour journey. We left at around 06.30 so we should get in around 13.00. The winds are very light and even though we have our full Genoa and Mainsail we are also motoring – it is very dull sailing Magic in light air as she is heavy and very slow. Magic needs wind!

As the time flows behind us and we move forward the shape of Dominica becomes clearer ahead of us. There is a perfectly blue sky with small fluffy clouds and the sea is gently rolling beneath our hull. As we sail we keep a careful watch for other boats – sailors and fishermen and motor cruisers – we are always watching to see their direction and speed to make sure we are clear of them and that we follow the Collision Regulations. Today a 16M yacht, Solitude was heading past us and we called her to check we could pass Port to Port – she confirmed that and then chatted to us on the VHF for 40 minutes about all the places in the North they had been, the people they met and recommendations for guides that are helpful and restaurants that are good. We reciprocated with our top tips for the South from Martinique to Union Island – it was lovely chatting with a fellow sailor and getting the inside info as we sailed past each other. I don't think we will ever actually meet Jerry and

Victoria as they have sold up everything in the USA and are planning on sailing forever towards New Zealand where they may stay. How exciting the people, you meet and how brave they are just to sell everything to live their dream. We watched as they sailed past us and south towards the unknown and their new life.

We are now close to the very South Western tip of Dominica – a tricky spot with an underwater pinnacle of rock that needs a wide berth. We are carefully watching our charts and keeping a look out. May is asleep in her bed.

As we near Roseau we are treated to the view of beautiful pink, yellow and blue houses nestled into lush, dark green tropical trees and bushes. A cockerel crows in the distance. We call Sea Cat- on Channel 16 he says he is at the Supermarket getting ice for another boat and will be with us in five minutes. What a strange world. As we close in on the beach – "Beans" arrives in a 'Sea Cat' market speedboat. He welcomes us warmly to 'his' tropical island and says, "follow me" he races off toward the beach and a buoy that we will call home for the next two nights. It is only 12.30 so we have made really good time on our crossing. I go on to the foredeck and hand the lines to 'Beans' and he helps me to secure Magic to the buoy. He is lovely – in his late 20s and with a huge warm smile and corn rows in his hair. He tells us he can take us on a tour tomorrow, asks if we have a permit for May (we do!) explains that Customs will be quiet now and he can take us. So, I grab a bag and put all our boat papers in it. I get the transom door down and step down the ladders onto it and into the 'Sea Cat' boat. Immediately we are off – skimming the surface at speed. It is weird because we have spent the last 15 months going at a maximum of 9miles an hour we find speeding cars or boats quite a shock to our senses. As we fly by palm trees and little shacks on the beach 'Beans' – tells me about his nickname. He is called Beans because as a boy he loved Bacon and Beans – his best friend did too but his friend got called Bacon and Beans was left with Beans. Fair enough. He shows me with pride the beach he played on as a child. We are moored just off his village and he tells me Sea Cat has a house overlooking the sea. We pass the local radio station (government owned) and the Government building – he shows me the palatial house that the Governor lives in and explains that they must pay 50% tax which means he must work twice as hard all the time – but he says he loves his job and loves visitors. Good pitch! We arrive at the stern of a ferry and an official helps me out of Bean's boat. I walk through the ferry and onto the dock steps. Then a very official and angry lady comes forward telling me that there is no point trying to clear in now, as there would be a very long wait. I ask when I should come back and she says, "up to you!" Great …then she explained that there was a queue of about an hour, then they will have lunch for an hour and then they close at 16.00. I talk to Beans and he says," let's go and come back at 14.30."So it's another exciting whizz back to Magic. I am not sure how much all this back and forth and moorings and tour will cost but we will find out soon enough! Back on the boat May was so excited to see me that she leapt right off the transom onto the platform – that's about five feet down – it was incredible she didn't hurt herself or fall in the sea – poor May. She is hot today and she doesn't really love the sailing bit. She can have some extra cuddles and a brush – she loves being brushed. We will have some salad for lunch and celebrate our arrival with some beer and then at 14.30 Mark can have a turn in Bean's speed boat to the Customs office – I know how much he loves the way those Eastern Caribbean women talk to him! – not!

Change of plan, as we put the dinghy in the water and decide to go to customs ourselves. Now we know where it is there it is easier. There is no wind and we skim across the sea towards the huge P&O Cruise ship dock. We tie our dinghy up by the dive center and Fort hotel. Every time we go to a new place we have new challenges with getting on and off the dinghy. This time a steel ladder built to get the divers out of the sea is there. We moor up alongside but of course we must climb over the handles of the ladder to get onto a step, as we are not in dive gear stepping out of the sea! We slip and slide on the wet metal but manage – very ungracefully to get on to the steps. I wish I felt more Lara Croft today!

We go and explore the town it is very Caribbean – lots of music blaring and bright colors on the house and the people. Locals cram into small vans that are buses – neat and tidy school children on their way home. As usual May is the center of attention – we had two offers to buy her, locals wanting to dance with her and lots of cruise ship passengers who were missing their dogs whilst on holiday. One lady introduced herself as – Jilly – she is from London but is half Dominican. She lives here and in London. She was telling us how good life is and how happy she is. She loves Dominica and tells us how safe it is and how beautiful. We end up going for a beer with her – lovely lady. Then we head back to Magic deciding that we will eat on board tonight – it's been a long day and we are tired – but wow, we're in Dominica.

We are going with 'Beans' tomorrow for a whole day tour 9-5 with some hiking and waterfalls – it will be wonderful to see more of the interior of an island. So often we only see the coast and local towns. Dominica is a wild, steamy wilderness so we are excited to meet her.

I hate hiking and getting caught with no pants on
MARCH 11

I don't know why I do it but a hike always tempts me. Seeing new things, the adventure and yes, even the exercise interest me. But then I never like it! I think it is the pace. I like to stop and look at things – a flower, tree roots or the view but it seems that the rule for a hike is that you must rush along precarious paths and the only thing you can see are your feet. Beans (our guide) had told us that we would be out all day and that we would have two hikes each 45 minutes. I do remember thinking – that will be ok!

On the morning of our adventure the clouds were coming in low over the hills and the rain was so heavy that it was like being in an expensive hotel shower with the setting on the highest power. It really was like a power shower as it switched on and then off in bursts.

As the shower turned off Beans collected us from Magic. Beans commented that I was brave wearing all white when going into the forest (I should have realised at that moment that this hike was going to be a big mistake) but we went with him to the dock.

We were introduced to Joe who would be our guide for the day. We got into his dusty van and we mentioned that we needed water filters and if we were passing a chandlery we would like to look for some. He drove us into town and we found ourselves being guided to what looked like a small version of Curry's. Joe had thought we needed water filters for a domestic water system. We explained that we needed a chandler, and as that was going to be in the 'too difficult' pile we were soon back in the van and off again. We drove up and up then stopped at a forestry office. The power shower in the sky had been turned on again and we hid under the covers in front of the office and watched as steam rose from the road – proving that there can be smoke without fire.

We needed a ticket each to go into the forest, which is a national park. Mark went in to get a ticket and I stayed outside (under cover) with May. I read a notice about a Cane Toad epidemic – I was thinking, "Aren't they the ones you lick and get high?" But the notice was warning how toxic these toads are and that the skin of the toads and their tadpoles were dangerous. I immediately thought of May and was becoming more concerned about this adventure.

Note: I just looked up Licking Toads and found this helpful note for anyone considering licking a toad.

A lot of people mistakenly think that the cane toad is the infamous licking toad, but it is not. Licking a cane toad will not result in a high, but rather some very serious illness and possibly even death. The licking toad is the Colorado River toad (Bufo alvarius), also known as the Sonoran Desert toad. Even with these, licking them can make you very ill and again, even possibly kill you. I've never done it, never will and don't condone it, but the way people get high from licking toads is to squeeze the warts on the toad, causing it to secrete the toxin, which is a white, creamy substance. They dry it and then smoke it in a glass meth pipe. I talked to guy who did it and explained this to me. He said the taste was horrible and the high lasts only a few minutes. He said it was extremely intense to the point where you are laying on the floor, drooling on yourself, and unable to remember your name. Doesn't sound like fun to me, but to each their own.

Mark found getting the permit a particularly Caribbean experience. The lady who was issuing the permits had no one else to serve but still Mark had to wait while she took her medicine before she served him! It took 20 minutes to get the permits which cost 13 EC which is about £3. This small fee goes towards the management of the forest. But we couldn't help wondering who set this fee and why it wasn't more as that amount would hardly cover the cost of the administration to print and sell the ticket. Caribbean bureaucracy defies logic.

Back in the van we headed up and up into the forest and then parked. Joe got out of the van and I was disturbed to note him changing into an old t-shirt and shorts and leaving his dry clothes in the van. No one had mentioned to us that it might be a good idea to have a change of clothes. I don't think I am good at rain forests.

We read a sign about all the bats and snakes and beetles that are in the forest and then headed off. I told Joe that I was not very sure footed and he said it was ok and that we would go at our own pace – right! We headed out at speed …

But wait. Just a change of direction for a moment while I tell you what just happened. To demonstrate that living on board you are always one moment away from something challenging happening. I was sitting writing to you about our hike in the rain forest and suddenly I heard Mark shouting for me – he was standing on the stern watching our new dinghy and outboard floating away! "you or me?" he said – I was wearing only a white linen shirt and excuse me for this – no pants!! Knowing I am the stronger swimmer and watching the dinghy float away I jumped in and swam hard. It is still windy and the waves were quite high and there is about a knot of current in the bay. I swam hard and soon caught up with the dinghy. Then I was thinking – urm how do I get in so I can start the engine. It is really hard to get into a dinghy from the water plus the 'no pants' thing was an issue. So, I grabbed the line and swam pulling the dinghy behind me – this was going to be tough. Just then I noticed a handsome guy from a neighboring yacht (Sea Biscuit) had seen what was going on and was in his dinghy coming to the rescue. He said,

"Hi, *I will tow your dinghy for you. Do you want to get in?*" I said, "thank you, but it is only a short swim" meaning – "*thank you but there is no way can I climb in your dinghy, I have no pants on!*"

I waved a thank you as he took 'Sparkle 2' (our dinghy) back to Magic where Mark was waiting. The lovely man then went back to Sea Biscuit and I then got out of the sea modestly intact and back on board Magic to dry. We had been so diligent with our beloved new dinghy. We were shocked to see that the rope that had tied her to Magic had come loose. What happens with wind and waves over time is that it seems to be able to undo bowlines or anything. We will be more careful.

Now dry and back to thoughts of Dominica! Where was I? Oh, yes – on a hike in the rain.

We headed out into the forest and within 5 minutes of pleasant walking along a good track past Ginger Lilies and gum trees we came to a river – May had been skipping along happily by our sides but she looked like she was thinking the same as me – "do we have to cross that?" Our guide just tripped across like a mountain goat and I thought I had better take off my trainers and socks to keep them dry. I took them in my left hand and Mark lifted May. One step onto the first rock and I was in – I slipped backwards and was on my bum in the river completely soaked. I got up and carefully managed to cross without falling again. This was the start. Perhaps some people are just not designed for trekking in rain forests. To cut the painful story short – we trekked in torrential train over slippery rocks and more rivers – up steep, muddy paths made of wet tree roots and down shale that slid – we did see the most incredible waterfalls and due to the rain, we saw them at their fiercest – thundering into the pools at their feet where we could have swum but not today as we would have died. What fun we had – soaking and bruised and cold. May was shivering. I thought, *"I don't like hiking!"* It's good to know what you like and what you don't – but I must remember next time to say "no!"

The rest of the day was spent going to swimming holes that we couldn't swim in and looking at the incredible scenery – the rain made it more dramatic. At one spot Joe stopped the van and got out a knife – he went up to a tree and took off some bark and brought it to us. "Smell this" he said. We did – it was cinnamon. Then he gathered some coffee beans and some lemon grass and wild thyme. All of it just by the road. Dominica is a wonderous, wild larder.

We ended up our day at a swimming place where we could swim without fear of death but I was so wet and tired I just sat and dried out in the hut with May while Joe our driver watched Judge Judy on the tiny TV. Mark went and sat in the muddy water that was the naturally heated hot tub. It was getting dark by the time we left and we were tired. What an incredible place Dominica is – just think Jurassic Park and you will be there in your mind. It is dense, green, steamy and wild. You can imagine you hear the squeak of things growing while you watch them.

Back on Magic for a rest and to plan the next day when we would fill up with water on the dock and then head North to Portsmouth.

The next morning, we slipped our mooring and went to the dock to get fresh water. It was straight-forward to moor alongside the dock. It was good to get water onboard as we had run out completely. Then we were off and sailing again. We put up our main and our genoa it was going to be a lovely sail. The wind was light and the sea state was calm – I like sailing like that.

Arriving in to Portsmouth we called for Providence – a boat boy whose actual name is Martin. He was recommended by 'Beans' in Roseau. Portsmouth bay is beautiful – natural horse shoe – calm and protected. There were several super yachts in the harbour – some with all their toys out – things I would love a go on include – the massive slide that goes from the side of the yacht to the sea and the jet boots that shoot you out of the water (although I think I would be scared in those)

We were met by Martin and he helped us onto a mooring buoy. He was warm and welcoming and he told us about PAYS. Portsmouth Association of Yacht Security was set up by a group of enterprising boat boys who realised that if the yachties were safe and happy then they would stay and spend. So, they all work together to ensure that everyone who stays feels safe and happy and it works well. We arrived on Saturday and Sunday was Mark's Birthday. Sunday is also when PAYS runs a massive Beach BBQ party for all the yachties as a fundraiser for PAYS. We had heard a lot about the Indian River Tour in Portsmouth so we asked Martin to take us.

He promised to be with us 7am Sunday morning. We went ashore to find out if there was anywhere for Mark to watch his beloved Manchester United on Sunday. We found a restaurant that had a big screen but it was broken – then we found another who said they would be showing the game at noon. Perfect. Mark's birthday was shaping up – 7am river tour, midday Man United and Beach BBQ in the evening.

Happy we went back to Magic and then out in the evening for sundowners and supper. At the local bar, we met some guys we had met in Saint Lucia. It is lovely to keep bumping into people who are also cruising up and down. We had supper with them and agreed that they would join us for the River Cruise in the morning.

It had been a full day – sailing from Roseau (4 hours) arriving and exploring, drinks and supper ashore. We went back to Magic tired and happy.

March 6th and it is Mark's Birthday – I found a card and some balloons (the sort of thing you have aboard when you live on your yacht!) He was surprised and delighted – oh the simple things in life are good – a yellow balloon and a kiss. I had written him a silly poem too and we laughed – today was going to be a good day. Our friends arrived to go on the tour and we waited for Martin – and waited and waited – we called him on the VHF but he didn't come – eventually Charlie another member of PAYS came and took us on the tour. We didn't mind, as we know all the guys know the river well. Charlie drove at speed from Magic to the mouth of the river. Then he turned his engine off and got his oars out. Nobody is allowed to use engines on the river – it is a wildlife sanctuary. It was a gentle and soporific experience being paddled up the river with Charlie like a gondolier skillfully steering his boat from the stern with one oar. He pointed out the wild life – shoals of fish dark shadows blurring under the milky surface, exotic birds watched us carefully as we sculled beneath them and huge crabs with beady eyes scuttled along the banks. The river had an eerie quality to it – swampy and quiet but deeply sensual and beautiful. It was like a film set and in fact it is where some scenes from

Pirates of the Caribbean were filmed. The ones that show the home of Jamaican Voodoo witch, Tia Dalma (played brilliantly by Naomie Harris – she is English but her father is from Jamaica and her mother is from Trinidad so her Patois in the film was perfection) She had a wooden house on stilts on the river and Cobra, one of the boat boys, has built a wonderful replica. At the end of the river we got out of the boat on a wooden jetty and walked through a bar. We walked past a skull (spooky) and into an orchard filled with bananas, coconuts and passion fruit vines – as we walked Joe cut fruit and gave it to us and explained what the trees and plants were. He showed us a weed that recoils if you touch it – mimosa pudica – locally called Morir-Vivir (Die and Live) it protects itself by recoiling when you touch it. Locals pick it, dry it and use it to make a drink that they say has the properties of Viagra.

Next to surprise us was a local guy running past us with a wheel barrow full of coconuts. He said, "I will climb the tree for you if you like" we said that was kind but he already seemed to have all the coconuts we would need. Mark bought one from him and he took his machete over his head and brought it down with alarming force on the nut to sheer its top off. He handed us a straw and while we drank the cool, delicious coconut milk he told us of the positive effect it would have on our reproductive organs. Every day is a school day. Then when were finished he used his machete again to open the nut and showed us how to scoop out the young, juicy coconut flesh. What a great birthday breakfast.

Back to the boat and gently we retraced our track back to the mouth of the river. It was a wonderful trip and we thanked Charlie.

Back on board we had a coffee and changed to go to see Manchester United play. We got the dinghy ready and headed ashore. We parked at the fisherman's dock and as we got out an official appeared and asked for May's papers – thank goodness, we had them with us. They do say that if you have a dog ashore with no papers they can have it killed. So that sharpens your focus when making sure the papers are all in order. It was an anxious moment but he seemed happy and we were on our way. We walked down the high street looking at the locals and their shops and houses. These people really have very little – we went to the chandlery and there was hardly any stock. The same was true of the supermarkets. Dominica is poor but very special – it is so un-spoilt and it has the last population of indigenous Caribe people living in the center of the Island. We walked to the restaurant that had promised the match would be on rather predictably it was shut. Mark was disappointed. We turned and walked back down the high street and as we passed a small general store we heard the match. Two locals, one wearing a Man U shirt were sitting on wooden stools watching the match in front of the counter. Mark and I stepped in and Mark asked if he could join them to watch the match. He was welcomed and we both sat in the shop and watched the game. It is a weird thing to be watching a football game in a tiny shop in the Caribbean. Weird but lovely and typical of the sort of welcome you get here. After the game, we walked back to the dinghy and went home to Magic. Next, we changed and got ready to go to the BBQ – life is fun.

The BBQ was fantastic and we met some people we had last met in Madeira – the cruising world is a small one. We ate and drank and danced in the sand and then we thought – early night.

The next day we had a five-hour sail to Les Saintes.

I am writing this from the French islands of Les Saintes and will tell you more about them soon but honestly today was mad! – it began with jumping off the stern and swimming after the dinghy – then in the middle we had an excellent French lunch and finally in the afternoon we decided – innocently enough – to walk to the petrol station and get some fuel for our dinghy outboard. Here is the tail of the trial …

We had read that there was only one fuel station on the Islands and that there was no road to it (odd) It was too rough to take the dinghy around the headland to the fuel station – and we didn't want to run out of fuel and be washed out into the Atlantic – even if it would make a fantastic story. Anyone who has been to The Saintes will now go "Oh no – you didn't walk to the petrol station did you?!" we walked and walked and walked and then the walk turned into a hike (didn't I say how I hate to hike) we were scrabbling up a hill on dusty rubble and spiky rocks – there were goats and the 'path' was confusing. We asked a local if we were heading to the petrol station and he said we were! I thought May was getting too hot (good excuse eh?) so I took a seat and Mark continued the steep steps to call it a path would be wrong.

He then said he arrived at a modern fuel station in the middle of nowhere. This is the only fuel station on the island and you cannot get to it by road – isn't that amazing. The fuel for the cars and scooters on the island is collected in cans by a local fishing boat and brought round to the town. Apparently, the fuel station was built and then road was never finished. Local people take their boats around to the fuel station. However, the reason we needed fuel was because the fuel in our dinghy was low so we didn't want to risk it as it is quite far.

Mark eventually turned up 45 minutes later – hot and dusty but with fuel. He had to walk down some broken steps and scramble through prickly bushes and more goats – amazing! Fuel in the tank we walked back to the harbour to get the dinghy back to Magic. It had only taken three hours to get the fuel. Nothing is ever straightforward when you are living aboard in the Caribbean.

What a bonkers day.

Tomorrow we have a five to six-hour sail from Les Saints north to Guadeloupe (I like saying Guadeloupe out loud – try it, it sounds and feels great!) We will stay in Deshaies tomorrow night – Saturday night in Guadeloupe – how exciting. We will stay there on Sunday as well as the wind is due to pick up on Sunday and calm again on Monday. We like to hide if it is blowing and we must cross from one island to another.

We plan to set sail for Jolly harbour, Antigua early on Monday morning – we have an appointment with the vet on Monday afternoon and want to prep the boat for our VIP guest Claire Archibald who arrives on Tuesday. It is £100 a night in Jolly Harbour so we won't stay long!!

Anchorxiety and playing with Nelson's toys in English Harbour – Why Not! MARCH 26,

Anchor -x·i·e·ty
noun
noun: **anchorxiety**; plural noun: **annchorxieties**
a feeling of worry, nervousness, or unease, typically about an imminent event or something with an uncertain outcome in relation to one's anchor. They felt a surge of anchorxiety"

I will tell you about our Anchorxiety in a moment but first a little more about Les Saints.

Apart from swimming around after our dinghy with no pants on and hiking with goats for fuel– all was quiet and wonderful. Les Saintes is a small archipelago of the French Antilles located just a stone's throw South of Guadeloupe. (I love saying Guadeloupe)

The food is French and mostly delicious and the sea is mostly turquoise and always warm – Turtles swim gently by and Pelicans look like carved statues sitting on the top of wooden posts. On one of the days we took our dinghy to a deserted beach – Mark went for a hike (I may have mentioned I hate hiking) and I played on the beach with May. May never goes in the water but suddenly she ran straight in. I couldn't believe it – then I noticed that she was chasing the crabs that she had disturbed. It was fantastic to see her running into the sea for the first time in her life. May loves sand but has never loved the water. On sand, she becomes her alter ego – a skippy, jumping running fool – it is lovely to see her joy. It was hot so soon she needed a rest in the shade of the dinghy. I sat beside her and watched a Pelican. They look far too heavy to fly and they have an awkwardness that makes you smile. They are not elegant birds. The one I was watching soared in circles and then suddenly folded its wings and smacked into the water to catch a fish. This dive would not have received many points in a diving competition – lots of splash and noise – but the Pelican had its fish. I watched the Pelican for an hour. What a pleasure... When we were at home the pace of life seemed to ever increase and we seemed to have an urge to stuff every spare moment with more and more stuff. So, watching a Pelican for an hour is bliss.

Sometimes a little Magic happens – We were on a mooring Buoy and it was banging on the hull in the night keeping us awake. Mark went on deck in the dark and used our special Buoy grabbing stick (technical term) to shift the buoy out of the way. The special Buoy grabbing stick has a yellow plastic 'thingy' on the end that is an amazing invention for threading a line through a hoop – that enables you to attach a line to a buoy quite easily. In the morning, I noticed that the plastic yellow 'thingy' was missing – Mark looked sheepish and said it had gone overboard in the night. I was disappointed as it was a very useful thingy and although we could order a new part I wasn't sure where or when. Resigned to the loss of the precious yellow thingy we went for a dinghy Safari to a distant beach.

The beach was down wind of Magic and the ride was fun surfing on the waves. We beached the dinghy and began a walk. Here comes the Magic. As we pulled the dinghy up the beach we ran over something yellow – yup it was our precious yellow thingy – washed up on this beach exactly where we had landed. Magic

Leaving Les Saintes we sailed to Guadeloupe (you must just savour that beautiful word) we were going to go to Pigeon Island, which is supposed to be fantastic and has a unique Jacques Cousteau Underwater Reserve. However, we wanted to ensure our trip to Antiqua was shorter so we decided to push on further North to Deshaies. Just as we arrived the wind picked up and it was funneling through the bay – we had sailed in beside "Ho!" A yacht we know – I have always wanted to hail them on the VHF as "Ho, Ho Ho – it's Magic –" – you should sing that... we were both looking for a secure Buoy but there were none available. "Rats "– we would have to use the bloody anchor.

The Bay was too deep where there was space but we had no choice. We dropped the pin and waited for it to drag – it did. We lifted it and dropped it again – this time it held. After a sleepless night, we found a Buoy and quickly we lifted our anchor and rushed over to it – then we could rest for that day and night.

The following morning, we had to leave for Antiqua and the weather looked good. And we had one of our rare perfect sails – we set off at 6am and arrived at 2pm. We had to clear in and we went to the customs dock. Mark went in and over an hour later came out looking very battered by Caribbean bureaucracy 1 – Mark - 0 – the bureaucracy and the attitude that goes with it is really wearing us down. Then we had to wait for the Government vet who was only 2 hours late. With all our paperwork finally complete we went into the harbour – Jolly Harbour was a welcome sight.

Great bars and restaurants, an amazing supermarket and a safe and secure marina add that to the fact that friends were all around us – perfect. I thought – let's stay here until the end of April. I have been admitting to Mark that I have had enough of sailing for a while. I think that living aboard for 16 months and sailing in some rough stuff has been like overeating a favourite food as a child. You love it and then have too much and then you are sick of it.

So now, ta dah! We have made a big decision. We have put Magic on the market to sell. We have still got our flights booked to come back to Antiqua on the 27th December and we are planning on doing another season to visit the BVI and other islands we haven't seen – but if she sells, she sells and we are putting that in the fickle hands of fate.

The next day Claire Archibald arrived – it is fantastic when you can share your adventure with loved ones. We confessed that we didn't want to sail as much … but we then decided we would sail a little and it was a good idea. We love Jolly Harbour – not least because of its great name – but we wanted to see English Harbour and Falmouth Harbour – famous sailing places. We had heard that English Harbour was tricky because you had to drop your anchor to moor up and the bay was tiny and the bottom is full of stuff – hurricane chains and anchors from Nelson's time – fascinating but also tricky for sailors. So, we were anxious (again!).

We wanted to be on the dock – actually on the dock where Nelson was – that is why they call it Nelson's Dockyard. You must go out turn around, drop your anchor and fall back to the dock. It is 'stern to mooring' like we were used to in Greece. But of course, there was an enormous gust of wind on our Starboard side just as we were dropping back that moved us out of alignment. We dropped the anchor and dropped back – Claire was ready with the stern Port line – she threw it to the guy on the dock but it fell short so Mark took Magic out again and tried once more. Why is it always gusty when we are doing a tricky mooring? Finally, we were tied up and the dock master said. "Your anchor is not in the right place. You will have to go out and lift it again and reset it" – My heart sank! So, the stern lines were slipped and I was on the bow clicking the anchor back up – after about 2 minutes it was clear that the anchor was firmly stuck on something. Magic was left swinging in the middle of the harbour. Our friends from 's/y Why Not' who had been watching came to our rescue. Richard and Tracey are sailor, sailors – they are so experienced and they know what it is like to be in a jam. They are kind and there is nothing they wouldn't do to help another sailor (or, I imagine, anyone) They are also great fun and love a drink – proper sailors. I would like to tell you about the pulling and pushing and lifting and dropping and bits of string that were employed to free our anchor from Nelson's toys but it is too dull. Suffice to say that after about 30 minutes of faff we were free to set our anchor down into the mess again! This time with the harbour master came on board Magic to direct proceedings. It is a good thing that Nelson's Dockyard is amazing!

We are now in Falmouth Harbour – when we left Nelson's Dockyard – we had treble trouble – a huge super yacht had dropped their massive anchor chains over the top of ours, the anchor was trapped on the bottom tangled in stuff and the windlass (the thingy that pulls up the anchor) was struggling. Once again Richard and Tracey came to the rescue but this time there was nothing they could do and we had to get a professional diver. The harbourmaster said – "you will have to pay a diver!" Mark was incensed –" you put us here, and you put the super yacht beside us" – it was resolved by the first mate on the Super yacht suggesting that they would pay the divers – $150 for them is small change. And it is 'the done thing' if you have put your chain over the top of someone else's chain. So, the divers came and untangled the mess. I hate anchoring. They helped us raise the anchor – and after an hour of mucking around in the mud with Nelson's toys his Dockyard finally let us go.

Now we are in beautiful Falmouth Harbour watching all the classic super yachts arriving for the famous 'classics' racing.

"Rowlocks!"
MARCH 30

We love being in Falmouth Harbour, Antiqua.

We are gently swinging on a secure mooring buoy, the wind is reducing, the sky is blue, the sea is turquoise and the sun is warm – we are surrounded by stunning classic and super yachts that make us go "ohhh" and "ahhh".

These yachts are beautiful things.

Their crew and armies of specialists – world-class painters and genius varnish wizards, who do such magical work, keep them in pristine condition. Everything on these classic yachts is something to be admired – the rigging, the steel, the wood and the paint – but most of all, the overall visual effect gives you a feeling similar to the feeling you get when you hit the perfect melting point of excellent chocolate on your tongue. You know what I mean.

But, apart from the natural and yachting beauty here, the best thing of all is the great fun we are having with lots of people who we know. It is often what any cruising sailor will tell you is the best bit. The people.

We must tell you about an amazing party. We got an invitation to Motor Yacht SKAT (we weren't special, they invited everyone who was on a yacht!) – the invitation said SKAT WARS and it was a Star Wars themed party. We turned up with a 'May the 4th (4:5) faux Tattoos one on Mark's T-Shirt and one on my right arm (we thought that was rather clever). We brought a bag of drinks and Val and Cliff from AWOL joined us. We were so surprised to find that there was a professional BBQ set up with chefs cooking up delicious burgers – all you can eat – also a dinghy had been filled with ice and cans of beer for 'all you could drink' and then they served trays and trays of delicious jelly vodka shots – How generous is that! They had invited *all* the yachts from Falmouth Harbour and Nelson's Dockyard. Amazing! I know the people who own these amazing yachts are wealthy but there is no rule that says they must be generous. We were moved and the following day delivered a thank you note.

The owner of SKAT is Charles Simonyi a billionaire one of the software designers of the Microsoft OFFICE package Charles Simonyi, Paul Allen and Bill Gates are all Microsoft buddies and they all have incredible yachts.

We have paid a fortune to Microsoft over the years so it was nice to get a free burger and a beer!

We do find it interesting looking at and finding out who owns the super yachts. Like Venus the motor yacht we saw in Rodney Bay – she was designed by Philip Stark and owned by Steve Jobs – he never saw her finished before he died. His wife now owns Venus and when the yacht was in Rodney Bay she was being chartered by Mark Zuckerburg – the guy who created Facebook.

The super-rich charter from the super-rich. We remembered also Octopus – we saw her in Gibraltar and she is owned by Paul Allen who owns Microsoft.

There are some fantastic places to eat, drink and hang out here in Falmouth and Nelson's Dockyard:

'Catherine's' on Pigeon Beach – stunning food, right on the beach with hammocks and cocktails

'The Pillars' – excellent art on the walls and a wonderful relaxed vibe and good food

'Le Cap Horn' – fantastic food and fun

'Abracadabra' – Southern Italian Food – go early for a peaceful, delicious meal or late for dancing and Disco

We balance eating and drinking ashore with eating and drinking on Magic – having reviewed that sentence I realise that the truth is that our eating drinking has no balance!!

Happy hour (s) are a must and we have also been going to the 'Tots" at 6pm with The Tot Club. This is a unique and eccentric organisation who do great work and you can find all about them at their website www.royal-naval-tot-club.com

We are beginning our initiation process. We were first introduced to The Tot Club and their work by Andrew and Susan from Andromeda in Lagos. They emailed the club and nominated us. While we are here Chris and Fiona from S/Y Four Seasons are 'hosting' us. That means they are introducing us. They crossed the Atlantic too and now they are enjoying Falmouth and pondering their next adventures. The initiation to The Tot Club includes a test on British Naval History and you must attend seven 'Tots" within 14 days. – The "Tots" are always at 6pm and are held on 6 out of 7 days a week in various watering holes and even yachts around Falmouth and English Harbour's, a gathering of members make a loyal toast – sip some water (to cleanse the palate) and down a 'Tot', a double, of Pusser's Rum. They also read out a, 'today in history', note from British Naval History. It is a special organisation with members all over the world. We will begin our initiation "Tots" when we return to Falmouth Harbour on the 12th April. We can then manage 7 'Tots" in 7 Days.

We are leaving tomorrow for Jolly, but we are returning for the Antiqua Classics race, which starts on the 13th April. We want to be back here so we can see or even participate in this race.

Tomorrow is Wednesday, 30th March and we are going to Jolly Harbour for 13 days. We have a lot to do there.

We have begun the decommissioning of Magic for the summer. It is a much bigger task than we thought. I was reflecting on how the plans we have had have been in bursts. When we set sail for the Med – that is all we had in our mind. We were thinking of The Bay of Biscay and Portugal. Then when we got there all we were thinking of was crossing the Atlantic. Then, when we got to the Caribbean we felt we had sort of fallen off the end of our plan – because the plan was to cross the Atlantic and we had done that. We hadn't thought a lot about the Caribbean. Then we enjoyed our Caribbean cruising but once again we were not really thinking about the time when we would put Magic 'on the hard' for the Hurricane season.

We had thought about it enough to ensure we had a place for her booked for here but we had no idea what the process was. As it turns out, it is another large project and, of course, as with all things on boats – it is going to cost more and take longer than we thought. The storage is just the beginning. Then there is the decommissioning of all the equipment – the water-maker and the generator, the engine, the fridge and the freezer – all the equipment needs to be carefully and professionally decommissioned to ensure it is all in good working order when Magic is put in the water again in December.

Then there is the huge task of considering all the 'stuff' on board. There is – safety gear, food, clothes, books and fun stuff like a BBQ and Hammocks. Mark and I are working through every locker, under all the seats and beds – cleaning and sorting as we go. We have a system – Charity Shop, Friends, Ship Home, Storage, Bin and Take home with us. We don't want to waste stuff so, for example, we are giving away our long voyage food to Cliff on AWOL for his trip home across the Atlantic. Food in Antigua is more expensive and we must get rid of all of ours. We have – as always – made life more complex for ourselves as we are planning for two scenarios. First, that we are flying back for another season on Magic – our flights are booked for the 27th of December and second that we sell Magic before December and we either don't return or we just return for a holiday and to finish the sale.

We suspect, and rather hope, that we won't sell Magic and that we have her for another season in the Caribbean. She is a wonderful yacht and everything works and is new. We have only just got everything working.

But, we are tired of living aboard, for now. However, we both know, that after a few days or weeks at home we will miss Magic, our new friends, the Ocean and the Caribbean. How much we miss it may make us make new plans. We are stressed out by the uncertainty but we are also addicted to it as it is exciting not to fully know what is next. At least we do now know that we will be moving into our beautiful converted chapel near Knaresborough, North Yorkshire. We had though it was going to be rented out but now it is not and that is good – so we at least are not homeless!!

Packing away and giving away all our stuff is emotional. I have had several weepy moments. I am not sure why. Perhaps it is the overwhelm of the amount of work we must get though. Perhaps it is change. I don't know why it makes me cry – it just does. I do, as always, keep reminding myself what a first world problem this is! Mark and I constantly remind each other how happy and lucky we are to be living life as we do.

As always – life on board is punctuated by events – some fun and some traumatic. Mark and I had been working on more sorting and Mark was taking a dinghy-load to the charity shop. I was cooking up a Spag Bol and Chili to freeze – we don't want to eat out every night in Jolly Harbour and we don't want to cook every night. I was also stowing things for tomorrow morning's sail to Jolly Harbour. I had Van Morrison blaring out and was in the zone of cooking and sorting. Then I heard a desperate sounding Mark – "Tina" "Tina" "It's a rescue" he was shouting. I have learned whilst sailing to just go to a calm place and deal with whatever is happening. I turned off the cooker and ran up the companionway ladder – through the cockpit and to the stern. I saw one dinghy with two crew pulling Mark in our dinghy (still full of our charity shop stuff) He looked a little sheepish. He explained that he had let a rope fall in the water and it had fouled the prop on the outboard. Then he had valiantly tried to row, hard against the wind and current in the harbour. However, the rowlock broke so he couldn't row. As he floated past S/Y Ayesha on his way out to sea – they asked, "Do you need any help?" Mark said "yes!" And they launched their Dinghy and went to his rescue.

We had met S/Y Ayesha further south when we had arrived into Mustique – They had radioed to us to tell us where the Harbour Master was. Here they were helping us again. This time more intervention was needed – they had to launch their dinghy and tow Mark in ours to Magic. They were so lovely – saying – "that's boats for you – there is always something!" That is true and I thought, "Bloody boats!!" – when a simple trip to the charity shop can become a life-threatening terror. I thought – there it is – that is why we are tired of living like this. Now we have a broken rowlock and Mark must dive under the dinghy to cut the rope free from the outboard's propeller.

I am sure there are people who love to live like this every day but I am sure they are under 50!

Don't get me wrong – I love the ocean and I love sailing but I love the sailing where we can sail in gentle breezes with dolphins and turtles. I love the fun and the friends. I love the sun and I love the ocean. I even love living in a confined space. But I do not love the constant jeopardy, the breaking of everything, the constant unexpected expense, the hanging upside down in impossible lockers trying to reach impossible seacocks and doing gymnastics to make the beds. I think I either need to win the lottery and have a super yacht with crew or I need to charter so that all the maintenance stuff is someone else's problem. I don't like it that you are supposed to be born with the knowledge of how to replace an impellor on a generator.

Line freed from the prop Mark headed off again – now with only one oar I suggested he took the other one as if anything happened again he would at least have it as a paddle. He said no it was fine – it wouldn't happen again. I reminded him as a joke not to talk to strangers and to keep the line on the dinghy away from the prop. He laughed and headed ashore to unload the stuff for the charity shop and to watch England play the Netherlands.

I stayed on board to write this.

I was enjoying the quiet and time to write when I heard Mark sounding stressed and calling my name again. I ran up on deck and looked over the transom. There was Mark in the dinghy only 3 metres away from Magic but drifting further away fast. It had happened again – the dinghy line had fallen in the water and drifted in the prop. Mark could not row as one oar was attached and one was on Magic. All he would have been able to do was row in a circle. I had no choice – fully dressed I dived in and swam to the dinghy. I was worried about May as she hates to be on Magic alone and she was on deck and could see I was in the water and Mark was in the dinghy. I had to will her not to jump. I swam hard towards the dinghy and grabbed the line. I swam and pulled and was soon at our transom door, which was lowered. I was thinking" Bloody Boats"

I was just starting to process in my head that this had happened twice in only a few hours when suddenly I was drifting out to sea with the dinghy. Mark had jumped off the dinghy onto the transom door and as he did the dinghy was pushed away and me with it. I lost it – I was swimming and pulling the dinghy and shouting at Mark – I got back to Magic and unfurled the line from the prop then I secured the dinghy and went to quietly fume. It would be a few hours before I could see the humour in it. We got changed and went ashore for that evenings 6pm Tot.

It was 35 Degrees but things were a little frosty.

Jolly times in Jolly Harbour
APRIL 13,

Scrubbing and Rubbing and Sorting

Who would have thought you could stuff so much stuff on a yacht? We have now spent two weeks – de-junking. Magic has been our home for 16 months and of course we have stuff on her for an Atlantic Crossing and for Cruising – for parties and for every day. We don't know if we will sell Magic between now and December so we are planning on clearing her completely so that if she does find some new owners she will be ready to go. That means all we can have is what we can fly home with! We will perhaps ship a few things home like our oilskins and boots – not sure. If Magic is still ours by Christmas we will be back to sail again in Antiqua (we have our flights booked for 27th December)

We know as soon as we land in the UK we will miss this.......

Magic sitting perfectly under the blue Caribbean Sky in beautiful Marigot Bay, Saint Lucia

We are very good neighbours at the moment as we are giving away lots and lots of things. We have made some lovely friends who are grateful for the stuff and so it goes in yachtie world – if someone wants to get rid of something there is usually someone who needs it.

Life is good in Jolly Harbour. We have a beach BBQ every Sunday on the stunning white sand. There is a lot to do here and great facilities – Mark is loving playing tennis and squash and I am loving swimming in the sea and the pool and singing and singing.

We have organized an art workshop and I am doing the Radio Net twice a week which seems to be going well. Today we – that is my new friend and music partner Nick and I are playing at The Crow's nest in Jolly Harbour and then tonight at Lyme in Falmouth Harbour. Staying in one place enables us to get involved in things more and to enjoy developing friendships. One of the negatives of cruising is that you are always moving on and so it is hard to make new friends. It is only when you slow things down that you can join in on-shore activities and get to know new people.

As we clean, polish, fix and tidy Magic we are reflecting on our time as 'live aboards'. We are thinking about all the people we have met and the places we have visited. We are thinking about all the good things and the challenges and how much we have learned.

Live on stage for one night only
APRIL 18,

Sometimes weeks go by and there doesn't seem to be much to say of any note and then there is a whole book to be written about just one evening! I want to tell you about one such evening. But before I do, a short diversion. I have said before that it is the people you meet when cruising that makes it so special – here in Antigua is no exception – there are so many people with amazing stories. Their stories reveal so many ways people have enabled themselves to live this life. Mostly what is behind the stories is a combination of talent, years of hard graft and a generous dollop of risk taking. People like Vlad and Olga – who had run away from the USSR – then with literally not a dime have made millions in the USA and then there is Simon and Holly   Simon was a Marine and served in Afghanistan before being medically discharged after he was blown up ....not everyday people and NOT everyday stories. There is a book to be written about the life stories of these extraordinary people. Nick and Teresa are amongst the extraordinary crowd. Nick was a world-class dentist and built his skill and business to the highest level and then sold his practice so came sailing. Like all sailors, we have met he is multi-talented and in addition to being a skilled sailor he is also an awesome musician. Nick has patiently coached me and supported me with my singing. I love singing but when I sing in public I feel very exposed and vulnerable – I don't feel the same when doing public speaking or presenting ideas but I do feel it when singing. So, during this process I have moved through the creative process:

1. This is amazing
2. This is tricky
3. This is shit
4. I am shit
5. This might be alright
6. This is Amazing

I am familiar with this process but living it in a short period of time has been an interesting adventure. When I have hit the 'This is shit – I am shit' correlation – Nick and Mark and friends have been there to help push me and support me towards to the final two pieces of the process 'This might be alright – This is amazing"

Initially singing with Nick on his boat, then on ours, then at the Beach BBQ. Then that led to going to an open mic night and finally creating a set and performing on Stage at the Antiqua Classics week. It has been fun to set increasingly stretching goals. Working with Nick has made this easy as he just says "right – we are doing a gig next week so we have to create a set and do it" There is no discussion or debate! The goal is set and we do it.

So, there we were – Saturday night in Falmouth Harbour. A professional stage was set with every manner of microphone, instruments and speakers. The organiser had told us the standard was high. It turned out to be a wonderful blend of singers and musicians from all over the world – folk singers from Falmouth in the UK and a local musician who was performing his own songs. It all seemed to be flowing well except there were two things wrong. Firstly, the organiser had booked a professional band to play in case there were gaps – but what happened was that the professional band hogged the stage and those who wanted an Open Mic were faced with a closed one. Secondly the sound engineer made the local band sound amazing and was variable on the support he was giving the other musicians. He got increasingly stroppy through the evening and ended up switching mics off. One of these occasions was when Nick and I were performing. I was trying not to take it personally. We had to stop performing. I turned my back on the audience and spoke to the guy. I put out my hand to shake his and said that we understood that it must be a frustrating evening but that we were not professionals. He looked at me with fury burning in his eyes and he refused to shake my hand. I felt this was getting out of hand. Then Terysa told Nick to just leave the stage and she flew on the stage to give the sound guy a good talking to!

Mark was delighted he said, "This evening just has everything!"

It was good fun and it was also a great experience.

There are only 11 more days to go before we fly home and I hope that we can get more singing done – several more gigs and an Album!

The transition is perfectly painted in the following three images

Chapter Seventeen

PLANE REFLECTIONS

MAY 9

Well that's it – MAGIC is on the hard in Jolly Harbour, Antigua – and we are in the airport about to board the plane and May is somewhere …we had to leave her at Cargo. I was distraught. We walked her, fed her and made sure she had plenty of water. But then we had to put her in her crate, shut the door on her and hand her to an incompetent Cargo guy who took her to his office. We can only hope that she will be taken great care of and that she will be put on our plane. This is no ordinary luggage this is May! I kept correcting the Cargo staff when they said 'it' will be put on the plane and 'it' will be well cared for – I said, "She is not an 'it' she is May!" They of course thought I was a weeping mad woman. The paperwork and vet visits have been a challenge (the previous word is a MASSIVE understatement) but we always knew we would make it and that we would eventually be clicking into our seats for the flight home.

We have met the kindest and the rudest people – we have seen the widest gap between competence and incompetence that is possible to have.

It has been a roller coaster getting to this point. Over the last three weeks we have sorted and wiped and polished and binned and repaired and scrubbed and painted and carried and scrubbed and scrubbed. We have had a lot of forms to complete and vets to see. We have had our feet in two worlds – one – the world of living aboard cruisers – joining in the fun of beach BBQs and meeting for sundowners. The other preparing to go home.

Sun going down, toes in the warm, soft sand, Beach BBQ with friends,
Dogs to cuddle – life doesn't get much better

We have been naïve about a lot of things to do with living aboard and sailing. Leaving Magic on the hard at the end of the season – or 'decommissioning' her is yet another steep learning curve. We didn't have a clue and have been given lots of hints and tips from other cruisers and from the team at Jolly Harbour. From 'pickling' the water maker to cleaning the bilges and blocking the seacocks – there was yet another long list. Then there is the cradle and crate we are storing her in – and then someone to check on her while we are away – and of course as with everything in sailing it costs a fortune – to leave Magic for eight months is costing us around £7000. But we know she will be in good hands and as safe as any boat can be if a hurricane does hit Antiqua.

We will be back on Tuesday 27ᵗʰ December and we hope we will be sailing for another season. I know we have put Magic up for sale – boats can (and often do) take a very long time to sell. So, we are planning on having another season in the Caribbean. We will 'do' the British Virgin Islands and around that area and aim to cross from Bermuda to take Magic back to Lagos in Portugal for Spring 2017. Mark has said he would sail her back – May and I will fly! But flying with May is not fun.

As we sat on the plane I asked the attendant if May was on the flight. She said "Yes, she is I heard her barking", I said thank you and then burst into tears. I was relived May was on the flight with us but I knew that if she is barking she was probably stressed. It is upsetting being separated from May and not knowing how she is but perhaps I was also tired and emotional as it was the end of an incredible adventure.

It is almost impossible to write about reflections on 18 months – it's too long a span of time and it has been too incredible. We bought our first boat, sailed across the Bay of Biscay in December, lived in Portugal for six months, sailed in the Med, crossed the Atlantic and cruised the Caribbean for five months. Each part of this adventure has been unique and we have learned more and spent more than we thought possible.

But it really is the people that have made our adventure memorable. We are so privileged to have met and become friends with so many outstanding people.

We are now back in the UK and although it was zero degrees and hail stones when we arrived it is now 27 degrees and sunny. We are seeing Yorkshire afresh, which is lovely. I went to Sainsbury's and was so overwhelmed that I thought I was going to have a panic attack! We are literally noticing everything and being grateful for what we have. Our home – The Old Church is stunning and as it is spring, there are lambs in the fields and blossom on the trees. We went to a fete in Knaresborough met the keeper of the Ravens, watched the Morris Dancers, had a pint of real ale in Blind Jack's pub and listened to the town crier announce what was next. Then we went to Harrogate to have roast lamb and Yorkshire pudding. We are really treasuring some simple things like having a lot of space, a large bed with beautiful covers, a kitchen that doesn't move and not having to check if the house is where we left it when we go out.

May is beside herself with joy – skipping and rolling around on the spring grass and running in and out of the hedgerows. Our diaries are filling up fast with friends and family catch ups and business meetings. And we are working on our hobbies – something we promised each other we would. Mark is painting again and I am learning the guitar, singing and writing.

We have had an incredible adventure.
But we are very happy to be home.
We have learned that we can live with less.
We are appreciating everything
and we have learned to take nothing for granted.

Reflections on being home after 18 months at Sea
Reasons to be Cheerful (part one) After several weeks on land we are now adjusting to a lot of things:

1. The house doesn't move - and it seems to be always in the same place when we come home.
2. The oven goes to the temperature you need it to and cooks stuff.
3. We don't get thrown about and bruised when we go to the toilet
4. We don't have to check the weather before we go anywhere
5. We don't have to worry that May will be in danger or too hot

6. We can get anything in the shops that we need (or want!)
7. We don't have to clean and tidy every day because the house is big enough to cope with a few days of clutter
8. We don't have to fix things all the time because things don't break all the time
9. We know what we are doing and feel competent
10. We know our way around and are not lost or disorientated - familiar faces and familiar places
11. There is food in the shops (and our fridge) that we recognise
12. We are never scared
13. Every time we park we do not think we are going to crash our car and bash into others - and no one is watching waiting for us to crash
14. We can do laundry whenever you like
15. We don't have to take two hours to pack everything we own away and check everything works before we travel anywhere.

But then

1. We are not rocked gently in our bed each night
2. The sky is not always blue
3. It is not constantly 30 degrees plus
4. There are no Sundowner Cocktails and Happy Hours with friends
5. There are no "OMFG can we do this?" moments
6. There are no physical challenges
7. There is no bonding from having experienced thrill and wonder together
8. There is no cultural stretch
9. There is no challenge when cooking on the level
10. There is no fear to overcome, no dolphins swimming by, no salt in our hair, no waves to watch, no pure open vistas with nothing but sea, no gulls, and no boobies.....
11. We cannot just slip the lines and disappear to another place and another adventure within 15 minutes
12. Having a roof over your head all day is just weird
13. We never sleep under the stars in awe
14. We don't see the sun go down in one place and arrive to watch it rise in another
15. We do not see rainbows most days

Readers Guide

Do you dream of having an adventure?

What adventure do you dream of?

How could you turn your dream into a reality?

What is the most adventurous thing you have ever done?

What are you prepared to risk for your adventure?

About the author

More about who we are

This is me – Tina, doing what I love

We have been asked to share some insights in to our Salty Sea crew so here we are – Mark and I are both in our early 50s – we are parents with two grown up children each of whom we love and of whom we are proud. In business we are entrepreneurs and have worked hard over the last 35 years building businesses and loving it (well mostly) We have an advertising agency www.outsidethebox.co.uk and an innovation management company www.thethinkteam.com We love working with the amazing teams and clients we have around the world. We are looking forward to continuing our work from our new watery home! I (Tina) am from Belfast and have been around boats since I was born – I learned to sail with the Ocean Youth Club – OYC and worked for them – sailing a 72ft Ketch from Holyhead to Bergen and back – via the Caledonian Canal and North Sea and around the fjords – I have experienced a force 10 gusting 11 in the North Sea and the calm cruising of the Greek Islands – Mark learned to sale when we got married and we love sailing together. Mark says he loves being on a yacht with me as it is the only place where I do what I am told!! I think that is true.

The other sailor in our crew is May. May is a six-year-old Maltese Terrier and is the Boss! May has not been to sea before and we have not sailed with dogs on board so this is a big adventure for all of us. We have a lot of concerns about her well-being (and ours) but we simply love her and cannot imagine leaving her, so here we go!

Epilogue

We were not sure if we would be using our return flight tickets to go back to Antigua and Magic in December but, thanks to our amazing yacht broker, Magic sold well. It is never a 'sure thing' that your yacht will sell and some yachts stay on the market for months or even years but Magic was a beautiful yacht and we had lavished her with love and technology so she was a good purchase for the buyer – a win – win.

We have now been home for almost a year. The British Spring is here and we are loving it. When you live in permanent sunshine you think that would be bliss but it is interesting that you do miss the lush green and the excitement of a change of season.

We are doing a lot of work again and, as we always do. we are planning an exciting future ahead. We don't think we will own another yacht but we do love sailing. So, the plan is to charter at least once a year and we are sure that as we will not be sailing all the time the costs of the charter will be less than ownership.

We are looking towards 2020 when we will have another adventure – perhaps buying a home in the sunshine which is something we have always dreamed of.

We are good at making dreams come true.

May is good at dreaming too

Printed in Great Britain
by Amazon